CHANGING WORLD

New Perspectives on Ageing and Later Life

Series Editors

Tony Maltby, The University of Birmingham, UK
Debra A. Street, The Pepper Institute on Aging and Public Policy
Florida State University, USA

This international collection of key research monographs provides a substantial outlet for the burgeoning body of research being conducted on ageing and later life issues. It brings to the wider academic and practitioner community both empirical and theoretical work in order to develop and refine policy and practice.

Encouraging both newly established and senior researchers alike, the series focuses on issues within social and behavioural gerontology with a direct practical application to the development of policy and practice in this field. Informative and wide-ranging, it will be of particular interest to academics, policy makers and practitioners working with older people.

Other titles in the series

Ageing and the Transition to Retirement:
A Comparative Analysis of European Welfare States
Edited by Tony Maltby, Bert De Vroom, Maria Luisa Mirabile and Einar Øverbye

Older Widows and the Lifecourse:
Multiple Narratives of Hidden Lives
Pat Chambers

Changing Worlds and the Ageing Subject

Dimensions in the Study of Ageing and Later Life

Edited by

BRITT-MARIE ÖBERG
ANNA-LIISA NÄRVÄNEN
ELISABET NÄSMAN
ERIK OLSSON

Linköping University, Sweden

Routledge
Taylor & Francis Group
LONDON AND NEW YORK

First published 2004 by Ashgate Publishing

Reissued 2018 by Routledge
2 Park Square, Milton Park, Abingdon, Oxon OX14 4RN
711 Third Avenue, New York, NY 10017, USA

Routledge is an imprint of the Taylor & Francis Group, an informa business

First issued in paperback 2018

A Library of Congress record exists under LC control number: 2003062726

ISBN 13: 978-0-815-38797-8 (hbk)
ISBN 13: 978-1-138-61904-3 (pbk)
ISBN 13: 978-1-351-16196-1 (ebk)

Contents

Notes on Contributors

Dr Els-Marie Anbäcken is Assistant Professor at the Department of Care and Welfare and at the Institute for the Study of Ageing and Later Life (ISAL), Linköping University, Sweden. She is a japanologist with an interest in research about older people and everyday life, family relations, social network and care systems. Among her recent writings is 'Sweden josei kenkyusha kara mita Sweden no josei' ('Swedish Women – a Swedish Female Researcher's Perspective') in 'Josei mondai-kaigai repoto, Sweden no josei', 2000.

Dr Jan-Erik Hagberg is Associate Professor at the Institute for the Study of Ageing and Later Life (ISAL), Linköping University, Sweden. His research interests concern technical changes and their impact on older people's daily life and old technology as cultural heritage. Among his recent writings is 'Tekniklandskapets vardagliga panorama' ('The Technological Landscape's Everyday Panorama'), in L. Sturesson (ed.) 'Spänningsfält: tekniken – politiken – framtiden' ('Domains: Technology – Politics – the Future'), 2002.

Dr Gunhild Hammarström is Professor in Sociology and Social Gerontology at Uppsala University, Sweden. Her research interests include intergenerational relationships, value change and continuity, welfare and ageing, ageing, loneliness and structural change and methodological issues. Among her recent publications are 'Hemtjänsten behöver mera hjälp!: Äldre hjälpmottagares erfarenheter av hemtjänsten' ('The Home Care Service Needs More Help!: Elderly Home Care Receivers' Experiences of the Home Care Service'), 2002, and 'Visioner eller realiteter? Generationsskillnader i synen på att ta hand om äldre' ('Visions or Realities? Generation Differences in Views on Taking Care of the Elderly'), 2000.

Dr Sarah Harper is the Director of the Oxford Institute of Ageing and a Senior Research Fellow in the Department of Sociology at the University of Oxford, UK. Her research interests include social implications of demographic ageing with particular emphases on intergenerational relationships and the family and the decisions and implications of early retirement. Among her recent writings are 'Families in Ageing societies', forthcoming and 'Ageing Societies', 2003.

Dr Phyllis Braudy Harris is Professor of Sociology and the Director of the Aging Studies Program, John Carroll University, Cleveland, Ohio, USA. Her research interests are Alzheimer's disease and care-giving, cross-cultural gerontology and gender issues and ageing. Her recent publications include 'The Voices of Husbands and Sons Caring for a Family Member with Dementia', in B.J. Kramer and E.H.

Thompson (eds.) 'Men as Caregivers: Theory Research and Service Implications', 2001, and 'Building Resilience through Adapting and Coping', in P.B. Harris (ed), 'The Person with Alzheimer's Disease: Pathways to Understanding the Experience', 2002.

Dr Kees Knipscheer is Professor of Sociology and Social Gerontology at the Free University in Amsterdam, the Netherlands. His research interests concern the issues of successful ageing and productive ageing strategies. Among his recent publications are 'The Effects of Environmental Context and Personal Resources on the Depressive Symptomatology in Older Age: a Test of the Lawton Model', 2000, and 'Family in the Aging Society', in Beets and Milteny (eds.) 'Population Ageing in Hungary and the Netherlands: a European Perspective', 2000.

Dr John Macnicol is Professor of Social Policy at Royal Holloway University of London, UK. His main research interests are the history of retirement, social policy and ageing, state pensions, age discrimination and the history of the idea of an underclass in Britain and the USA over the past hundred years. Among his recent publications is 'Age Discrimination', forthcoming and he has also recently edited 'Paying for the Old: Old Age and Social Welfare Provision', 2000.

Dr Anna-Liisa Närvänen is Associate Professor of Social and Cultural Analysis at the Department of Thematic Studies and at the Institute for the Study of Ageing and Later Life (ISAL) Linköping University, Sweden. Her research interests concern time, space and identity, life course and generations, gender, and illness experience. Among her recent writings are 'Time, Space and Identities: a Dramaturgical Approach', 2003, and 'Childhood, Generation or Life Phase?', forthcoming.

Dr Britt-Marie Öberg is a Manager of the Research and Development Center of Ageing in Östergötland, Linköping, Sweden. Her research interests are gender and employment in the later years and ageing and communication. She has published 'Arbetsvärdering och lokala löneförhandlingar' ('Job Evaluation and Local Pay Negotiations'), 1999, with Elisabet Cedersund and 'Skratt, skämt och ironi som kvinnlig strategi i diskussioner mellan arbetsgivare och arbetstagare' ('Laughter, Joke and Irony as a Female Strategy in Discussions between Employers and Employees'), 2001.

Dr Birgitta Odén is Professor Emerita at the Department of History, Lund University, Sweden. Professor Odén is one of the pioneers and forefront figures within research about ageing in Sweden. She has carried out many research projects about ageing, for instance 'Older People in Society; in the Past, Now and in the Future', 1983. She has been involved in several official reports concerning ageing, for instance 'Research about Older People', 1988. Among her later publications is 'Growing Old in Sweden', 1993.

Dr Isabella Paoletti is a Senior Researcher at the Department of Communication Sciences, University of Bologna, Italy. Her research interest is gender, ageing and communication. Among her recent works are 'Membership Categorization and Time Appraisal in Interviews with Family Cares of Disabled Elderly', 2001, and 'Caring for Older People: a Gendered Practice', 2002.

Foreword

Changing Worlds and the Ageing Subject

Dimensions in the Study of Ageing and Later Life

Britt-Marie Öberg

Countries across Europe as well as outside Europe, e.g. Japan and the USA, have recently been experiencing great demographic changes, a decline in the birth rate and a significant increase in the numbers of old people, especially those over 80 years old. These demographic changes are prophesied to have critical consequences for the world's economy and the lives of young and old. The demographic changes are running parallel to changes in other areas, which also have a deep impact on people's everyday life regardless of age. Important and deep-rooted changes infallibly attract the attention of researchers from different disciplines. This book describes from different perspectives how the conditions for old people's lives are changing and how this in its turn is changing the aims and conduct of research about ageing and later life.

A Changing World

During the last centuries the world has changed considerably and it is still changing at an ever-increasing speed in many areas. The inventions and discoveries in technology, medicine, biology, physics and other natural sciences increase and the development regarding issues such as political democracy, gender equality, religious freedom etc have changed the living conditions for human beings in different ways. In particular the fast development within the area of information technology is conspicuous. Not only has it given us an easy access to all types of information as well as to culture in all forms from different parts of the world, it has also made it possible for almost everyone to stay in contact with other people at any place (even the moon!) but also to be reachable themselves within seconds. The words of the 17th century poet John Donne 'No man is an island'[1] are more relevant than ever.

Recent changes in the world which have been discussed in terms of late modern or postmodern society include changes such as the weakening of the welfare state, weakening collective identities, changing conditions of production and accelerating globalization (Giddens, 1991; Bauman, 1998; Senett, 2000).

The globalization of the world is both a result of the many changes as well as the cause of some of them. Globalization has created new challenges not only in economy, politics and culture but also in people's everyday life, the life world of the old being no exception (Phillipson, 2003).

Migration, for example, flowing in different directions plays an ever-greater role in the globalized world. Old people are an important part of these flows whether they grow old in a foreign country, move back and forth, or remain in their native country and yet communicate and interact in different ways with their children and other relatives that have immigrated to different parts of the world. In either case they together form transnational communities within which the members are connected through social, economical and symbolic ties that are maintained over time and across space in complex patterns of exchange and support (Faist, 2000). Another flow of migration consists of an increasing amount of wealthy people who choose their place of residence in old age according to their different interests in leisure or preferred climate.

Postmodern times have also meant a 'transformation in the meaning associated with the traditional bonds of family, work and community' (Phillipson, 2003). Beck describes it as follows:

> We live in an age in which the social order of the nation state, class, ethnicity and the traditional family is in decline. The ethic of individual self-fulfilment and achievement is the most powerful current in modern society. (Beck. 2000:165)

These and other changes, which characterize the present world, have consequences for research on ageing. One consequence of the previous institutional approach to ageing and later life was a strong medical focus and the tendency to describe old age in relation to society's problems with health and social care. But in such research old people often tend to be conceived as a homogeneous group irrespective of their differences regarding gender, social class, ethnicity and state of health. Moreover, the research may contribute to the stereotyping of old people as a group constituting social problems associated with illness and functional incapacity. It may also be argued that a sanctioned form of research conditions and facilitates research of the same kind and therefore, new research projects often proceed along old ruts.

However, new conditions generate new questions. Mainstream research on ageing will be challenged when other aspects of the ageing process are focused on. Other dimensions in research about ageing that include new theories and new methods will gain ground. This will lead to more nuanced perspectives on older people in society and on ageing as a cultural and social phenomenon.

How then should the perspective on old age used in research based on health and social care be complemented? What are the new theoretical and methodological questions concerning research about ageing that are raised in a changing world? These issues were discussed in February 2001 in Norrköping, Sweden. Scholars from Europe and the US, who are involved in research about ageing and later life, were assembled for discussions with members of the newly established Institute for Studies on Ageing and Later Life (ISAL). Thoughts and ideas were put forward as to how to reduce the bias for medical and social care studies and how to inspire and encourage to new and different approaches within this field of research.

When summing up the discussions, four different dimensions within research about ageing, based on four, to some extent complementary perspectives, were described: the importance of seeing old age and ageing as a part of the whole life, i.e. from a life course perspective; the importance of making old people's own ideas, experiences and opinions the startingpoint of studies of the ageing process; the heterogeneity principle, that is to observe the fact that old people are as varied as individuals as middle-aged and young people are; and finally, the humanistic-historical dimension.

New Dimensions in Research on Ageing and Later Life

One important discussion during the conference dealt with the fact that the ageing process is related to all socially defined life phases, childhood, youth, middle age and old age and their meanings. Consequently it is important to pay attention to the whole life course of an individual as well as to the changing social structures during the same historical period and their mutual influence. This dimension becomes even more important when considering the radical changes in lifestyle and perception of identity and sense of self that are considered to be characteristic of the changing world of today.

For example, a more extensive education induces young people to remain longer in their parental home, and to postpone marriage and children in comparison to earlier generations. Changing value systems have also made it possible for young people to co-habit instead of marrying, or divorce and enter new relationships and form different types of stepfamilies (cf. Harper in Chapter 1). On the other hand, longevity may have similar consequences for an old person. When becoming a widow, widower or divorcee and thus facing a long period of living alone, an old person may consider repartnering, which then also changes family relationships (de Jong Gierveld, 2002).

As these examples show, new life patterns are formed by both young and old subjects. Their choices are influenced by their intergenerational relationships and their definitions of the meanings of the life course as well as of the different life phases but also by the interplay between their individual lives and the social structures with their built-in cultural values. Continually these structures are changing just as they vary from one society to another (Kertzer and Schaie, 1989). An analytical framework emphasizing a life course perspective will help to clarify these interdependencies and help to elucidate how people experience the ageing process.

A second dimension that was raised in the discussions was the fact that older people are not a homogeneous group. To grow old has different meanings for different persons, depending on differences regarding gender, social class, cultural background and state of health. Women's and men's life experiences are different in many aspects. It is a well-known fact, for instance, that in most cases the economic situation for men is better than that for women at retirement. However, there is also research that indicates that men and women in old age perceive their own health status and feelings of loneliness differently (Knipscheer, ISAL lecture in April 2002). Thus it is important to observe the gender dimension in research about ageing. Membership of different class and groups as well as having a different cultural or ethnic background may account for other diversities in research results.

Studies about ageing according to a humanistic-historical dimension is a line of research in its own right. As the gerontologist Thomas R. Cole points out:

> Because the humanities emphasize description, interpretation, explanation, and appreciation of the variety, uniqueness, complexity, originality and unpredictability of human beings striving to live and know themselves they offer a valuable lens through which to view the phenomenon of aging. (Cole, 1992:xi, xiii, in Deats and Lenker, 1999)

Moreover, in interdisciplinary projects this third dimension of research about ageing can also fortify life course research and gender, – class- or ethnic-geared research. Literature, the arts and history bear witness about our traditional mores regarding ageing and our attitudes towards old age and old people during previous times, in other cultures and in different classes or subgroups in society. The images of old age we meet in humanistic-historical research not only show how old age was perceived in another time or in another culture, these images also helped to create and sustain these perceptions. They may have contributed to the construction of the stereotypes of ageing. Studying these 'portraits' of ageing can give us a better understanding of the development of negative and positive conceptions of ageing. By studying this process we can become more aware of the mechanisms of negative stereotyping and learn how to deconstruct them (Deats and Lenker, 1999:2).

Taking the starting point in people's own interpretation and understanding of the changing world and the ageing process is another important dimension in studies about ageing. How does the changing world appear in the eyes of old people? How does it affect them? What does it mean to grow old in a new context with new techniques that can give old people new possibilities in spite of changed functional capacities but that can also threaten to exclude them if they cannot or will not make use of the new possibilities and adapt to new ideas? What does it mean to grow old in a world that is more mobile and flexible and where, for many individuals, a sense of belonging and identity no longer can be built on the categories of nation, class or gender? What does it mean to grow old in a context where more emphasis is put on issues of diversity and difference than on traditional values and priorities? How do old people themselves experience and talk about their daily lives and how do they organize their lives and interactions in relation to others?

Thus taking the perspectives of older people means that studies on the macro level of a changing world and its impact on people's lives have to be complemented by studies on the micro level of how old people make sense of the changes in their daily lives. To this end a qualitative approach is preferred. 'Everyday life and its world of meanings is too complex, socially mediated and locally differentiated to be adequately captured by a quantitative approach, such as laboratory experiments and social surveys.' (Gubrium and Holstein, 2000:9). As is shown in this book such an approach can take several research directions, for instance open-ended interviews, participant observation, narrative analysis and even osteological analysis (cf. Odén in Chapter 5). Several of the book's authors use qualitative methods but it is also claimed that a combination of qualitative and quantitative methods will have a unique strength as they can complement and build on one another (cf. Knipscheer in Chapter 10). Evidently, to include one or more of these dimensions in new approaches to research within ageing and life in later years, will also easily result in studies where analyses on the micro and mezzo levels and as well as on the macro level complement one another.

To pay attention to these four dimensions not only leads to diversified research methods, it also opens up for studies about ageing and later life in other areas than the, up to now, more common studies within medicine and health and social care. Living in a more globalized world will lead to interest in ethnographic and social-cultural anthropological studies. A rapid development within technology will lead to studies about how old people cope with the new technological surroundings. To be able to understand how old people make sense of the present world and the different changes in their daily life and how we, young and old, talk about and describe these phenomena both in everyday life and in institutional and political contexts, we need different kinds of interactional studies.

There are groups of researchers over the world working in these and similar areas but we need to emphasize these, often interdisciplinary, studies and make the results more known and available to reduce the bias for medical and social care studies.

This book is one step in that direction. In the following chapters the authors show what can be achieved through studies in areas previously not considered for studies about ageing. In this way the book is fulfilling its aim to strengthen the efforts of renewing and expanding the research in ageing and encouraging both established and new researchers to new and different endeavours to reach new horizons.

In the latter part of this introduction the contents of the book will be presented. However, it is necessary to first account for some of the difficulties in defining the core concept 'being old'. What and who is an old person and how old is an old person?

Old People, Older People, the Elderly and Older Elderly?

When is an individual old? How do we define old people? When people are talking in general about old people or the elderly they may have different chronological ages in mind and the exact meaning of the word is not often explained. Many consider the retirement age as a doorway to old age and to be retired is to be labelled as elderly. But the retirement age is different in different occupations and it is different in different countries. It has also been different in different times. In working life one can be considered too old as early as at the age of 35-40; compare the third team of the Dutch Ballet Company described by Professor Kees Knipscher in his chapter in this book. Some decades ago Swedish authorities took the average age of 70 as a starting point when planning for the amount of health and social care needed by older citizens. Today, when people not only live longer, but also are healthier and more active the age of 80-85 is considered as a more relevant starting point. In the material from the British Office for National Statistics (ONS) elderly people is a general term used for all people from the age of 65 to over 100. By old people is meant people between 65 and 75 and by older elderly all people over 75.[2]

In research literature the confusion is often greater. Some British scholars claim that the word elderly has a derogatory overtone and contributes to ageism, therefore they avoid using it. Thus all the words, old, older, elderly, or older elderly people are relative and their meanings are dependent on context.

Chapter Contents

Dramatic demographic changes in the Western part of the world are the main reason why the interest in research about ageing has rapidly increased. In the first chapter 'Some Implications of Population Ageing for Societies and Individuals', Sarah Harper discusses demographic change on a structural as well as on an individual level and their interrelatedness. She points out that there are two ways of approaching the implications of a mature society. Either one considers the national and international implications of these demographic changes or one examines what it means to the individual that there is a possibility that she or he will live well into the 9th or even the 10th decade (see Harper, p. 1 of this book). But she also points out that it is important to see not only the problems but also the opportunities that are offered by a maturing society.

In her chapter she discusses in particular two issues that affect both individuals and society as a whole; 'Changing Family Roles, Relationships and Transitions' and 'The Emergence of Mass Retirement'. In the first case she discusses how the changing trends in marriage patterns (divorce rates, co-habitation, and delayed first child birth) affect people's living arrangements and lead to changes in kin care and support. The new trends also affect how society has to plan and arrange the health and social care for its older citizens. The second issue Harper takes up is the increase in early retirement and how it affects individuals and society. She mainly takes into account the first dimension discussed above i.e. she puts the demographic changes into a life course perspective. But she also touches on the dimension of heterogeneity when she compares the conditions for men and women.

The problems of early retirement are also brought up by John Macnicol in his chapter 'Analysing Age Discrimination'. The fact that those taking early retirement include two distinct groups, those with well-funded pensions voluntarily withdrawing to a life of rest and leisure and those with low levels of education and involuntarily withdrawing to a life of scarcity makes the author discuss ageism, its origins, manifestations and possible correctives. He also compares the ongoing discussions about ageism in the UK and the USA. In this chapter the dimension of heterogeneity comes clearly into play as the author analyses how working and retirement conditions are different for men and women and blue- and white-collar workers. In comparing the UK and the USA he analyses how the difference in cultural background as well as in background history have fostered a different development of ageism in the two countries.

As has been pointed out above, theoretical and methodological issues as well as contents were also discussed in the call for new perspectives within the research about ageing and later life. In the chapters the authors also make theoretical reflections and comment on their choice of methods. In the chapters by Gunhild Hammarström and Anna-Liisa Närvänen theoretical issues is the main focus.

Hammarström scrutinizes the concepts of generation and cohort in research on old age, ageing and old people. In line with Närvänen, she demonstrates the conceptual problems in earlier research and turns back to Mannheim's seminal work in order to clarify the differences between the concepts and to argue in favour of the theoretical as well as empirical relevance of a Mannheimian research approach in these areas today.

Based on a thorough review of recent literature in the social sciences and humanities, Närvänen summarizes the critique concerning theoretical vagueness and ambivalence in the empirical studies in the field and contributes to the clarification of the conceptual mess. With others she strongly proposes some limitations in the way specific concepts are to be used and logically linked to one another. She discusses ageing as a social phenomenon and argues in favour of a broad life course perspective on the social and cultural processes of ageing.

To emphasize old people's own interpretation and understanding of the ageing process is an important dimension in the research about ageing and later life and Phyllis Braudy Harris and Isabella Paoletti make a particular point in using this dimension. In her chapter 'The Sense of Self in Alzheimer's Disease: The Person's Perspective' Harris lets us listen to the voices of people with Alzheimer's disease (AD). She has interviewed persons in an early stage of AD in order to investigate what happens to their sense of self. In the excerpts from the interviews we can experience their emotional reaction as they struggle to maintain their sense of personal identity and we are told what coping strategies they develop. Harris shows that by using the dimension of listening to the patients' own words about their experiences of fighting AD she extracts new and valuable knowledge which might not have been possible in more traditional research about patients with dementia.

Paoletti strikes a similar note in her chapter 'The Social Construction of Older Women's Identities and Institutional Intervention', when she shows through her discourse analysis how women in their discussions at video recorded committee meetings in a group for older women use the membership categorization 'old' in varying ways. She shows how the women project positive personal identities, differentiating themselves from old age categories and from related category-bound activities. The images of the older women emerging from her analysis are ones of busy and effective adults. On the other hand they construct stereotyped identities through images of dependency, sickness and loneliness for the 'other', the very old or institutionalized elderly. This way she shows how the varying use of the membership categorization 'old' has different implications for their identity construction. Paoletti also let the dimension of heterogeneity inform her work. This is done by the contrasting pictures she gives of the women and the old men that also took part in the work at the club.

The historian Birgitta Odén highlights another experience particular to women, namely that of old women's ailments. Are these ailments talked about or silenced? By whom and in what way were the old women taken care of before welfare systems were common in most western countries? Together with the author we explore sources of information as different as archaeological findings among prehistoric skeletons and written sources, starting with quotations from the Bible and ending with excerpts from diaries and literature written by women in the 19th century. The scarce information sifted out paints a picture of women not talking about their problems but carrying on their duties till they are too ill to leave the bed. However, the many sources also tell us that there is a difference in how much care each woman is receiving due to the fact that they belong to different social classes. Birgitta Odén plays skilfully with almost all the dimensions. As she writes about old women's ailments in historical time the humanistic-historical dimension is naturally dealt with. She compares the situations for women from different classes and in different times and places. In this way the dimension of heterogeneity is paid attention to. As she sources some of her information from diaries and private letters we hear the voices of old women telling about their ailments in their own words. All in all her text paints a fascinating picture of a part of old women's everyday life that hardly would be possible to depict without resorting to what can be found through using all the dimensions.

The variety of the experiences of ageing and being old is not only due to gender and social class but also to different cultural background. In her chapter 'Researching Home Help Services for the Elderly in Japan and Sweden: How Cultural Concepts Affect the Research Design', Els-Marie Anbäcken compares how filial duty is perceived in Japan and Sweden. She also analyses how the concepts of independence and autonomy in Sweden and the concept of 'Amae', the Japanese kind of dependency, are informing the countries' official policies for old age and the ways individuals view the ageing process. She points out how this difference in thinking also affects the co-operation between Swedish and Japanese scholars involved in the same project about ageing and later life.

All the chapters introduced so far have been more or less interdisciplinary in nature. An obvious interdisciplinary perspective can also be found in the chapter by Jan-Erik Hagberg who examines the role in and the affect of old and new technology in old people's lives. Hagberg clearly shows that it is not enough to be an engineer and to invent some technical gadget with the potential to increase the life quality of old persons. One must also find ways to make the gadget accepted, used and appreciated by the old person. In this work an intimate co-operation between representatives of both technology and social sciences and perhaps also representatives of health care or social care is needed.

In many of the chapters different concepts of time are proposed by the authors. The distinction between chronological time and social time makes it possible to discuss ageing not only as a biological but also as a social phenomenon. Ageing is also discussed in terms of biographical time and its relatedness to historical time. In the chapter 'Biographical and Strategic Issues in Research about Ageing', Kees Knipscheer parallels his biographical time and his own lifetime career, with historical time, in this case the history of the development within research in ageing. He tells us how he as a young man in the 1960s was asked to write about the sociological role and meaning of age, a concept that at the time seemed very abstract to him. Limited to a sociological approach in the beginning he slowly through the years arrives at a more interdisciplinary approach to research and gains more diversified perspectives on ageing. Through the years, he confesses, he felt more and more limited, even frustrated by the use of quantitative research methods and advocates today the use of a combination of quantitative and qualitative methods. Knipscheer clearly has a life course perspective but as it is his own life he is telling us about, he is also using the fourth dimension, that of letting old people give their on views on the ageing process.

Being a nestor in this research field Kees Knipscheer concludes his chapter by giving young scholars advice about research methods and suggesting possible research projects in areas that he has found sparsely researched. We found it appropriate for him to end this book, thereby underlining the line of development and continuous change within a field of vital research.

Summary

To these ten chapters, scholars with varying academic backgrounds bring with them their experience of different methods and characteristic perspectives in order to contribute to a deeper and more comprehensive understanding of what it is like to grow old and be old today, as well as in the past. One of the points in this introductory chapter is that research foci can contain several dimensions and when analyzing data it is important to consider the relevant dimensions. It is important that people's own experience is the starting point for research that aims to examine the ageing subject's position in a rapidly changing world. Previously researchers have realized that events in the early years influence the way we experience life in old age. We argue that local and global changes, whether historic or contemporary, also influence the way we experience our individual lives and influence how younger people perceive old people and vice versa. People's memberships in different groupings also influence how they experience their lives. Moreover, it is an advantage if the research is interdisciplinary and builds on knowledge from different sources and use methods from different academic traditions. By turning to new areas for research and analysing the empirical material according to one or several relevant dimensions scholars will manage to draw a richer and more multi-facetted picture of old age and later life. With this book we hope to inspire and encourage scholars to new efforts in exploring a field of research that to some extent is still virgin soil.

Notes

1 John Donne 1624, *Devotions upon Emergent Occasions* no 17.
2 Official Swedish documents use a similar division. People over 65 are called 'yngre äldre' (younger old people) and people around 75-80 and above are called 'äldre äldre' (older old people). However, the division is less fixed at the chronological age as 'äldre äldre' also has the connotation of being in need of care and perhaps living in a home for the elderly.

Bibliography

Bauman, Z. (1998), *Work, Consumerism and the New Poor*, Open University Press, Philadelphia, Pa.

Beck, U. (2000), 'Living Your Own Life in a Runaway World: Individualisation, Globalisation and Politics', in W. Hutton and A. Giddens (eds.), *On the Edge: Living with Global Capitalism*, Jonathan Cape, London, pp. 164-174.

Cole, T. R. (1992), 'The Humanities and Aging: An Overview', in T.R. Cole, D.D. Van Tassell and R. Kastenbaum (eds.), *Handbook of the Humanities and Aging*, Springer, New York.

de Jong Gierveld, J. (2002), 'The Dilemma of Repartnering', *Ageing International*, Vol. 27 (4), pp. 61-78.

Deats, S.M. and Lenker, L.T. (1999), *Aging and Identity: A Humanities Perspective*, Praeger Publishers, Westport.

Donne, J. (1624), *Devotions upon Emergent Occasions no 17.*

Faist, T. (2000), *The Volume and Dynamics of International Migration and Transnational Social Spaces*, Oxford University Press, Oxford.

Giddens, A. (1991), *Modernity and Self-identity: Self and Society in the Late Modern Age*, Stanford University Press, Stanford.

Gubrium, J.F. and Holstein, J.A. (2000), *Aging and Everyday Life*, Blackwell, Malden.

Kertzer, D.I. and Schaie, K.W. (1989), *Age Structuring in Comparative Perspective*, Lawrence Erlbaum, Hillsdale.

Phillipson, C. (2003), 'Cultural Perspectives, Globalisation and the Reconstruction of Ageing Communities: Methodological Challenges for Gerontological Research', in K. Lumme-Sandt, J. Outi and N. Mäkinen (eds.), *The Cultural in Gerontology: Challenges, Approaches and Methods: Proceedings, 4th International Symposium on Cultural Gerontology*, 24-27 May, 2003, Tampere, Finland.

Sennett, R. (2000), *The Corrosion of Character: the Personal Consequences of Work in the New Capitalism*, W. W. Norton, New York.

Acknowledgements

The editors gratefully acknowledge the support of Linköping University and the Institute for Studies on Ageing and Later Life which made the production of this book possible. However, the completion of the book would not have been possible without the help of many colleagues making suggestions, criticism and elaboration. In particular we thank Els-Marie Anbäcken, the Institute for Studies on Ageing and Later Life, Linköping University, Sweden and Christine E. Swane, the Danish Institute of Gerontology, Hellerup, Denmark. We also thank Lindy Gustavsson for conscientious translations and Grace Rose for conscientious proofreading and indexing. We thank Anna Mercer-Högsten who provided valuable feedback on the first and second draft and also added original thoughts of her own. Special thanks to Anita Stenberg for superb technical support and turning the written manuscript into camera-ready copy.

Linköping and Norrköping
July 2003

Britt-Marie Öberg
Anna-Liisa Närvänen
Elisabet Näsman
Erik Olsson

Chapter 1

Some Implications of Population Ageing for Societies and Individuals

Sarah Harper

Introduction

The population of the world is ageing. Following a rapid increase in the number of younger people over the past century, we are now entering a mature demographic profile. The common public concept of 'ageing' has been one of an increased requirement to provide health and social service delivery to older people per se. Yet demographic change will also result in nearly half the population of Western Europe being over 50 within 30 years. This will have significant implications for labour supply, family and household structure, health and welfare service demand, patterns of saving and consumption, provision of housing and transport, leisure and community behaviour, networks and social interaction, and even, it has been suggested, the geopolitical order of the new century.

As Figure 1.1 demonstrates, population ageing will over the next quarter century affect all regions of the world. Fertility and mortality rates have fallen in most developed countries over the last 150 years or so. In less developed countries, these declines occurred later in the last century. The combination of a decline in offspring, with a lengthening of life of those already born, is the power behind this demographic change. This process is set to spread throughout the world this century, with increasingly ageing populations, until equilibrium is reached as we approach the 22nd century, when a more balanced profile will, it is predicted, emerge and be maintained. The challenges, or we should say opportunities, presented by this mature society will be with us for but a short period.

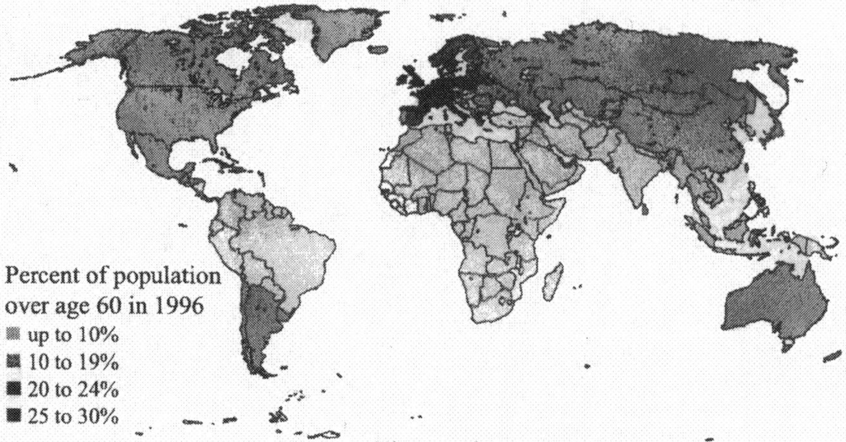

The numbers of older people vary widely among nations ….

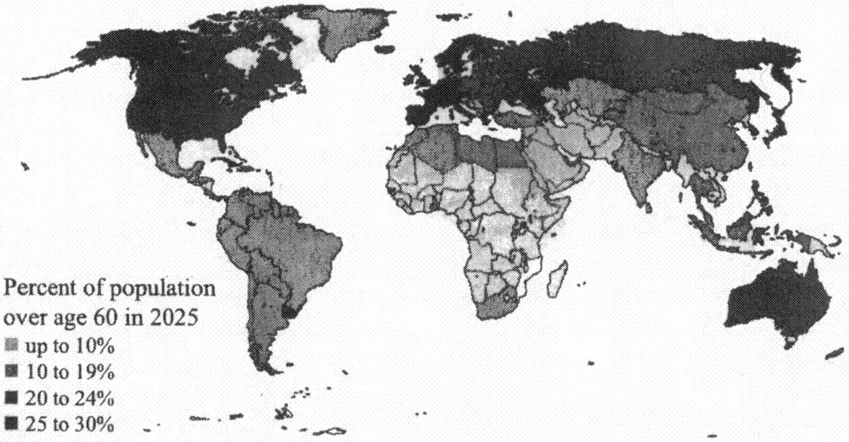

… but will have increased significantly in many countries by 2025.

There are two ways in which we can approach the implications of this. On the one hand, we can consider the national and international implications of these demographic changes. What are the social, economic, and political implications of this mature age structure? What might be the impact upon labour and consumer markets and upon political and civic behaviour, of having over half a nation's population aged over 50? On the other hand, on an individual level, life expectation has risen significantly over the past few decades. Current European Union (EU) predictions suggest a rise in healthy active life expectancy, forecasting that both men and women in their early 70s can expect to live well into their 80s, enjoying most of those years disability-free. What is the impact on individuals as they realize the potential of life spans, which may take them well into the 9th or even 10th decade.

In this chapter I wish to consider some key questions addressing both societies and individuals as they age. I will here focus on two broad themes which impact upon the life experiences of all adults and can be viewed from both societal and individual perspectives – kinship roles and relationships, and access and contribution to economic activity. My stance is that we should not consider late life as a separate entity. One would sometimes believe that late life was a stage beyond adulthood. Older adults are just that – adults who are older. Changes across the life course impact upon later life, just as period and cohort effects impact upon individual experiences of later life. Questions, which pertain to older adults, also pertain to all adults. These include: the requirements for full adult participation in a particular society and how the ageing process across the adult life course affects an individual's ability to fulfill these requirements; the access adults have to social and cultural resources within their societies, and how these are affected by socio-economic, ethnic, gender and age variables; the manner in which adults acquire social and cultural capital over the life course.

It is possible to argue, however, that chronological age has little relevance in the 21st century. Clearly to have one's first child at 20 is different from having one's first child at 45; to lose a job at 55 is different from losing it at 25. However, is the difference between chronological ages that much greater than that between socio-economic groups, or genders? It surely is the life transition – such as for example to parenthood, which is the significant issue. The individual's age, gender or cultural group are but moderators of that experience. Chronological age should therefore be perceived as merely one of many factors impacting upon individuals as they pass through life's transitions. In many cultures that is the case. Rarely it seems that contemporary Western cultures view age in this way. I believe we need to change this.

Changing Family Roles, Relationships and Transitions

In most Western industrial societies the shift from a high mortality/high fertility society to a low mortality/low fertility society has been accompanied by the ageing of family transitions, with these ageing societies also displaying an increase of age at first marriage, at first childbirth, and at leaving the parental home. The first set of demographic trends results in an increase in the number of living generations, and a decrease in the number of living relatives within these generations. Increased adult longevity may increase the duration spent in certain kinship roles, such as spouse, parent of non-dependent child or sibling. A decrease in fertility may reduce the duration of other roles, such as being a parent of dependent children. It may even remove the opportunity for some roles, such as that of sibling. The ageing of some family transitions, in particular birth of first child, leads to long intergenerational spacing, and a transition to both parenthood and grandparenthood at a later age than has been the recent historical norm.

Perhaps the major impact on the 21st century families is rapidly changing trends in marriage (Harper, 2003b), for the marital status of a person is a dimension of family structure that deeply affects their living arrangements, support systems and individual well-being. Cohabitation and divorce are increasing at all adult ages. Individuals are marrying later, facing a greater possibility of divorce, and are increasingly less likely to remarry following marital dissolution. Historically, marriages ended due to the early death of the wife, usually through childbirth or related reproductive complications, with the average length of early 20th century marriages likely to be less than 25 years. Now, due to divorce, many 21st century marriages are dissolved much earlier (Anderson, 1982). However, those marriages which do not end in divorce are likely to be longer than at any other historical time, owing to lengthening life expectancy for both men and women.

In most Western industrialized nations, *marriage rates* are declining, with marriage occurring later in life, or not at all, accompanied by a growing trend for a period of cohabitation first. In addition, throughout the Western world, rates of remarriage, following divorce or widowhood, are also falling. This last fall is particularly of note as it mainly involves older cohorts who seem no more tempted to remarry than their younger compatriots. *Cohabitation* is increasing, both for never-married couples and for those who were formerly married (Ermisch and Franceseconi, 1996, 1998). At the turn of the century, around 10 per cent of all couples living in the EU for example, were cohabiting, and despite cultural and cohort/age differences, there is a slow trend throughout Europe for couples of all ages and in all countries to undertake a period of cohabitation before legal marriage (Kiernan, 2000). We still know little about the impact of a period of cohabitation on later life, or on wider family relationships (Haskey, 1992; Delphy and Leonard, 1992). Perhaps the potentially biggest impact is the growth of cohabitation in later life, particularly following divorce, as these unions are less likely to end in marriage. Given that it is generally acknowledged that cohabitation has a higher likelihood of separation than legal marriage (McRea, 1993; Popenoe, 1993; Nock, 1995), it may be argued that such late life alliances do not provide the stability for the extensive cross-kin interactions and relationships supported within marriage-based families or step families. This may be particularly important in terms of reciprocal care in late life. However, the assertion that these relationships are less stable is based primarily on evidence from younger cohabiting couples. As older adults move to this form of mid- and late-life union the picture may be very different.

In terms of both *crude divorce rate*[1] and the *total divorce rate*,[2] England and Wales rank highest in Europe, with around 40 per cent of marriages currently ending in divorce. However, while families in all industrialized nations have faced an increase in marital divorce over the past century, at the same time they have also faced a reduction in marital disruption due to death. There is a range of cross-cultural evidence which indicates that, in comparison with the non-married, married people have an advantage which may be measured across both health and socio-economic variables (Verbrugge, 1979; Gove, 1973; Waite, 1995). As Waite (2000) has argued, intact husband-wife families provide a multiple support system for spouse in terms of emotional, financial and social exchanges, and married people tend to enjoy higher levels of health and survival, social participation and life satisfaction than persons who are not married. Indeed, the rather limited empirical evidence we have suggests that divorce tends to be associated with lower economic wellbeing among elderly people. Thus, US data on both income and wealth indicate that older persons who are married enjoy much higher standards of living than non-married persons, with the highest rates of poverty being experienced by those who are divorced, as much as three or four times the married rate.

It has long been recognized in the United States that married people have an advantage in terms of both health and longevity (Verbrugge, 1979; Gove, 1973) with these figures being substantiated outside the US in a cross-national study of 16 countries (Hu and Goldman, 1990). This is particularly the case for men. Divorced men are at an extra disadvantage over widowed men however, in that they frequently also lose social support networks (which appear more likely to be retained by both widowed men and widowed or divorced women); and an increasing number may find themselves without support from offspring in later life. Women generally have stronger and more multi-faceted networks than men, and are able to retain stronger social support following divorce (Hyman, 1983); children currently have a higher propensity to remain with the mother after a marital divorce or cohabitation split. Thus while both death and divorce have an impact on the wider family structure, and may lead to varied reconstituted family forms, there are significant gender differences in the experience of each. Women thus face economic decline through both widowhood and divorce, but are able to maintain strong family and other relationships; men, however, are cut off from personal relationships through divorce to a far greater degree than through being widowed (Hughes and Waite, 2000). In addition, under a regime of low fertility both men and women will have fewer children and in all Western industrialized countries increasing geographical mobility results in more separation from children.

Marital dissolution clearly also has implications beyond those for the couple themselves. Dissolution in younger life often leads to remarriage or cohabitation by one or both partners, introducing a variety of complex reconstituted family structures, which impact upon both reciprocal family care, and intergenerational transmission. In the United Kingdom, for example, there has been limited research on the role of reconstituted or step families in caring for older adults (Finch and Wallis, 1994; Finch, 2003; Bornat et al., 1999; Dimmock et al., 2001). The broad conclusions from all these studies are that the complexities of the ensuing relationships do not lend themselves to any particular pattern or structure of care. However, the dominant care relationship of blood-related daughter for mother, found within non-reconstituted families, seems to remain central. As an extensive qualitative study by Dimmock and colleagues on the role of step-families in later life relationships concludes, whilst there is a growing awareness of the possibilities of looser-knit, divorce extended families, when it comes to 'the crunch' the availability of care will usually depend on access to close 'blood ties' (Dimmock et al., 2001).

These general trends in adult union formation and dissolution are being accompanied by a general trend for an increase in the age at various family transitions, in particular those associated with marriage and childbirth. As indicated earlier, concurrent with the fall in marriage rates has been an *increase in the age of marriage* and remarriage for both men and women.[3] Both delayed marriage and remarriage are clearly associated with the growth in cohabitation. Thus it may be argued that they only represent a shift from one form of adult union to another. However, other life transitions are also being delayed, in particular age at first childbirth and age of leaving the parental home. Despite an increase in out-of-wedlock births, delayed marriage is still associated with *delayed first child birth*, with both the average age at birth of first child and median age for childbearing rising throughout the Western industrialized world. Average age at birth of first child thus rose from 24 in 1970 to 26 in 1995 for European Union women. The increasing delay of first childbirth highlighted above has the potential to create a family structure with long intergenerational spacing. This may well create difficulties in the development of bonds across the life course, especially as this may result in simultaneous demands from adolescent children and ageing parents, the 'sandwich generation', or 'women in the middle phenomenon' (Bengtson, 1995). The delaying of this first childbirth, impacts upon subsequent family structure, particularly on the age at which subsequent life transitions occur. These include, for example, grandparenthood and the *empty nest syndrome*, the extended post-parental period following the departure from the family home of the child/children. Running alongside the general fall in fertility is a specific increase in voluntary childlessness. Latest figures reveal that one-third of the female UK 1964 birth cohort had yet to reproduce at age 35 (Office for National Statistics (ONS), 1999). This is the lowest fertility rate recorded, and even if a large percentage of 1964 birth cohort decide to bear children, the rate of secondary infertility among the UK population (infertility arising naturally as fertility declines in late maternal reproductive life) is such that the fertility rate of this cohort will be significantly lower than that of cohorts. While childless adults establish bonds with extended or fictive kin, building such connections will become more difficult as the frequency of such kin declines with falling fertility.

There has also been a rapid and recent increase in the age at which young people leave the parental home. Within Europe, for example, every EU member state, with the exception of Denmark and the Netherlands, saw an increase between 1987 and 1996 in those aged 20-29 remaining within the parental home. A similar picture emerges in the US. This may be an artefact of measurement, but it may also indicate a growing trend to delay the commitment to full independent adult living, as opposed to an extended form of independent adolescent living. A range of factors are associated with this postponement of flying the nest, including remaining in education, financial uncertainty and peer example. This additional increase in age of leaving home not only increases the age at which parents experience the empty nest syndrome, but also prolongs the time that children and parents live close in non-dependent adult relationships.

Indeed, as populations age, so the child-parent dyad shifts from one of dependency to one primarily experienced as an adult relationship. Many parents and children will soon experience 60 years of joint life, of which under one-third would be spent in the traditional parent/dependent-child relationship (Grundy, 1999). However, not only will parents and children spend a longer time in non-dependent relationships, but the time spent as a child with a dependent parent is also increasing. There is evidence, for US women at least, that the time spent as the daughter of a parent over 65 now exceeds the time spent as the parent of a child under 18 (Watkins et al., 1985). Indeed, given that it is now not until after age 80 that the crucial stage for relying on children for assistance is reached, we should perhaps be comparing ages over 80 with those under 18. What then becomes apparent is that adult US women now spend more time without a dependant – be it a dependent child or potentially dependent parent – than with one.

As the common experience of parenthood moves to more than 50 years of shared life, parents and children are adjusting to spending most of their relationship as independent adults. Similarly husbands and wives are spending less of their joint lives as parents of young children. Clearly, the association between marital and parental roles becomes less rigid. Relationships which have been historically based on a hierarchy which existed in part to support successful reproduction must move to greater equality, both child-parent, and husband-wife, as traditional roles based on parenthood give way to companionate relationships.

For the past twenty years it has been generally accepted that many people alive today in Western industrialized nations will spend some time as part of a four-generation family. These, however, will have increasingly fewer members, and longer gaps between the generations (Hagestad, 1988; Shanas, 1980), and family members will spend longer time occupying intergenerational family roles than before. Data from the US indicates that a fifth of all women who die after 80, will spend some time in a five generation family as great-great-grandmothers (Hagestad, 1988). The *bean-pole family*, or the *verticalization* of family structure has been well recognized, in the US in particular (Bengtson and Dannefer, 1987; Bengtson et al., 1990; Hagestad, 1986; Goldman, 1986). Two recent national surveys, the Health and Retirement Survey, and the AARP Intergenerational

Linkages survey, show that more than half of the respondents reported membership in four generation families (Soldo and Hill, 1995; Bengtson and Harootyan, 1994; Bengtson, 1995).

More recently, however, the full extent of this verticalization has been questioned by Farkas and Hogan (1995). Analysis of cross sectional data from the International Social Survey Program (ISSP) covering the US, Australia and five European countries (Austria, West Germany, Great Britain, Hungary and Italy) (Table 1.1) revealed that, at least at the end of the 1980s, only a very small percentage of individuals lived in a complex multigenerational family. Just under half of the 10,000 respondents were living in a two generation family, 43 per cent had three living generations, but under 3 per cent were part of a four generation family. An individual in the US was more likely to have both a surviving child and surviving parent than one in any of the European countries. However, such findings put the verticalization debate in perspective. While it is likely that during an individual's lifetime, he or she will experience a period of complex, possibly four or even five generational living even if for only a short portion of the life-course, at any one time the percentage of such long-chain multigenerational families within a society is still low. Clearly we do not as yet have sufficient longitudinal data to claim the bean-pole or vertical family as the common norm in Western industrialized societies.

Table 1.1 Multigenerational families by age, in percentages

	18-24	25-44	45-64	65+	Total
One generation	0.6	5.6	9.3	15.9	7.4
Two generation – Youngest	27.4	52.1	8.3	1.2	29.1
Two generation – Oldest	0.1	2.6	41.9	31.7	17.4
Three generation – Youngest	69.7	28.5	0.3	0.1	22.3
Three generation – Middle	0.6	9.4	29.1	1.9	12.7
Three generation – Oldest	0.0	0.1	7.3	46.8	8.7
Four generation	1.6	1.8	3.7	2.4	2.4

Absolute number of respondents 10,131.

Source: International Social Survey Program (ISSP) covering the US, Australia, Austria, West Germany, Great Britain, Hungary and Italy; adapted from Farkas and Hogan, 1995.

Impact of These Changes for Kin Care and Support

Early work on ageing and the family predicted that increasing longevity equalled increasing older people requiring care. At the same time, declining fertility was perceived as shrinking the reservoir of family care for the old, and placing increasing pressures on the middle-aged coping both with dependent children and ageing parents. The complexity of the equation is now clearer. In addition, there has been a recognition that the environments, which were producing ageing societies were also producing new family situations, and that the demise or shrinking of the family was too general a concept; rather more heterogeneous family forms were emerging. Despite the growth in individual household living and individualistic values, many Western families remain committed to care for and support their parents, cross-kin and children/grandchildren. Those defined as closest to the care recipient, are most likely to provide maximum support, typically spouse or child, most likely daughter. Work by Harper and Lund (1990), for example, suggests that family structure, (including number and proximity of children) and cultural values, (which determine the kin relationship, gender, or numerical positioning of the selected child), are primary variables in many societies. These are followed by family history and personal influences. Intergenerational transfer of care and services are thus both age- and gender-related. However, while these transfers generally flow from older to younger generations, they decline during the life course, and transfers from younger to older generations increase and dominate, though our understanding of the transfers from grandparents to children and grandchildren is still not well understood in the European context. These care relationships are clearly heavily dependent on the health and economic resources, commitments and life stages of the individuals, and increasingly on changing family structure and networks, and whether this is wholly or partially a reconstituted kin network, including a complex pattern of biological and step-relationships. Yet, as we have discussed, the changes in marital experiences suggest that elderly people in the future will be reliant on networks with highly divergent levels of connectedness and commitment to each other. Henretta (2001), for example, has drawn on data from the US Health and Retirement Survey to illustrate how the context of kin care giving in the US includes both changing mortality, fertility and marriage patterns that shape the size, age structure and kin connections of families.

In order to achieve full understanding of the implications of these demographic changes we must also take into account a broad range of historical, cultural and cohort factors (cf. Hammarström in Chapter 3). At one end of the spectrum, families are organized into corporate descent groups through clans and lineages, with individuals gaining access to resources by virtue of being born into the lineage, and the extended family providing both material and emotional support. The nuclear family lies at the other extreme, with kin operating as individuals living independently within a family group, seeking both economic and emotional security from others beyond that group. Most Western industrial societies tend to support nuclear-style families. As Keith (1995) points out, this can be problematic in later life, as the ideal of the nuclear makes living in an independent household an indicator of full adult status, something which young people strive for and older people resist giving up. This results in problematic re-entry into an extended family household on widowhood or increasing frailty. Viewed from a temporal perspective, there has long been both evidence that this shift from extended to nuclear family occurred as part of the emergence of modern societies. However it is important here to distinguish between the individual or family as a social and economic unit, and the individual of family as a focus of life-course transitions. As Hareven's (1982) detailed analysis of New England families at the turn of the 19/20th centuries explores, economic insecurity dictated that kin support was the only constant, and therefore individual choices were subsumed by necessity to family needs. Hareven's work in the US, and Laslett's (1973) in the UK have also indicated limited evidence that extended kin actually cared for older relatives, the adult child being accepted as the primary caregiver of the parent. Clearly history, culture and cohort interact to add another dimension to our understanding.

To explore this in more detail I should like to revisit more closely the work of the American historian Hareven. Her work on New England families (among others Hareven 1978, 1982) highlights the considerable diversity in cultural obligations to family members, and that these family obligations change over time. Following a life course and historical perspective, she argues that we need to unravel the three connected times in an individual life; *historical time* – historical circumstances such as migration, war, social and cultural change, economic collapse or boom; *individual time* – an individual's timetable of life transitions such as marriage, childbearing and retirement; and *family time* – the manner in which the individual timetables of family members are woven together to optimize family circumstances. Hareven's key study, based on life history interviews with two cohorts of New England children who were born between 1910-19 and 1920-29 reveals how both of these cohorts were to some degree transitional between a milieu of deep involvement with extended kin, reinforced by strong family orientated values, and the more individualistic ways of life and values that emerged after World War II. Yet neither cohort was free from the complexities of caring for elderly parents; the older cohort accepted their lot with resignation, the younger cohort with guilt. This work clearly highlights the complexity of decisions regarding the needs of family members. These are not only set obligations and responsibilities defined by cultural norms, but are also based on individual judgements which take into account both personal needs and resources, as well as those of other family members. In addition, Hareven provides a method of understanding how inter- and intra-generational mutual support develops over a person's lifetime, and how these are shaped by historical circumstances. Exploration of experiences across the life course thus enables us to consider patterns of support achieved in old age in the light of the social, economic and cultural conditions that the respective cohorts encountered over their lives.

The Emergence of Mass Retirement

The second broad area I wish to discuss is the historically unprecedented spread of mass retirement at a broadly fixed chronological age. In most Western industrial countries modern mass retirement began in the 20th century to cope with specific health and socio-economic needs of the then older population, and in response to the changing administrative and personnel management demands of growing corporations (Harper, 1988; Harper and Thane, 1989). Indeed the acceptance of mass retirement for all at increasingly earlier ages in order to carry out a fulfilled leisure and consumption based healthy period of late life is historically very new with current retirement expectations emerging in the post-1960s. As late as the 1950s in the UK, there was a widespread public perception that abrupt retirement was detrimental for male health, supported by some rather inconclusive health and medical research. Such labour market withdrawal at state pension age has been extended over the last 30 years through the spread of early retirement. For example, in the UK one-third of those aged between 50 and state pension age do not work with the proportion of men of this age (50-64) who are not working doubling in the last 20 years (cf. Macnicol in Chapter 2). This decline in male economic activity has occurred in all Western industrial countries, as indicated by the eleven nation study directed by Gruber and Wise (2000), with most countries seeing a percentage

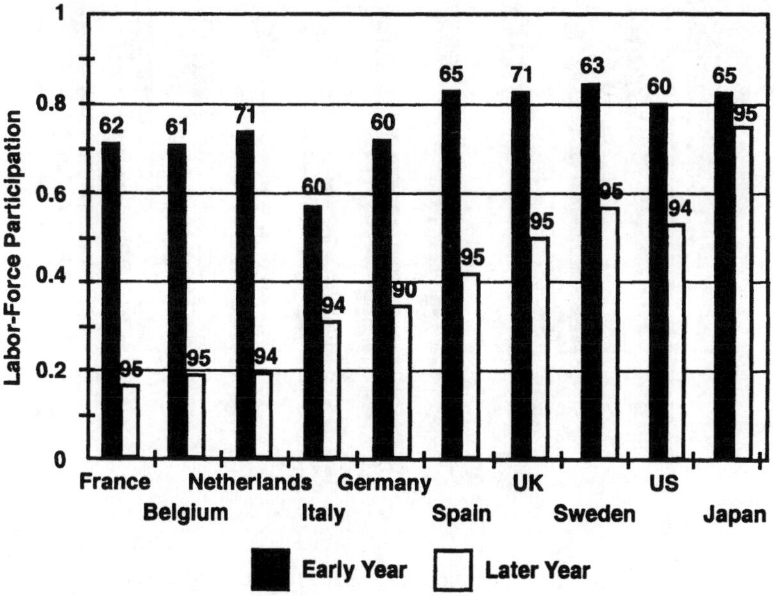

Figure 1.2 Decline in labour force participation

Source: Gruber and Wise, 2000.

fall over the past 30 years (Figure 1.2). Indeed each successive cohort of older men has lower employment rates than the preceding generation.

This has led to considerable concern over the human resource waste, both in terms of unused productive capacity and a perceived increasing skills shortage. Alongside this run economic concerns, both for older people as individuals, with research consistently indicating a relationship between poverty in old age and withdrawal from economic activity (Johnson and Stears, 1996; Bardasi et al., 2000), and also at the national level, with regard to the question of whether nations can afford to support increasing numbers of older people as a growing proportion of their population. For example, by 2030 all G7 countries, with the exception of the UK, will face dramatically raised tax burdens or large budget short falls. Indeed, Börsch-Supan (1998) estimate that Germany will require an increase in social security contributions from 21 per cent to 34 per cent by 2035, in addition to increasing contributions to mandatory health and long-term care insurance, an increase which, they argue, is politically unsustainable. Similarly projections by the OECD (Roseveare, 1996) suggest that France will have to double the proportion of national income to cope with its ageing population over the next couple of decades.

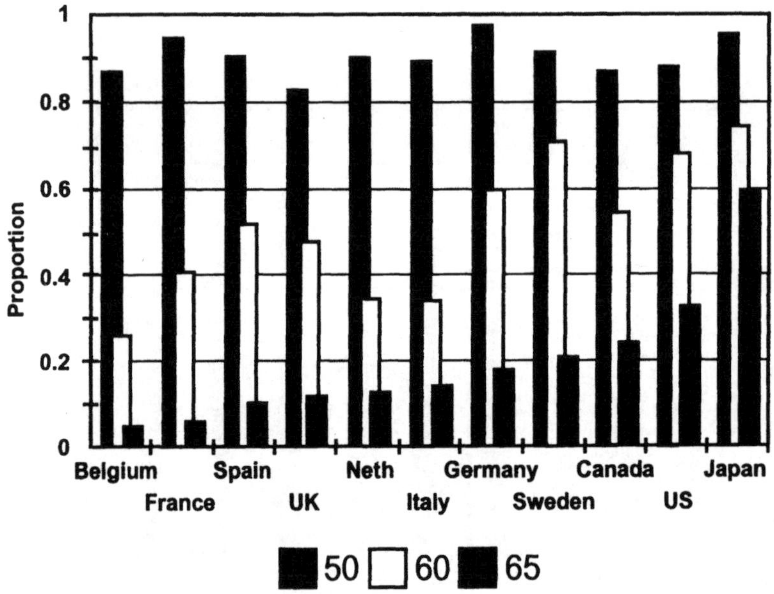

Figure 1.3 Current labour-force participation by country and age

Source: Gruber and Wise, 2000.

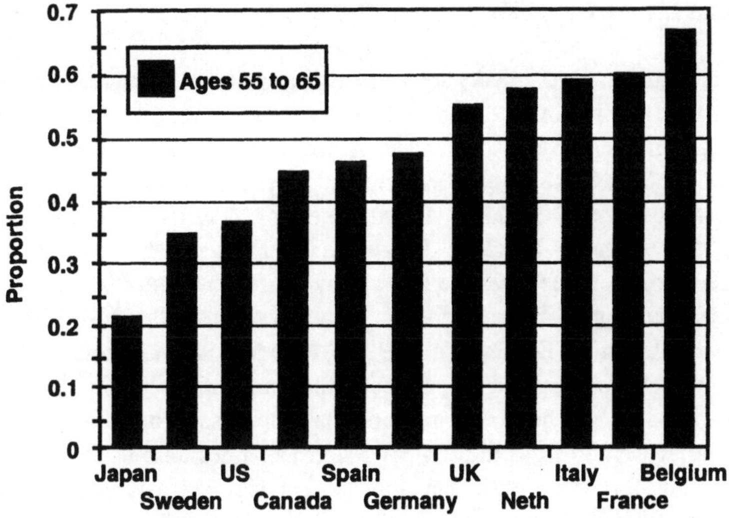

Figure 1.4 Unused productive capacity in eleven industrialized nations

Source: Gruber and Wise, 2000.

Gruber and Wise (2000) use a measure of forgone productive capacity. Drawing on national data of current labour force participation at ages 50, 60 and 65, they estimate the measure *unused productive capacity*, this being the proportion of men not working at a given age, i.e. 1 – LFP where LFP is the labour force participation. As described by Figure 1.3, this ranges from 0.95 in Belgium to 0.4 in Japan. Summing up unused capacity over all ages in some range, the area above the LFP curve in that range is calculated. When divided by the total area above and below the curve for that age interval, and multiplied by 100, a rough measure of unused capacity over the age interval, as a percentage of the total labour capacity in that range is produced. This is then plotted for the 55 to 65 age group. As is clear from Figure 1.4, the unused capacity varies significantly between developed countries, ranging from some 67 per cent in Belgium to 22 per cent in Japan.

There appear to be three broad forces driving this phenomenon. Firstly, there exists within most national pension systems incentives to retire early. Secondly, recent structural, sectional and technological changes within the work environment and labour market have encouraged employees to withdraw from work. In addition, there is evidence that employers retain ageist attitudes towards older workers (cf. Macnicol in Chapter 2). Finally, attitudes and expectations, and the growth of leisure and consumption have created a conducive peer environment to retire while still physically and mentally active without apparent loss of self-esteem.

Retirement Incentives within Current Pension Plans

The broad argument presented here is that state pension plans can have a very significant role to play in determining the modal age at retirement and in encouraging early retirement. State social security provision in some countries may offer considerable incentives to early retirement and may account for a significant part of the long-term decline in economic activity rates for older men. In many European countries, for example, Belgium, Italy and the Netherlands disability and unemployment programmes have provided early retirement benefits well before the official retirement age (Gruber and Wise, 2000; Kapteyn and de Vos, 1998).

A variety of studies (Disney et al., 1998; Mitchell, 1988; Luzadis and Mitchell, 1991) have also demonstrated that the retirement incentives within occupation or employee-based plans, and private pension plans are also strong and may go some way explaining some of the differential retirement rates among the occupational groupings. Furthermore, while pensions and social security systems provide incentives for the population at large to retire, different occupational groups have access to different types of provision and thus are affected in different ways. This has thus led some to argue that professional, managerial workers are pulled out of the labour force by economic incentives and enhanced opportunities for leisure and consumption, whereas those in skilled and unskilled occupations are pushed via untenable working conditions and employer attitudes.

Changes in Labour Markets and Working Environments

Another causal factor is that economic, industrial and organizational changes within both the public and private sectors have provided the circumstances for the decline in labour force participation among older people. Within the public sector, the privatization of utilities and the introduction of compulsory competitive tendering have altered employment practices, in particular threatening the opportunities for over 50s (Burgess and Rees, 1997). Similarly within the private sector, the globalization of markets and the resultant increased competition has led to workforce reduction, which has particularly affected older workers, with some studies indicating that older workers are targeted for early retirement or redundancy packages (Leppel and Clain, 1995; Arrowsmith and McGoldrick, 1996) supported by evidence that, once unemployed, older workers find it disproportionately less likely to find new work.

Finally, there is the debate over the impact of technological change. While many argue that the requirement for new skills, particularly abilities in information and communication technologies increasingly exclude older workers, especially men (Briscoe and Wilson, 1991), others propose that technological innovation and flexible working patterns will increase opportunities for older workers (Casey, Metcalf and Millward, 1997), allowing them the possibilities of post-career employment (Arrowsmith and McGoldrick, 1996). I suggest that the inherent training component of new technological labour means that future cohorts of older workers will be used in continual training and skills updating.

There is also evidence that this early withdrawal from the labour market is both directly and indirectly encouraged through age discrimination by employers (McKay and Middleton, 1998; Lumsdaine, 1996; Scales and Scase, 2000), and that *push factors*, such as redundancy or fixed retirement ages, are responsible for a large percentage of early retirements. There are clearly two questions here: are these negative attitudes supported by any firm evidence? And, regardless of the answer to this, do such perceptions influence how employers treat older workers? In answer to the first question, little practical evidence supports the view that those over 50 are consistently less able to perform modern economic activity than those who are younger. Such simple associational analysis, however, is likely to be reflecting proxies for more fundamental issues within the workplace. Walker and Taylor's (1998) contention that employers are ageist, is too simple a contention, and hides multiple complexities. As Casey et al. (1992) has argued, with long-term contracts the wages of some older workers may simply exceed their marginal productivity, and it may be considered more cost-effective for the organization to dismiss them. A similar argument may be made regarding the American *Age Discrimination in Employment Act*, 1967, which from 1986 allowed no upper limit on employment. It has been problematic because it was based on the notion of stereotypical age discrimination as the driver behind employer motivated retirement, and not on the relationship between wages and age. In addition, employers may also be making moral judgements, such as that it is preferable for those without young dependants to face redundancy. Or we can return to the argument promulgated by Hannah (1986), that large companies in particular desire to manage the retirement process in order to control their own internal labour markets.

Evolving Expectations of Workers

Europe has currently such a paucity of late life longitudinal data that the question of whether the increase in life expectancy has been accompanied by equivalent increases in disability-free life expectancy cannot yet be concluded, though US indications are promising. However, as earlier discussed, recent UK ONS-data does indicate that for men, the ratio of disability-free life to total life expectancy is increasing. Average life expectancy for UK men aged 65 now stands at 80, with disability-free life expectancy reaching 79 (ONS, 1999), a near 3-year increase over 15 years. Given that disability benefits are commonly used as a source of pre-retirement age income for the over 50s, it may be argued that increases in disability are driving late life employment withdrawal. While heavy manual labour has decreased, mental stress has grown over the last few decades. Yet early studies by, for example, Walker (1985), which stressed the importance of ill-health as a factor in retirement, have been criticized for their definitions of health. In particular, as Casey (1998) has pointed out, respondents giving retrospective answers may offer ill-health as a socially acceptable reason for retirement. Beyond the definitional struggle, it would seem that the contention produced by Maule (1996) is sound, that health may be best regarded as a dichotomous – conditioning – variable. If someone suffers ill-health this can be a major factor influencing their decision to retire. If not, health status probably does not enter the equation. Given this, a broadly generalized conclusion is that there does seem to be consistent evidence that between one fifth and one quarter of retirements prior to the age of 65 can be assigned to the category of being promoted by 'ill-health' (Maule, 1996).

Then there is evidence that the current older cohorts have internalized the notion of retirement, including early retirement, as an extended period of funded leisure and consumption and post-economic activity, and expectations of this are considerably entrenched (Scales and Scase, 2000). Such expectations are now strongly held, not only by the employee, but also by his or her partner and wider family. Henretta, O'Rand and Chan (1993), reported that male retirement was nearly twice as likely if the spouse had retired. This suggests that social factors are also significant at the individual level of choice. While it might appear counter-intuitive, given that on economic grounds one spouse might be more able to retire if the other was still working, clearly couples in this study were perceiving retirement as a time of leisure, in which they could carry out jointly shared activities. This is compounded by the growing responsibilities that many of these cohorts have for kin care and support, especially for their parents (Anderson, 2001; Kodz, Kersley, and Bates, 1999). Again, we need further research here into the role such commitments play on the decision to withdraw from economic activity, particularly for men. Finally, the understanding of the interaction of all of these factors with health status and disability at older ages is at present limited, though this may account for more than a third of early retirements (Smith, 2000).

It is, however, a complex story, in that it is clear that different groups are choosing, or not choosing, to withdraw from economic activity for a range of reasons. There is now considerable evidence that those taking early retirement thus include two distinct groups (Quinn et al., 1998; Uccello and Rix, 1998; Ozawa and Wai-On Law, 1992; Mutran, Reitzes and Fernandez, 1997). Professional and managerial workers, with high levels of education, and secure well-funded pension plans have a higher-than-average likelihood of withdrawing from economic activity before the age of 65, especially if their pension plan includes a defined benefit component. This may be tempered by a restraining factor of high enjoyment of work, but also encouraged by increasing levels of stress in these high level occupations. A second group of early retirees comprise those with low levels of education, and manual or semi-skilled occupations, who may be being encouraged or forced to take early retirement through employer instigated redundancy schemes. These may be involuntary or nominally voluntarily but set in a context of discriminatory and uncomfortable working conditions. Maule et al. (1996), for example, distinguish between salaried and hourly paid employees, suggesting that those who are hourly paid are more likely to take involuntary retirement due to push factors – negative aspects of current job and ill-health – while those who are salaried are more likely to choose retirement voluntarily due to pull factors – positive potential of new career, jobs, activities.

The Notion of Retirement

As Costa (2000) has demonstrated, there was a steady withdrawal from employment at earlier ages throughout the 20th century. However it is necessary conceptually to separate the retirement growth of the period before the 1960s, which was primarily based on health and welfare issues and the growth of state support of older people in the form of pensions; from that post-1960 which was more the result of private pensions, a desire for leisure, good health in late life and a leisure-based expectation of retirement. Within the wider national contexts of a general rise in income and the growth of consumption and leisure across the industrialized world, the improvement in late life health status, and the spread of private pensions and the occupational pensions encouraged the growth of late life consumption and leisure activities. The notion of retirement thus moved from one of *rest* in the 1950s and 1960s through *reward* in the 1970s to a *right* by the 1980s. Thus the health and welfare framework which operated in the first half of the century has now been replaced by a different context, which is primarily driven by an economic paradigm: the increasing level of pension provision due to the introduction of occupational and private schemes, the increasing opportunities to purchase leisure goods appropriate to late life, and the market pressure on employers which lead to rationalization of the workforce with detrimental effects on older employees.

What is clear, however, is that the attitudes and experiences of older people today will not necessarily remain unchanged in the future. Younger cohorts, currently in early and mid-life, will have very different labour market and health experiences. They are already growing accustomed to a less rigid labour market (Gallie et al., 1998) with greater access to part-time and flexible working patterns, and the need for continual skills updating and retraining. These individuals may have different aspirations in later life, and the financial incentives and disincentives for economic employment will undoubtedly have changed. Alongside this is the growing evidence, mainly from the US (Manton and Land, 2000) that these cohorts are healthier, and that this cohort effect is likely to continue into old age. The economic and social attitudes towards late life employment and retirement are thus likely to be different, possibly very different, for these younger cohorts who are approaching late life work and retirement decisions over the next three decades.

In Conclusion

As we approach the historically unprecendented population pyramids of the early to mid 21st century, it is clear that we need to shift our focus of interest away from late life and older people per se. Population ageing will affect us all. For the majority of us in the Western World who were born last century, this will comprise membership of a very large extended cohort who will experience much of their lives within a demographically mature society, with the challenges and opportunities that this will bring. Those born in the first half of this century will probably follow-through at the end of this, and those who follow, experience the emergence of balance demographic profiles, with approximately 20 per cent of the population in each of the five 20 year age quintiles between birth and 100. In addition, dramatic advances in medical technology and drug therapy may mean that chronological age will increasingly become irrelevant for many physical and mental health status transitions. It is of growing importance that chronological age thus also becomes increasingly irrelevant for most socio-economic transitions. Over a lifetime we pass through physical, mental and social life transitions. The medical, health, economic, social and environmental advances that have enabled the lengthening of this life span are also able to support the change of emphasis from chronological age to life transitions as a marker of that lifetime.

Notes

1 Ratio of the number of divorces to the mean population.
2 Mean number of divorces per 100 marriages.
3 Within all industrialized Western countries, those registered within manual and semi-skilled socio-economic groups generally marry earlier than those in professional and managerial occupations, see Waite, 2000.

References

Age Discrimination in Employment Act (1967), Public Law (PL) 90-202, Washington D.C.

Anderson, R. (2001), 'Working Careers', in S. Harper (ed.), *The Family in an Ageing Society*, Oxford University Press, Oxford.

Arrowsmith, J. and McGoldrick, A. (1996), *Breaking the Barriers: A Survey of Managers' Attitudes to Age and Employment*, Institute of Management, London.

Bardasi, E., Jenkins, S. and Rigg, J.A. (2000), *Retirement and the Economic Well-Being of the Elderly: A British Perspective*, Institute for Social and Economic Research, University of Essex, Colchester.

Bengtson, V.L. (1995), 'Six Controversies in Current Research on Adult Intergenerational Relationships', in V.L. Bengtson, K.W. Schaie and L.M. Burton (eds.), *Adult Intergenerational Relations: Effects of Societal Change*, Springer, New York, pp. 333-35.

Bengtson, V.L. and Dannefer, D. (1987), 'Families, Work and Aging: Implications of Disordered Cohort Flow for the 21st Century', in R.A. Ward and S.S. Tobin (eds.), *Health in Aging: Sociological Issues and Policy Directions*, Springer, New York, pp. 256-289.

Bengtson, V.L. and Harootyan, R. (eds.) (1994), *Intergenerational Linkages; Hidden Connections in American Society*, Springer, New York.

Bengtson, V.L., Rosenthal, C. and Burton, L. (1990), 'Families and Ageing: Diversity and Heterogeneity', in R.H. Binstock and L.K. George (eds.), *Handbook of Aging and the Social Sciences*, 3rd ed., Academic Press, San Diego, pp. 263-87.

Bornat, J., Dimmock, B., Jones, D. and Pearce, S. (1999), 'Stepfamilies and Older People: Evaluating the Implications of Family Change for an Ageing Population' *Ageing and Society*, Vol. 19, pp. 239-261.

Börsch-Supan, A. (1998), *Incentive Effects of Social Security on Labour Force Participation: Evidence in Germany and Across Europe*, National Bureau of Economic Research, Working Paper w6780.

Burgess, S.M., Pacelli, L. and Rees, H. (1997), *Job Tenure and Labour Market Regulation: a Comparison of Britain and Italy Using Micro Data*, CERP Discussion Paper no 1712, Centre for Economic Policy Research, London.

Casey, B. (1998), *Incentives and Disincentives to Early and Late Retirement*, Working Paper AWP3.3, OECD, Paris.

Casey, B., Lakey, J. and White, M.R.M. (1992), *Payment Systems: A Look at Current Practice*, England Employment Department, Sheffield.

Casey, B., Metcalf, H. and Millward, N. (1997), *Employers' Use of Flexible Labour*, Policy Studies Institute, London.

Costa, D.L. (2000), 'Understanding the Twentieth-Century Decline in Chronic Conditions among Older Men (in Chronic Conditions and Older Populations)', *Demography*, Vol. 37 (1), pp. 53-72.

Delphy, C. and Leonard, D. (1992), *Familiar Exploitation: A New Analysis of Marriage in Contemporary Western Societies*, Polity Press, Cambridge.

Dimmock, B., Bornat, J., Peace, S. and Jones, D. (2001), 'Intergenerational Relationships among UK Stepfamilies', in S. Harper (ed.), *The Family in an Ageing Society*, Oxford University Press, Oxford.

Disney, R., Mira d'Ercole, M. and Scherer, P. (1998), *Resources during Retirement*, Working Paper AWP4.3, OECD, Paris.

Ermisch, J. and Franceseconi, M. (1996), *Partnership Formation and Dissolution in Great Britain*, WP 96-10, ESRC Research Centre on Micro-Social Change, Institute for Social and Economic Research, University of Essex, Colchester.

Ermisch, J. and Franceseconi, M. (1998), *Cohabitation in Great Britain: Not for Long but Here to Stay*. WP 98-1, ESRC Research Centre on Micro-Social Change, Institute for Social and Economic Research, University of Essex, Colchester.

Farkas, J. and Hogan, D. (1995), 'The Demography of Intergenerational Relationships', in V.L. Bengtson, K. Schaie and L. Burton (eds.), *Adult Intergenerational Relations*, Springer, New York.

Finch, J. (2003), 'Inheritance and Intergenerational Relationships in English Families', in S. Harper, (2003b) (ed.), *Families in Ageing Societies*, Oxford University Press, Oxford.

Finch, J. and Wallis, L. (1994), 'Inheritance, Care Bargains and Elderly People's Relationships with Their Children', in D. Challis, B. Davies and K. Traske (eds.), *Community Care: New Agendas and Challenges from the UK and Overseas*, Arena, Aldershot, pp. 110-20.

Gallie, D., White, M., Cheng, Y. and Tomlinson, M. (1998), *Restructuring the Employment Relationship*, Oxford University Press, Oxford.

Goldman, N. (1986), 'Effects of Mortality Levels on Kinship', in *Consequences of Mortality Trends and Differentials*, United Nations, New York.

Gove, W.R. (1973), 'Sex, Marital Status, and Mortality', *American Journal of Sociology*, Vol. 79 (1), pp. 45-67.

Gruber, J. and Wise, D. (2000), 'Social Security and Declining Labour-Force Participation: Here and Abroad: Social Security and Retirement: An International Comparison', *The American Economic Review*, Vol. 88 (2), pp. 158-163.

Grundy, E. (1999), 'Intergenerational Perspectives on Family and Household Change in Mid- and Later Life in England and Wales', in S. McRae (ed.), *Changing Britain: Families and Households in the 1990s*, Oxford University Press, Oxford.

Hagestad, G.O. (1986), 'The Family: Women and Grandparents as Kin-Keepers', in A. Pifer and L. Bronte (eds.), *Our Ageing Society: Paradox and Promise*, W.W. Norton and Company, New York, pp. 141-161.

Hagestad, G.O. (1988), 'Demographic Change and the Life Course: Some Emerging Trends in the Family Realm', *Family Relations*, Vol. 37 (4), pp. 405-410.

Hannah, L. (1986), *Inventing Retirement: The Development of Occupational Pensions in Britain*, Cambridge University Press, Cambridge.

Hareven, T. (1978), 'The Dynamics of Kin in an Industrialised Community', in J. Demos and S. Boocock (eds.), *Turning Points: Historical and Sociological Essays on the Family*, University of Chicago Press, Chicago.

Hareven, T. (1982), *Industrial Time and Family Time*, Cambridge University Press, Cambridge.

Harper, S. (1988), 'The Impact of the Retirement Debate on the Emergence of Retirement', in M. Bury, *Social and Economic Change in Britain*, Royal Holloway.

Harper, S. (1990), 'The Emergence and Consolidation of the Retirement Tradition in Post-War Britain', in M. Bury and J. Macnicol, *Aspects of Ageing and Social Policy*, 12-29 RHBNC.

Harper, S. (2003a), *Ageing Societies*, Arnold, London.

Harper, S. (ed.) (2003b), *Families in Ageing Societies*, Oxford University Press, Oxford.

Harper, S. and Lund, D. (1990), 'Wives, Husbands and Daughters Caring for Institutionalised and Non-Institutionalised Dementia Patients', *International Journal of Aging and Human Development*, Vol. 30 (4), pp. 241-62.

Harper, S. and Thane, P. (1989), 'The Social Construction of Old Age', in M. Jeffreys, *Growing Older*, Routledge, London.

Haskey, J. (1992), 'Pre-Marital Cohabitation and the Probability of Subsequent Divorce', *Population Trends*, 68, pp. 10-19.

Henretta, J. (2001), 'The Availability of Children to Provide Support in Later Life' in S. Harper (ed.), *The Family in an Ageing Society*, Oxford University Press, Oxford.

Henretta, J.C., O'Rand, A.M. and Chan, C.G. (1993), 'Joint Role Investments and Synchronization of Retirement: A Sequential Approach to Couples' Retirement Timing' *Social Forces*, Vol. 71 (4), pp. 981-1000.

Hu, Y. and Goldman, N. (1990), 'Mortality Differentials by Marital Status: An International Comparison (in Mortality)', *Demography*, Vol. 27 (2), pp. 233-250.

Hughes, M.E. and Waite, L.J. (2000), *Health in Household Context: Living Arrangements and Health Trajectories Among Black, White and Hispanic Adults*, Paper presented at Meetings of the Population Association of America, New York.

Hyman, H.H. (1983), Of Time and Widowhood: Nationwide Studies of Enduring Effects, Duke University Press, Durham, N.C.

Johnson, P. and Stears, G. (1996), *Why Are Older Pensioners Poorer?*, Institute for Fiscal Studies, London.

Kapteyn, A. and De Vos, K.D. (1998), 'Social Security and Labour-Force Participation in the Netherlands (in Social Security and Declining Labor-Force Participation: Here and Abroad)', *The American Economic Review*, (Papers and Proceedings of the Hundred and Tenth Annual Meeting of the American Economic Association, (May, 1998), Vol. 88 (2), pp. 164-167.

Keith, C. (1995), 'Family Caregiving Systems: Models, Resources, and Values C', *Journal of Marriage and the Family*, Vol. 57 (1), pp. 179-189.

Kiernan, K. (2000), 'European Perspectives on Union Formation' in L. Waite, C. Bachrach, M. Hindin, E. Thompson and A. Thorton (eds.), *The Ties that Bind: Perspectives on Marriage and Cohabitation*, Aldine and de Gruyter, New York.

Kodz, J., Kersley, B. and Bates, P. (1999), *The Fifties Revival*, IES Report 359, Institute for Employment Studies, Brighton.

Laslett, B. (1973), 'The Family as a Public and Private Institution: An Historical Perspective', *Journal of Marriage and the Family*, Special Section: New Social History of the Family, Vol. 35 (3), pp. 480-492.

Leppel, K. and Clain, S.H. (1995), 'The Effect of Increases in the Level of Unemployment on Older Workers', *Applied Economics*, 27 (10), pp. 901-06.

Lumsdaine, R. (1996), 'Factors Affecting Labour Supply Decisions and Retirement Income', in E. Hanushek and N. Maritato, (eds.), *Assessing Knowledge of Retirement Behaviour*, National Academy Press, Washington D.C.

Luzadis, R.A. and Mitchell, O.S. (1991), 'Explaining Pension Dynamics', *The Journal of Human Resources*, Vol. 26 (4), pp. 679-703.

Manton, K.G. and Land, K.C. (2000), 'Active Life Expectancy Estimates for the U.S. Elderly Population: A Multidimensional Continuous-Mixture Model of Functional Change Applied to Completed Cohorts, 1982-1996', *Demography*, Vol. 37 (3), pp. 253-265.

Maule, A.J., Cliff, D.R. and Taylor, R. (1996), 'Early retirement decisions and how they affect later quality of life', *Ageing and Society*, Vol 16, pp. 177-204.

McKay, S. and Middleton, S. (1998), *Characteristics of Older Workers: Secondary Analysis of the Family and Working Lives*, DfEE Research Report 45.

McRea S. (1993), *Cohabiting Mothers: Changing Marriage and Motherhood*, London Policy Studies Institute, London.

Mitchell, O.S. (1988), 'Worker Knowledge of Pension Provision', *Journal of Labor Economics*, Vol. 6 (1), pp. 21-39.

Mutran, E.J., Reitzes, D.C. and Fernandez, M.E. (1997), 'Factors That Influence Attitudes Toward Retirement', *Research on Aging*, Vol.19 (3), pp. 251-273.

Nock, S. (1995), 'A Comparison of Marriages and Cohabiting Relationships', *Journal of Family Issues*, 16 (1), pp. 53-76.

ONS (1999), *Population Trends*, The Stationery Office, London.

Ozawa and Wai-On Law (1992), *Income Status of Older Women: A Briefing Paper for the National Eldercare Institute on Older Women*, George Warren Brown School of Social Work.

Popenoe, D. (1993), 'American Family Decline, 1960-1990: A Review and Appraisal', *Journal of Marrriage and the Family*, Vol. 55, pp. 527-542.

Quinn, J.F., Burkhauser, R., Cahill, K. and Weathers, R. (1998), *Microeconometric Analysis of the Retirement Decision: United States*, OECD Economics Department Working Papers 203, OECD Economics Department, Paris.

Roseveare, D. (1996), *Ageing Populations, Pension Systems and Government Budgets: Simulations for 20 OECD Countries*, OECD, Paris.

Scales, J. and Scase, R. (2000), *Fit and Fifty? A Report Prepared for the Economic and Social Research Council*, Economic and Social Research Council, Colchester.

Shanas, E. (1980), 'Health of Older People. A Social Survey', in *Growing Old*, New York.

Smith, A. (2000), *Age of Retirement and Longevity*, Government Actuaries Department Position Paper for Pensions – the Big Issues, Institute of Actuaries, London.

Soldo, B.J and Hill, M.S. (1995), 'Family Structure and Transfer Measures in the Health and Retirement Study', *Journal of Human Resources*, Vol. 30 (Suppl.), pp. S108-S137.

Uccello, C.E. and Rix, S.E. (1998), *Factors Influencing Retirement: Their Implications for Raising Retirement Age*, Public Policy Institute, AARP, Washington D.C.

Verbrugge, L.M. (1979), 'Marital Status and Health', *Journal of Marriage and the Family*, Vol. 41, pp. 267-285.

Waite, L.J. (1995), 'Does Marriage Matter?', *Demography*, Vol. 32, pp. 483-507.

Waite, L.J. (2000), 'The Family as a Social Organization: Key Ideas for the 21st Century', *Contemporary Sociology*, Vol. 29 (3), pp. 463-469.

Walker, A. (1985), *The Care Gap: How Can Local Authorities Meet the Needs of the Elderly?*, Local Government Information Unit, London.

Walker, A. and Taylor, P. (1998), *Combating Age Barriers in Employment – Examples of Good Practice*, Office for the Official Publications of the European Communities, Luxembourg.

Chapter 2

Analysing Age Discrimination

John Macnicol

Introduction

Since the Enlightenment, western societies have moved towards a firmer conception of individual rights. This process formed the basis of T.H. Marshall's celebrated account of the formation of welfare states in conjunction with the development of civil, legal and social rights, and it remains an attractive, if much-criticized, thesis (Marshall, 1963). The classic social democratic narrative of welfare development would argue that equality of individual rights has gradually been bestowed upon populations of western societies, such that complete equality under law is assumed to exist in theory, if not always in practice. However, the move towards stronger individual rights is also a product of the growth of competitive individualism in western societies. With the emergence of 'post-industrial' labour markets since the mid-1970s this tendency has become even more pronounced. Welfare states have become increasingly underpinned by a public-private partnership in the provision of services, and the prevailing expectation is that citizens must purchase their own welfare support through the private market, and must engage in paid labour in order to do so.

Today, social rights appear to have been confirmed by legislation against sex, race and disability discrimination. Yet ageism is often omitted from the catalogue of discriminations, and many passionate campaigners against ageism maintain that it remains the last great discrimination to be tackled. Arguably, age is the most virulent of discriminations, since it is the least acknowledged, and thus most likely to be accepted as 'normal' or 'inevitable'. Surely it ought to be possible to construct laws to make 'incitement to age hatred' a crime, just as 'incitement to race hatred' is a crime in Britain,[1] and to protect the employment rights of older workers? This chapter will explore some of the conceptual and practical difficulties that might make the attainment of such a goal problematic.

Ageism and Age Discrimination in Employment

As a starting-point, it is useful to distinguish between ageism in social relations and attitudes, and age discrimination in employment. The former was first defined by the eminent gerontologist Robert Butler as 'a process of systematic stereotyping and discrimination against people because they are old, just as racism and sexism accomplish this for skin colour and gender' (1995:35), and can be thought of as the application of assumed group characteristics to an individual, regardless of that individual's actual personal characteristics. Ageism permeates popular attitudes, and manifests itself in subtle ways, which are difficult to detect and eradicate. It may also occur at any point in the lifecourse. Thus the British pressure group Age Concern suggests that

> Age discrimination occurs when someone makes or sees a distinction because of another person's age and uses this as a basis for prejudice against and unfair treatment of that person. It is something that can affect everyone, regardless of their age. It is just as easy to discriminate against someone because they are too young as it is to say they are too old: both are equally pernicious. (Age Concern, 1998:4)

Much of the current concern is over age discrimination in employment against older men (since they are suffering more labour market problems than women), and therefore this chapter will focus more on men. However, it is important to remember that age discrimination can compound, or accelerate, race and sex discrimination. Hence Susan Sontag has pointed out that women suffer a 'double jeopardy' of ageing. Prevailing images of beauty and desirability tend to be those of young women; society is more tolerant of ageing in men, who are 'allowed' to age, where women are not (Sontag, 1978). And in the USA, it is well established that ethnic minority older women may suffer from 'multiple discrimination' or 'compounded discrimination' (United States Commission on Civil Rights, 1977:13).

By contrast, age discrimination in employment refers to those personnel and managerial policies that discriminate unfairly against employees, regardless of age, by assuming that they possess, at an individual level, the assumed characteristics of their age group. Most often, it occurs in hiring, firing, promotion, retraining and redundancy: one particular age group – say, all aged over fifty – may be targeted in workforce downsizing, or an older employee may be replaced by a younger one, merely on the basis of assumed workplace performance. In age discrimination in employment, crude 'age proxies' tend to be used where individualized testing for job competence would, it is argued, be fairer. The result is said to be both personally unjust and economically dysfunctional, by 'throwing out the good with the bad'.

Where does ageism originate? A variety of answers have been offered. Some suggest psychological explanations: ageism arises because of deep-rooted, subconscious fears of our own ageing, and our revulsion at the prospect of physical and mental decrepitude. Hence Butler declares that

> Age-ism reflects a deep seated uneasiness on the part of the young and middle-aged – a personal revulsion to and distaste for growing old, disease and disability; and fear of powerlessness, 'uselessness', and death. (Butler, 1969:243)

At the other end of the extreme are broadly economic explanations: modern capitalist economies have marginalized older people into enforced retirement, involving a lowering of economic and social status (Phillipson, 1982). Anti-ageism activists believe that legislation against ageism (enforced, say, by a Commission for Age Equality) could work, and could gradually change public opinion, like existing legislation against race and sex discrimination. They hold up the ideal of an 'age-blind' or 'age-neutral' society, in which citizens would be judged by the content of their character, rather than by their chronological age.

The case against ageism thus rests upon powerful social justice arguments. It appears an affront to the dignity and self-worth of an individual to categorize them merely on the basis of their age. As Erdman Palmore puts it,

> The democratic ideal is that each person should be judged on the basis of individual merit rather than on the basis of group characteristics such as race, sex and age. (Palmore, 1990:7)

Ageist assumptions are also inaccurate and misleading, since old people are as different from each other as are their fingerprints. Heterogeneity in health status, personality, cognitive ability and socio-economic position increases as individuals age; thus a random sample of seventy-year-olds contains a vast array of individual differences, far more than can be encapsulated by the blanket term 'old person'. Worse, ageism manifests itself in linguistic expressions of contempt that are commonplace in everyday life – terms like 'pensioner', 'old codger', 'old biddy', and so on – and in ageist jokes. Such language would be quite unacceptable today if applied to an ethnic minority.

Problems Inherent in Ageism

No reasonable person could but applaud any effort to mitigate the corrosive effects of ageism in social relations, and to help older workers. However, ageism does contain some inherent difficulties, which would make the designing of anti-discrimination legislation problematic. The ideal of an 'age-neutral' society may in practice be impossible to achieve, given that human beings inevitably use age divisions to make sense of the world. 'Age-appropriate' behaviours are widely accepted and internalized, and many age restrictions are unquestioningly accepted as rational and sensible. These would include: minimum ages for obtaining a driver's licence, for consensual sexual intercourse, attending 'adult' films, or drinking alcohol; age-based tax reliefs; juvenile justice systems; age-based school curricula; concentrated screening for certain diseases, such as breast cancer, on particularly susceptible age groups; and so on (Schuck, 1980:82). The distinguished social gerontologist, Bernice Neugarten, has thoughtfully explored this problem in a number of publications: she argues that expectations regarding age-appropriate behaviours form an elaborated and pervasive system of norms governing behaviour and interaction, a network of expectations that is embedded throughout the cultural fabric of adult life.

All of us, she maintains, live according to 'social clocks' that govern our behaviour across the lifecourse (Neugarten, 1996:24, 60).

Another difficulty is that social policy in most advanced industrial societies involves a subtle balance of positive *and* negative age discriminations (Palmore, 1990:7). Modern social security and health care systems spend a disproportionate amount of resources on those aged 65+: in Britain, for example, retirees consume fully one-half of the entire social security budget, and social security makes up one-third of total government expenditure; the proportion of total National Health Service resources devoted to those aged 65+ rose from 20 per cent in 1951-2 to nearly 50 per cent in 1988 (Appleby, 1992:64). Yet there are persistent – and justified – allegations of negative discrimination against older people in health care.[2] A real difficulty is whether such positive discriminations by age would be permissible in a truly 'age-neutral' society.

Many campaigners view ageism as akin to sexism and racism. However, it has been suggested that it is in fact fundamentally different, and would thus be difficult to combat with legislation. The oft-repeated truism is that we all grow old, but we will not all become black or female. Hence in civil rights legal cases in the USA, race has been defined as an 'immutable characteristic', whereas age is a 'continuous variable' (O'Meara, 1989:93). However, if age discrimination can operate at any point in the life course, and by any age group against any other, defining the 'protected' group in civil rights legislation would be very difficult. (For such legislation to work successfully there must be a plaintiff and a defendant.) Again, ageism does not have the same tragic historical legacy as slavery, and thus has not been the focus of freedom marches, sit-ins, civil disobedience protests, and so on. Hence the US Supreme Court ruled in 1976 that, unlike race or sex discrimination, older people had not suffered a history of 'purposeful unequal treatment' (Eglit, 1981:884). Nor is it the case (as, say, with women one hundred and fifty years ago) that at some point in history old people suffered second-class legal status. It is thus more difficult to construct philosophical doctrines of recompense in favour of one particular group, upon whom harm was once inflicted.

It would be fair to say that the philosophical implications of ageism and age discrimination have hitherto not been explored with much sophistication in Britain, despite some interesting studies.[3] However, one philosophical conundrum has been explored by the moral philosopher Norman Daniels. Deploying a cross-sectional view of society, argues Daniels, it does indeed seem that the old suffer negative discrimination in certain policy areas (such as age-based rationing of health care) and in cultural values. But this perspective is based upon a 'synchronic' or 'time-slice' view of society, in which the moral claims of different age groups are pitted against each other at any one time. By contrast, a 'diachronic' or lifespan perspective views the old as the same persons as the young, but at a later stage in their lives. An old person may experience some negative discrimination when old, but this will be balanced by (presumably) having experienced positive discrimination when young (Daniels, 1988). There are, of course, some problems inherent in Daniels's view: for example, it seems merely an elegant version of those crude 'human capital' arguments that view the young as worthy of investment, but the old as unworthy. However, it is a valuable counter to the view that intergenerational justice could be easily achieved.

There has also been considerable debate over the question of whether age discrimination in employment is rational (deriving from age-based generalisations that are correct in the aggregate, even if there may be individual cases of injustice) or irrational (based upon 'false stereotypes', and perhaps deriving from subconscious and deeply-rooted prejudices that have little foundation in reality) (Levine, 1988). In most current discussions in Britain, the 'irrationality' model predominates. For example, a representative of employers' opinion has stated that age discrimination in employment

> does not generally occur as a result of deliberate malice or prejudice, but rather as a result of a quite complex set of different attitudes which combine to form an often unconscious but nevertheless potent exclusion of older people from opportunities in employment. (Worsley, 1996:80)

However, employers may have perfectly rational reasons for preferring a thirty-year-old over a sixty-year-old – notably, a longer working life expectancy. Alternatively, an employer may accurately perceive older workers to be less employable, not because of their diminished productivity, but because they possess outmoded skills compared with younger workers (Disney, 1999). Again, the age profile of a firm is likely to be attributable to factors other than discrimination per se: for example, newly established enterprises always have youthful age structures. This makes the application of the doctrine of 'adverse impact' – in which intent is deduced from outcome – highly problematic: in a case of sex discrimination, it would be convincing proof if a firm had never hired a woman; but a firm might have an extremely youthful age structure simply because it was new.

Finally, the labour market problems of older workers need to be considered. Throughout history, older men have experienced unemployment rates only slightly higher than younger men; but once unemployed, they remain out of work longer, and tend to become economically inactive 'discouraged workers'. Thus in late 1998, 13 per cent of unemployed men in Britain aged 16-49 had been unemployed for three years or more, compared with 43 per cent of those aged 60-4. As would be expected, economic activity rates fall with rising age: by the age of 60, only 58 per cent of men are employed, and only 34 per cent of those aged 64 (Office for National Statistics, 1999:25-30). By contrast, in the early 1950s some two-thirds of men reaching the pensionable age of 65 continued working. What we are witnessing is the slow spread of involuntary retirement down the age structure. This trend to male 'early' retirement actually commenced in Britain over one hundred years ago: the economic activity rates of men aged 60-4 began to fall in the 1880s, continued in the inter-war years (exacerbated by economic recession and industrial restructuring), stabilized in the 1950s and 1960s, and then fell precipitously from the early 1970s. Thus, 88.7 per cent of men aged 60-4 were classified by the census as economically active in 1921, 87.2 per cent in 1931, 87.5 per cent in 1951, and 91.0 per cent in 1961 (Clark, 1966:35). (No census took place in 1941, because of war.) However, the massive transformation of the British economy that has taken place since the early 1970s has involved the shedding of older labour. Thus by the mid-1990s only 76.1 per cent of men aged 55-9, and 51.2 per cent of men aged 60-4 were economically active. By the late 1990s, nearly one-third of British men aged 50-64 had no paid work. Many have been moved onto invalidity/incapacity benefits and face the prospect of never working again. (In the last thirty years, there has been a steady increase in apparent work-disability, with the numbers claiming invalidity or incapacity benefits rising threefold in the 20 years to 1998, reaching a total of about 1,750,000. The causes of this are complex, but rising levels economic inactivity clearly play an important part.) Older women, by contrast, have increased their levels of economic activity, consequent upon the growth of feminized jobs (many of them being part-time). Age discrimination may be a contributory factor in the decline of older men's employment, but it is minor compared with the effect of structural changes in the British economy. As a recent government publication rightly emphasises, age discrimination in employment 'is a complex issue', for which 'there is no simple solution': there is even now no clear evidence on how widespread the problem is (Department for Education and Employment, 1998:2, 6, 12).

Some commentators have viewed mandatory retirement as the institutionalisation of age discrimination. For example, Alan Walker suggests that 'retirement may be seen as an age discriminatory social process designed to exclude older people en masse from the workforce'(Walker, 1990:58). But we must bear in mind that there are many 'social justice' arguments in favour of mandatory retirement: it facilitates a just sharing-out of jobs; it removed blockages to promotion; it enables employers and employees to plan careers; it makes the design of pension schemes easier; it offers a rough-and-ready system of employment termination, without all the difficulties (and possible unfairness) of individualized testing; on an existential level, it forces human beings to accept the inevitability of ageing and death.

All these difficulties mean that constructing legislative action against ageism in social relations and age discrimination in employment is not straightforward. Further problems arise when one tries to establish what such legislation would achieve. These problems become evident when we look at the recent British debate, and the experience of legislation in the USA.

The Recent Revival of Interest in Britain

In the last ten years, there has been increasing interest shown by successive British governments in policies to combat age discrimination in employment. This began under John Major's Conservative administration (1990-7), and has continued under New Labour. The emphasis so far has been on persuasion, and a number of official reports have been published, culminating in the *Code of Practice: Age Diversity in Employment* (1999). Legislation is promised (in response to the European Directive on Equal Treatment) by the year 2006, and further measures will be forthcoming to persuade employers to retain and hire older workers. This has been accompanied by much upbeat, positive rhetoric that 'ability is ageless', 'grey is good' and so on (including the establishment of a Government website, *Age Positive*). Action against age discrimination has been placed firmly in the context of the Labour government's 'welfare-to-work' New Deal programme. The aim is to encourage economically inactive older workers back into the labour market, and much publicity has been given to the small number of 'success stories' where retail supermarkets have specifically employed older men, allegedly to great advantage.

Space does not permit a full analysis of the official justifications offered for this governmental initiative. It is sufficient to note that, at the moment, the age discrimination debate in Britain is intriguingly balanced between two opposed arguments. On the one hand, there is a powerful social justice case based upon the rights of older workers which is related to a wider debate over all forms of 'unjustified' discrimination. This case is argued by pressure groups working on behalf of older people, such as Age Concern. On the other, there are hard-nosed economic arguments derived from concerns over the supply of labour in the new economic conditions of postindustrial capitalism; these are being articulated by employers (most notably, by the Employers Forum on Age).

Why has there been a revival recently? The first point to note is that there has been a debate over age discrimination in employment for much of the twentieth century. For example, during the 1930s recession, British trades unionists frequently complained that, in the high-unemployment depressed areas, older workers aged 65+ receiving the old age pension were discriminated against by having their wages reduced by exactly the amount of the pension (which at that time carried no retirement condition) (Macnicol, 1998). In the early 1950s, there were considerable governmental efforts to encourage the postponement of retirement, against a background of fears over an ageing population and the need to maximize the supply of available labour. The reasoning was uncannily similar to the arguments of today: older people were healthier and fitter than ever before, at higher ages; a considerable proportion of them expressed the desire to continue working past retirement age; remunerative activity in old age was good for people's self-esteem and psychic well-being; demographic, labour-supply and other macroeconomic considerations necessitated as much postponement of retirement as possible. Remedial action seemed tantalisingly easy: more flexible retirement ages, the removal of compulsory, fixed-age retirement, alteration of occupational pension regulations, more enlightened personnel policies, and so on, to remove the 'unjustifiable' age barriers to employment. The 'prejudices' of employers and others were to be dispelled by a campaign to achieve a better understanding of the issues

(Ministry of Labour and National Service, 1955). However, these governmental initiatives achieved little.

The resurgence of interest in age discrimination in Britain has arisen from complex causes, but we can immediately identify two obvious ones. First, there is the problem of joblessness among men aged 50+, already referred to. There is growing governmental concern about the economic cost of supporting male 'early' retirement, in terms of social security expenditure, lost income tax revenue and a depleted workforce (Campbell, 1999). One estimate is that the cost to businesses amounts to around £16 billion per annum (Cabinet Office, 2000:30). But the human consequences are equally important: for many working-class men, enforced joblessness in one's fifties and sixties involves a traumatic loss of identity in a culture where work still defines one's social status.

The second reason is the anticipated ageing of the British population after the second decade of the twenty-first century, as the 'baby boomers' move into retirement, and the pension costs associated with this. Whereas in 1991, 15.8 per cent of the British population was aged 65+, this is projected to increase to 20.5 per cent by 2031 (a rise of roughly 30 per cent). It is easy to become over-alarmist, and lapse into crude demographic determinism: previous forty-year periods have seen faster increases, without being followed by economic catastrophe. For example, between 1911 and 1951 the rise was of the order of 100 per cent. However, the future ageing of the population has heightened concerns over the implications of lengthening chronological life but a shortening working life. Crude, age-based dependency ratios are misleading unless other factors (such as age-specific economic activity rates) are taken into account. But Britain undoubtedly faces a problem, as shown by the following official calculation:

Table 2.1 Number per 100 people of working age

	Child	*Old age*	*Overall*
1994	34	30	64
2021	28	30	58
2041	28	43	72
2061	29	44	73

Source: Tim Harris, 'Projections: a Look Into the Future', in Office for National Statistics, *Social Trends 27* (1997), p. 17.

However, these two very obvious factors must be considered in their economic and labour market context. The last thirty years have witnessed a major economic transformation of the British economy. There have been several inter-related changes in the structure of the labour market: a shift from manufacturing to service- and information-based jobs (exacerbated by the need to maintain competitiveness in the face of globalization); an increasing segmentation into highly-paid, technology-intensive 'core' employment on the one hand, and a hypercasualized periphery of insecure jobs on the other; and a growth of part-time and feminized jobs (in 1951 the ratio of full-time to part-time jobs in the British economy was 23:1; by 1996 it was 3:1).[4]

There has been much comment recently about the emergence of a new, reconfigured lifecourse in which childhood and education at one end, and retirement at the other, occupy an inexorably-lengthening proportion of chronological life, with the working life shrinking (Hancock, Jarvis and Mueller, 1995:36). Retirement may now span thirty to forty years. Is this sustainable? Can any remedial action be taken? Since the trend to male 'early' retirement is a long-run one, it is potentially a serious problem. However, a few cautionary notes need to be expressed about this theme of shortening working lives. First, it is odd that higher education should not be defined as 'work': it is work – even though it is so badly paid that, in Britain, one ends up seriously in debt. In today's information- and service-based economies, higher and further education have become the equivalent of working apprenticeships. Likewise, retired people are not passive 'consumers' of national wealth: they contribute much in the way of informal economic activity (notably, child care of grandchildren). Women have always been informal workers, and older women are no exception. Second, only looking at the shortening working life of some men is deceptive. An alternative way of looking at things is to ask the question: by the end of its life, which would have contributed more 'full-time equivalent years of work' to the British economy – a baby born in 1900, or one born in 1970? The exercise involves a complicated calculation, but it has been done for the USA by Robert Khan (1984:91). And the answer is, of course, the baby born in 1970 – because of improved survival and more women working. So in some ways, we are working *more*. Third, another rather different way of looking at what has happened is to say that, over the past thirty years, there has essentially been a 'redistribution of work' – from older men to women of all ages, from industrial jobs to service jobs, from full-time work to part-time, and from some regions to others. It is not, of course, the same work, but it is, nevertheless, a redistribution of employment on the one hand, and unwaged dependency on the other. If there has been a 'redistribution of work', caused by sectoral and gendered shifts in labour market demand, then there ought to be a redistribution of income to support the growing number of workless men at the upper age range. Unless households develop a 'female breadwinner model' in the next decades, and they are supported by their working wives, these jobless men will need financial support. One positive development is the New Deal for those aged 50+, which may lead on to more in-work benefits.

The question, therefore, is: what policies might stem this long-run trend to earlier retirement? A variety of suggestions have been made in Britain, and some counter-measures – of a piecemeal, guerilla-warfare kind – are being taken: final-salary occupational pension schemes are being altered to money-purchase ones; certain occupational early retirement schemes (for example, for school teachers) have been cut back; age discrimination measures are under discussion, including educating employers in the value of an 'age-diverse' workforce and the framing of legislation; there may be further extensions of the welfare-to-work 'New Deal' for those aged 50+; there is to be encouragement of more retraining of older jobless workers; and so on.

However, if the principal problem is declining labour market demand then these policies will have little effect. A recent government report has acknowledged that no more than one-third of the increase in older men's joblessness since the 1970s can be attributed to 'voluntary' factors, such as early exit incentives (Cabinet Office, 2000:22). The New Labour government has shown a marked disinclination to intervene in the labour market and mitigate the effects of globalization, and thus action to 'protect' older workers' jobs (even if this were practicable) is not on the political agenda. The most radical solution of all is the one that is hardly mentioned: the introduction of a Basic Income or Citizen's Income for all aged 50+, to subsidize diminishing income from employment. This would, of course, be enormously expensive and administratively complex, but it may be that, just as social commentators of the 1880s and 1890s discussed the desirability of state old age pensions for all aged 65+, so today a similar debate should take place about the financial support of those in late middle age.

Could Legislation Work? Lessons from America

In considering both the dilemmas inherent in the concept of age discrimination and the viability of possible remedies, it is instructive to examine the working of perhaps the most famous piece of remedial legislation, the USA's 1967 Age Discrimination in Employment Act (ADEA). What conclusions can be drawn from the American experience?

As in all advanced industrial societies, the economic activity rates of men in the USA aged 65+ fell steadily from the late nineteenth century onwards, from 68.3 per cent in 1890 to 16.3 per cent in 1990. This slow deindustrialisation process began to be noticed by America's small band of social reformers in the early years of the century: for example, in a study published in 1912, Lee Welling Squirer calculated that some 1,250,000 of the 4,000,000 US citizens aged 65+ were dependent upon public and private charity, being the 'worn-out, indigent veterans of the industrial army' (Squirer, 1912:3-4). Far from extending the working life, new labour-saving machinery appeared to be hastening the onset of industrial obsolescence, in contrast to the farm economy where the aged still retained a labour market niche.[5] The 1930s depression greatly worsened conditions for older workers. Little relief was provided by those pension schemes administered by states, which had poor coverage and low benefits (Quadagno, 1988:72). Federal old age pensions were introduced in the USA by the 1935 Social Security Act, and were underpinned by old age assistance.

The labour market problems of older workers came under scrutiny in the 1930s, with several commentators suggesting that age discrimination in employment was a growing problem (Barkin, 1933). Some discussion of legislation against age discrimination did occur in one or two states (notably, Massachusetts and New York)

('Causes of Discrimination Against Older Workers', 1938), but there was a reluctance to introduce any regulation in America's labour market. By the 1950s, most commentators realized that long-run trends were slowly deindustrialising older workers: as one observer put it, 'as obvious as Cyrano's nose, the main barrier to the employment of older workers is simply the lack of available jobs' (Abrams, 1952:65). When the US economy experienced the temporary stimulus to its heavy manufacturing occasioned by the Second World War and the Korean War, the economic activity rates of older men rose. But low unemployment and a tight labour market in the 1950s failed to arrest the inexorable spread of male 'age-65' retirement. Paradoxically, it was because of this operation of demand-side economic forces that commentators turned their attention to those factors over which policy might have some control, notably mandatory retirement and age discriminatory employment practices. By the 1950s, there was a burgeoning debate on the problems of older workers, with much discussion of such 'modern' topics as flexible retirement, individualized testing, the value of an 'age-diverse' workforce, and so on (Abrams, 1955; Drake, 1958).

Why did the 1960s produce federal legislation against age discrimination in employment? The conventional explanation is that action against age discrimination succeeded in the USA because of the success of the wider civil rights movement: that is, it was logical to cover race, sex and age discrimination together. (Age was at one point to have been included in the coverage of the 1964 Civil Rights Act, but was temporarily dropped, made subject to an official investigation, and then included in separate legislation three years later.) However, other factors were at work. There was pressure from America's growing 'gray lobby', concern over the jobless older worker, and compelling evidence of the poverty of older people: Bureau of the Census statistics showed that, in 1958, 60 per cent of Americans aged 65+ had incomes of less than $1,000 per annum, where the federal standard of adequacy for a retired couple in an urban area in 1959 ranged from $2,681 to $3,304 per annum (Harrington, 1962). But perhaps most important of all was the fact that the US economy was experiencing a major technological revolution. Blue-collar industrial jobs were disappearing, white-collar and service jobs were expanding, and together these were worsening the labour market prospects of certain marginal groups (such as unskilled African-American men). Improving the technological proficiency and per capita productivity of the US workforce became a key theme in the 1960s. This meant not only raising educational and skill levels of the young, but also modernising personnel policies so that productive workers, regardless of their age, were retained. Increasingly, the use of crude 'age proxies' – seemingly based upon irrational, 'false stereotypes' of older workers' industrial obsolescence – and the imposition of mandatory retirement at age 65 were seen as economically dysfunctional, leading to a loss of valuable workers and diminishing the productive power of the economy, as well as forcing growing numbers of older citizens to live in poverty on a low pension.

The 1967 Age Discrimination in Employment Act

As in the recent debate in Britain, there was an intriguing combination of social justice and labour-supply reasons in the debates leading up to the 1967 ADEA. President Lyndon Johnson's 'Older Americans Message' of 23 January 1967 stressed both the economic loss to the nation caused by the under-utilisation of older workers' skills and the damaging impact joblessness had on such workers and their families (United States Equal Employment Opportunity Commission, 1981). Ageism in social relations was not to be tackled (though some hoped that the ADEA would gradually change attitudes and behaviour), and there was general acknowledgement that age discrimination in employment was fundamentally different to race and sex discrimination, since it was often rationally related to ability to perform a job. The aim was thus to combat that 'irrational' or 'arbitrary' age discrimination which was economically dysfunctional. Hence the Chair of the Senate Committee on Aging, looking back in 1986, pointed out that the Act

> does not require employers to keep unfit or unproductive employees. All that the ADEA requires is that the employer make individualized assessments where it is possible and practical to do so.[6]

The ADEA had three explicit aims: to promote the employment of older persons; to prohibit 'arbitrary' age discrimination in employment; and to assist employers and workers to find ways of solving problems arising from the impact of age on employment. Of these, the first was never really achieved, and most focus was upon the protection of older workers' employment rights with regard to hiring, firing, retraining, promotion, workplace harassment, and so on. The most obvious prohibitions introduced by the ADEA were on age stipulations in job advertisements, and age-discriminatory personnel policies within firms. The protected group was initially those aged 40-65: thus in its original form the Act was essentially a job-protection measure for middle-aged workers, and was not about old age as such. However, in 1978 the upper age limit was raised to 70, and in 1986 it was abolished for nearly all occupations (with some notable exceptions). This uncapping was largely irrelevant, given the small proportion of men and women aged 65+ who were economically active in 1990. Other extensions occurred in the years after 1967, and a major change took place when enforcement was handed over to the Equal Employment Opportunity Commission (EEOC) in 1978. Aggrieved individuals who feel that unlawful discrimination has taken place have to file a charge, and then there are a set of 'procedural wrinkles' (Friedman, 1984:20) which reflect the Act's attempt to build in a measure of 'conciliation, conference and persuasion' between the parties involved. The EEOC only becomes involved at a late stage; the final resort is in the courts of law, and several 'landmark' cases have established interpretation of the Act.

The Principal Defences

Anti-discrimination legislation in the USA has traditionally been drafted in fairly general language, with clarification coming from legal decisions (Northrup, 1980: 51). Thus the three principal ADEA defences engendered much litigation. These were: (1) Where age is a bona fide occupational qualification (BFOQ) reasonably necessary to the normal operation of the particular business, or where the differentiation is based on reasonable factors other than age (RFOA); (2) To observe the terms of a bona fide seniority system or any bona fide employee benefit plan such as a retirement, pension, or insurance plan, which is not a subterfuge to evade the purpose of the Act, except that no such employee benefit plan shall excuse the failure to hire any individual; (3) To discharge or otherwise discipline an individual for good cause.

Of these, BFOQ and RFOA have occasioned the most controversy. Acceptable instances of the former have over time been steadily whittled down to examples where public safety is crucial (for example, airline pilots, helicopter pilots, police officers, bus drivers, firefighters and prison guards), or where age is necessary for authenticity (actors and actresses, and persons promoting products to a particular age group). A series of important cases hinging upon medical evidence and performance testing have helped reduce the scope of permissible BFOQ categories, as did the virtual elimination of mandatory retirement in 1986. One interesting aspect of ADEA is, therefore, the interface between legal arguments and medical evidence on the biology of ageing – for example, the ability of clinical examinations to predict heart attacks in airline pilots, or the validity of simulation tests for firefighters.

As noted, one purpose of the ADEA was to maximize labour supply. Legal rulings have confirmed that, if a test of employment is job-related, it can be a rational basis for compulsory retirement. For example, in Massachusetts Board of Retirement v. Murgia (1976), an uniformed policeman's objection to compulsory retirement at age 50 was rejected on the basis that physical ability *does*, in the aggregate, decline with age. 'Justified' age discrimination was permissible (Player, 1992:75). Again, the RFOA defence can cover inability to meet certain job-performance targets.

The Age Discrimination in Employment Act: Success or Failure?

What verdict is to be pronounced on the ADEA? Much depends upon what one judges to have been its aims. As an employment rights measure, it has given much-needed protection to the older worker in America, who forty years ago was subject to age-limited job advertisements, summary dismissal, non-promotion, ineligibility for re-training programmes and even workplace harassment on grounds of age. (We cannot, of course, identify how far the ADEA has been responsible for eliminating these, and how far they would have disappeared with changing cultural values.) It may also have made the American public more aware of ageism in social attitudes and inter-personal relations. Advocacy groups such as the American Association of Retired Persons (AARP) (1999) believe that much work still needs to be done in this area.

However, two powerful critiques have been directed at the ADEA. The first is that – as far as we can tell – it has failed to arrest the trend to earlier retirement that has occurred in all Western economies. (This is often cited as a reason why legislation in Britain would be pointless) (Cabinet Office, 2000). Thus whereas in 1970, 83.0 per cent of American men aged 55-64 were economically active, by 1990 this had fallen to 67.8 per cent. The primacy of labour market demand over legislative protection can also be illustrated by the fact that the continued expansion of feminized jobs increased the economic activity rates of American women aged 55-64 from 43.0 per cent to 45.2 per cent over the same period (United States Census Bureau, 1999:411). The ADEA's inability to influence labour market changes was also demonstrated during the wave of workforce downsizings that occurred in the 1980s. By one estimate, some 43,000,000 jobs were lost between 1976 and 1993 – not only blue-collar, manufacturing jobs but white-collar corporate jobs – as a consequence of industrial restructuring and outsourcing of production overseas (Uchitelle and Kleifield, 1996). The American workforce continued to expand, but these new jobs tended to be more insecure, low-paid, service industry-based, and filled by young workers (often women) (Report of the Secretary of Labor, 1989). Employers managed to get rid of older workers using the 'reductions in force' provision of the ADEA, but to comply with the Act they had to persuade employees to leave voluntarily by generous early exit incentives. Essentially, employers were using crude age proxies, much as they had done in the 1950s. The events of the 1980s demonstrated that age discrimination was only one part of the set of problems faced by older workers (Sandell, 1987).

The second criticism levelled at the ADEA is that it has been essentially a 'litigation bonanza' for white, middle class, middle-aged corporate executives. In the Reaganite 1980s, many conservatives attacked the ADEA for being a piece of ill-considered, liberal legislation that did little more than make life increasingly difficult for employers in their personnel policies by permitting incompetent middle-aged executives to seek lucrative payouts through the courts (Schuck, 1980), and this criticism has dogged it ever since. Even one scholar broadly sympathetic to it concludes that it is, in many respects,

> a piece of well-intentioned legislation of the 1960s that has ultimately failed in its primary purpose, the reduction in long-term unemployment among older workers ... the primary impact of the ADEA has been as a wrongful discharge statute for white male professionals and managers. (O'Meara, 1989:93)

This criticism appears to be borne out by analyses of ADEA cases (which show such plaintiffs to be the majority) (Friedman, 1984; O'Meara, 1989). Women and minorities who feel themselves to be the victims of employment discrimination will be more likely to take legal action under the sex and race discrimination provisions of the 1964 Civil Rights Act. But it is likely that the ADEA has not been a sensitive enough instrument to tackle the especial problems of women. One reason for women being a small minority of ADEA plaintiffs is that women are least likely to bring a charge relating to termination: they are most likely to encounter discrimination in hiring, promotion, remuneration and fringe benefits (Shaw, 1988).

Finally, we cannot really pronounce a verdict on whether the ADEA has succeeded in maximising workforce productivity by retaining good workers, regardless of age, and only permitting the bad to be dispensed with. This rather controversial 'labour supply' motivation was strongly evident in the discussions during the 1960s, but it is impossible to assess since we do not know how much better or worse the US economy would now be functioning without the ADEA.

Conclusion

This necessarily brief essay has suggested that age discrimination is a particularly difficult and troubling form of discrimination to identify and counter – more so than sex or race discrimination. There is substantial anecdotal evidence that ageism is widespread in social relations and attitudes, but it is so closely bound up with strongly internalized ideas of 'age-appropriate' behaviour that remedial action would be problematic. So far, the recent age discrimination debate in Britain has been highly masculinist in orientation, since it has focused mainly upon the labour market problems of older men. It is to be hoped that the social and economic disadvantages experienced by older women will also be addressed.

An examination of the working of the USA's Age Discrimination in Employment Act reveals that anti-discrimination legislation produces uncertain outcomes. The recent revival of interest in Britain owes as much to the new economic conditions of postindustrial capitalism – particularly the need to maximize the supply of low-grade, cheap labour – as it does to abstract ideas of social rights and justice. In current British political discourses, the language of rights is counterbalanced by a powerful language of 'responsibilities' and 'obligations' – notably the obligation to work in the labour market. Effective action to alleviate the growing labour market problems of older workers could take the form of more re-training programmes, flexible retirement policies and even a guaranteed citizen's income benefit system for all aged 50+. On the other hand, it could involve the forced re-enlistment of jobless men aged 50+ back into the hypercasualized, low-paid sectors of the labour market. If action took this form, it would not be in the best interests of older people.

Notes

1 Recently, there has been consideration of whether 'incitement to religious hatred' should be a crime in Britain.
2 See, for example: John Grimley Evans, 'Challenge of Ageing', in Richard Smith (ed.), *Health of the Nation: the BMJ View* (1991).
3 See, for example: Bill Bytheway, *Ageism* (1995); Eric Midwinter, *Citizenship: From Ageism to Participation* (1992); Eric Midwinter, *Ageism, Discrimination and Citizenship* (1991).
4 For a summary of trends, see Paul Gregg and Jonathan Wadsworth (eds.) *The State of Working Britain* (1999).
5 See, for example: Abraham Epstein, *Facing Old Age: A Study of Old Age Dependency in the United States and Old Age Pensions* (1922).
6 Quoted in O'Meara, *Protecting the Growing Number of Older Workers: the Age Discrimination in Employment Act*, 1989, p. 345.

References

Abrams, A.J. (1952), 'Barriers to the Employment of Older Workers', *Annals of the American Academy of Political and Social Science*, Vol. 279 (Jan.), p. 65.

Abrams, A.J. (1955), 'Discrimination Against Older Workers in Various Countries', in *Old Age in the Modern World*. Report of the Third Congress of the International Association of Gerontology, Edinburgh 1954, E + S Livingstone, London.

Age Concern (1998), *Age Discrimination. Make It a Thing of the Past*, Age Concern, London.

American Association of Retired Persons (1999), *The Public Policy Agenda 1999*, AARP, Washington, DC.

Appleby, J. (1992), *Financing Health Care in the 1990s*, Open University Press, Buckingham.

Barkin, S. (1933), *The Older Worker in Industry: A Study of New York State Manufacturing Industries*, J.B. Lyon Co., Albany.

Butler, R.N. (1969), 'Age-Ism: Another Form of Bigotry', *The Gerontologist*, Vol. 9 (4), pt. 1.

Butler, R.N. (1995 edn.), 'Ageism', in G.L. Maddox (ed.), *The Encyclopaedia of Ageing*, Springer, New York.

Cabinet Office. Performance and Innovation Unit (2000), *Winning the Generation Game. Improving Opportunities for People Aged 50-65 in Work and Community Activity*, TSO, London.

Campbell, N. (1999), *The Decline of Employment Among Older People in Britain*, LSE Centre for Analysis of Social Exclusion, London.

'Causes of Discrimination Against Older Workers' (1938), *Monthly Labor Review*, Vol. 26 (6), pp. 1138-43.

Clark, F. Le Gros (1966), *Work, Age and Leisure. Causes and Consequences of the Shortened Working Life*, M. Joseph, London.

Code of Practice: Age Diversity in Employment (1999).

Daniels, N. (1988), *Am I My Parents' Keeper? An Essay on Justice Between the Young and the Old*, Oxford University Press, Oxford.

Department for Education and Employment (1998), *Action on Age: Report of the Consultation on Age Discrimination in Employment*, TSO, London.

Disney, R. (1999), 'Why Have Older Men Stopped Working?', in P. Gregg and J. Wadsworth (eds.), *The State of Working Britain*, Manchester UP, Manchester, pp. 25-30.

Drake, J.T. (1958), *The Aged in American Society*, Ronald Press Co, New York.

Eglit, H. (1981), 'Of Age and the Constitution', *Chicago Kent Law Review*, Vol. 57 (4), pp. 859-914.

Friedman, L.M. (1984), *Your Time Will Come: The Law of Age Discrimination and Mandatory Retirement*, Russel Sage Foundation, New York.

Hancock, R., Jarvis, C. and Mueller, G. (1995), *The Outlook for Incomes in Retirement. Social Trends and Attitudes*, Age Concern Institute of Gerontology.

Harrington, M. (1962), *The Other America: Poverty in the United States*, Macmillan, New York.

Harris, T. (1997), 'Projections: a Look Into the Future', in Office for National Statistics, *Social Trends*, 27, p. 17.

Khan, R.L. (1984), 'Productive Behaviour Through the Life Course', in *The Ageing Society Project*, Human Resource Implications of an Ageing Work Force, The Ageing Society Project, New York.

Levine, M.L.(1988), *Age Discrimination and the Mandatory Retirement Controversy*, Johns Hopkins University Press, Baltimore.

Macnicol, J. (1998), *The Politics of Retirement in Britain, 1878-1948*, Cambridge University Press, Cambridge.

Marshall, T.H. (1963), 'Citizenship and Social Class', in Marshall, T.H., *Sociology at the Cross-roads and Other Essays*, Heinemann, London, pp. 104-22.

Ministry of Labour and National Service (1955), *Employment of Older Men and Women* (1952); National Advisory Committee on the Employment of Older Men and Women. First Report, Cmd. 8963, 1953 and Second Report, Cmd. 9628.

Neugarten, D.A. (ed.) (1996), *The Meaning of Age: Selected Papers of Bernice L. Neugarten*, University of Chicago Press, Chicago.

Northrup, J.P. (1980), *Old Age, Handicapped, and Vietnam-Era Antidiscrimination Legislation*, University of Pennsylvania, Philadelphia.

Office for National Statistics (1999), *Social Focus on Older People*, TSO, London.

O'Meara, D.P. (1989), *Protecting the Growing Number of Older Workers: The Age Discrimination in Employment Act*, University of Pennsylvania, Philadelphia.

Palmore, E.B. (1990), *Ageism. Negative and Positive*, Springer, New York.

Phillipson, C. (1982), *Capitalism and the Construction of Old Age*, Macmillan, London.

Player, M.A. (1992), *Federal Law of Employment Discrimination in a Nutshell*, West Publishing Co., St Paul.

Quadagno, J. (1988), *The Transformation of Old Age Security. Class and Politics in the American Welfare State*, University of Chicago Press, Chicago.

Report of the Secretary of Labor (1989), *Labor Market Problems of Older Workers*, Columbus, OH.

Sandell, S.H. (ed.) (1987), *The Problem Isn't Age. Work and Older Americans*, Praeger, New York.

Schuck, P.H. (1980), 'The Graying of Civil Rights Law', *The Public Interest*, no. 60, Summer.

Shaw, L.B. (1988), 'Special Problems of Older Women Workers', in M.E. Borus, H.S. Parnes, S.H. Sandell and B. Seidman (eds.), *The Older Worker*, Industrial Relations Research Association, Madison, pp. 55-70.

Sontag, S. (1978), 'The Double Standard of Aging', in V. Carver and P. Liddiard (eds.), *An Ageing Population. A Reader and a Sourcebook*, Open University Press, Milton Keynes, pp. 72-80.

Squirer, L. Welling (1912), *Old Age Dependency in the United States: A Complete Survey of the Pension Movement*, Macmillan, New York.

Uchitelle, L. and Kleifield, N.R. (1996), 'The Price of Jobs Lost', in *The New York Times*, The Downsizing of America, Times Books, New York.

United States Census Bureau (1999), *Statistical Abstract of the United States: 1999*, US Government Printing Office, Washington DC.

United States Commission on Civil Rights (1977), *The Age Discrimination Study*, US. Commission on Civil Rights.

United States Equal Employment Opportunity Commission (1981), *Legislative History of the Age Discrimination in Employment Act*, US Government Printing Office, Washington DC.

Walker, A. (1990), 'The Benefits of Old Age? Age Discrimination and Social Security', in E. McEwen (ed.), *Age: The Unrecognised Discrimination*, Age Concern England, London.

Worsley, R. (1996), *Age and Employment. Why Employers Should Think Again About Older Workers*, Age Concern England, London.

Chapter 3

The Constructs of Generation and Cohort in Sociological Studies of Ageing: Theoretical Conceptualizations and Some Empirical Implications

Gunhild Hammarström

Introduction

The aim of this chapter is to discuss the generation construct in relation to the cohort construct as structural, analytical categories in sociological studies of ageing. The reason for doing sociological research into generations and cohorts is related to a wish to study social change by connecting individual biographies with the history of society. A weakness of some sociological research on ageing is that it often only considers the individuals' life course, or age groups, without relating them to the history of society. Age groups represent a certain point in time, as for example people of 20 years of age or 65 years of age, meaning that membership is changing with the ageing process. The constructs of cohort and generation, on the other hand, refer to aggregates of individuals born during a specific period of time. The membership is permanent throughout life, and the two constructs can be said to be age categories 'stretched out over time', and are thus related to the history of society and to structural and social change.

A particular benefit from generation and cohort studies is the possibility to map and compare the collective life course patterns of people born at different periods of time, and to include a historical dimension in the analysis. People born in the same historical period are not only exponents of shared historical experiences, they also go through life passing certain life stages at more or less the same chronological age. They will therefore differ not only in their historical experiences but also in life course experiences from, for example, those born 30 years earlier or 30 years later. Studying generations and cohorts thus enables us to grasp history and biography and their intersections within society. This presupposes that also the individual life course is included in the analysis. However, because of the lack of space, the life course perspective will not be addressed in this chapter.

Studying generations and cohorts as aggregates of individuals follows the sociological traditions of Linton (1942) and Parsons (1942), who pointed to age as a differentiating factor in the social structure, and identified age-grading as a way of classifying individuals as group members. In contemporary sociology, generation differences and relationships between generations are widely studied, and to mention only a few examples: the discussions of intergenerational solidarity, intergenerational equity, and the fairness of the distribution process (Laslett, 1992; Walker, 1990, 1993), and also John Rawls' (1971) work about the obligations of future generations. In youth research it is mostly generations as life-styles that are in focus. According to Schaie (1996), much of the literature on generation differences written by sociologists deals with issues of generation conflicts and the transmission of values.[1]

Social gerontology studies of generations deal mainly with family generations; otherwise the cohort construct is preferred. This might be due to the recommendation in American handbooks on ageing to avoid the term 'generation', because of confusion with the term 'cohort', and to reserve the term generation for parent-child or other kin relations (see for example, Uhlenberg and Riley, 1996). A reason for this recommendation is that the generation construct is viewed as a more imprecise and diffuse construct than the cohort construct. Whereas the term cohort is originally a purely demographic construct, referring to an aggregate of individuals born during a specific time period, the term generation, on the other hand, is an everyday-language word. It is commonly used in various ways, such as family generations, generations as birth cohorts, artist generations, author generations, welfare generations, etc. Bengtson et al. (1997) also talks about generations of theories in social gerontology. The term generation also denotes successive groups referring to historical periods, such as earlier generations, the generations of today, and future generations etc.

Although the two constructs of cohort and generation have certain similarities, and sometimes are seen as synonymous constructs, they are in other respects conceptually distinct from each other. This is however, a result of the way in which we choose to define concepts, which is only one of many possible ways, and not in accordance with some natural order (Tornstam, 1992: 322). My position in this respect is constructivist, meaning that the nature of social reality is linguistically constructed. Social categories, such as 'the aged' or other categories, such as 'generations' and 'cohorts', are rendered realities achieved in linguistic practices of naming, describing, classifying, referencing, and the like. This constructivist approach means that our understanding of reality is socially constructed in language use – not that reality in itself is socially constructed; that is, 'it does not deny that ageing people exist' (Green, 1993: 1-13, 15). It is of significance however that there is some kind of general agreement with the meaning of the used constructs.

This chapter is not meant to be an inventory study with a complete bibliography. My intention is rather to give a basis for further discussion and future research. One of the sources of inspiration for this chapter is the concept of generation elaborated by Karl Mannheim in his classic essay *The Problems of Generations* (1952/1928).

Written about 75 years ago, some reasoning might seem obsolete today. Nevertheless, his essay still includes fruitful ideas which avail themselves of elaboration, especially his concept of 'generation units', which seems to have been neglected in earlier research. As the characteristics of Mannheim's generation construct are quite distinct from those of family generations, the article also includes a short description of what signifies family generations, and other so-called life course generations. The discussion of the cohort construct departs from Ryder, and Riley and her colleagues, who have developed this originally demographic construct into a more sociological construct (Ryder, 1965; Riley, 1971, 1988, 1994; Riley et al., 1972). Since one of the implications of theoretical conceptualizations is how to determine the constructs in empirical research, this will be discussed with the aid of examples from earlier empirical studies. Issues related to analysing cohort and generation data and the limitations of cross-sectional designs in relation to longitudinal studies will not however be outlined, as these problems are widely discussed in other works, for example in Hardy (1997) and Riley et al. (1972). The present article concludes with some ideas for future research.

Historical Change and Individual Diversity

The view that history is an integral part of people's experience is to be compared with Mills' statement that 'man is a social and historical actor who must be understood ... in close and intricate interplay with social and historical structures' (Mills, 1959: 158). Among others, Ryder (1965), and Riley and Riley (1999) call our attention to the importance of understanding the dynamic interplay between social structures and the lives of individuals.

Because of the presumed relationship with history, the inclusion of time is seen as a basic condition for the constructs of cohort and generation. The age structure in society is viewed from at least two parallel time dimensions, namely chronological time and historical time, each of them including a present, a past, and a future. Whereas *chronological* time refers to years of age as applied to the life course of people, that is, individual biographical time, *historical* time applies to the history of society in which people live (Riley et al., 1972: 19). Historical time is indexed by calendar years, and is thus also chronological in its character.

To Mannheim, as well as to Riley and her colleagues, the chronological dimension serves as an indicator of life course experiences, as well as of age-related biological changes, and they see life course experiences as more sociologically important than chronological age as such. In this respect it could be relevant to refer to *social time*, in the sense Neugarten and Datan (1973) give it, meaning the processes that intervene between the social structure and the individuals. That is, the process through which chronological age categories are socially defined, or constituted. The social time dimension is thus of another character than the chronological and historical time dimensions. Chronological time and social time have their correspondences when talking about age, such as chronological and social age.[2] As the term life course is more common than the term social time when describing the social process of ageing nowadays, I will in the following also use the term 'life course', which often refers to the set of positions that people occupy at certain points in time.

The significance of considering time when studying the intersections between the individual and society is in accordance with the view of Berger and Luckmann. They state that the world of every day life on the individual level is structured temporally, as well as spatially, and the temporal structure of everyday life determines the human being's situation in the world of everyday life (Berger and Luckmann, 1967: 26-28). This view has however been questioned lately. Lynott and Lynott, for example, are resistant to social systems' structuring of biographical time. Further, they set aside belief in the reality of age and age-related concepts, such as age cohorts and life stages: 'One can hardly attempt to study such objects as stages, cohorts, and the like, without taking for granted their existence' (Lynott and Lynott, 1996: 756). Murphy and Longino express a similar view: 'In the post-modern world, age does not represent a place on a temporal trajectory or historical timeline ... Life represents an array of choices, not necessarily arranged *ad seriatim* with old age at the end' (Murphy and Longino, 1997: 90). According to the constructivist approach, stated in the introductory section, I see the time dimensions as analytical constructs, not as existing in a metaphysical sense. The time dimensions could be claimed to serve as different theoretical conditions for the various constructs of generation and cohort.

However, there are great variations within a society concerning social events, which are not formally defined by chronological age, such as work experiences, length and type of education, marriage, parenthood etc. These differing experiences denote variability between individuals, and it is often argued that shared life course positions, determined by social age, give rise to a sense of community to a higher degree than similar chronological age. These examples of differing experiences underline the importance of making an analytical distinction between chronological age and social age. In cases where chronological age, by legislation defines life course position (for example when children are allowed to begin school, when people are allowed to vote or leave work because of retirement etc.), chronological age and social age of course coincide.

However, when studying aggregated categories, such as generations and cohorts, individual diversity and variations are toned down in favour of the collective characteristics. Intergenerational (intercohort) differences are focused at the expense of variations within a generation (intracohort differences). That is, categorizing individuals in order to make reality understandable leads to oversimplifications, because of a tendency to focus on homogeneity and central tendencies in studies of ageing, rather than on variance and heterogeneity (Tornstam, 1992: 321; Dannefer, 1988).

The preference for treating generations, as well as cohorts, as age homogeneous categories is heavily criticized, not least among scholars working within the frameworks of political economy and gender theory (among others, Kohli, 1988; Minkler and Estes, 1999; Ray 1966). As Uhlenberg and Riley express this: 'treating cohort patterns as averages that refer to the aggregate or collective lives of individual cohort members facilitates comparison. These average patterns can however obscure wide variations that reflect the marked heterogeneity of older people' (Uhlenberg and Riley, 1996: 301). A similar view is that with increasing individualization, the social significance of age classification, and of age as such, lessens (Hazelrigg, 1997: 110). Treating generations and cohorts as age homogeneous categories could however be avoided, if sub units of generations and cohorts are taken into consideration. With regard to this, Mannheim's concept of generation units is of theoretical interest, which will be discussed further on in this chapter.

Generations and Cohorts as Theoretical Constructs

As mentioned in the introductory section, the term generation has multiple meanings. Although the meaning of family generation is the best known, this section will start with an overview of the construct of generation developed by Mannheim. Mannheim could be said to talk about generations at two different 'levels', or 'stages', a) generation as birth cohort, or 'generation location', and b) generation 'as actuality', or generation as actors. This latter stage has in recent works been referred to as generations as social movements; other terms are political, socio-political, or idea generations, and nowadays they are often named cultural generations. In comparison with Mannheim's generation constructs, the characteristics of family generations are outlined. The discussion of cohorts departs, as mentioned earlier, from the conceptualizations elaborated by Norman Ryder and Riley and her colleagues. My aim in this section is to clarify some of the distinctions between the various meanings of the cohort construct and the generation construct.

Karl Mannheim's Construct of Generation

The origin of Mannheim's interest in generations was the impact which the continuous flow of generations had on social change, and how society affected generations. In his essay *The Problem of Generations*, he tried to identify the link between the biological process of generation replacement and social change. Central concepts in his discussion are 'generation location', 'generation as actuality', and 'generation unit', and according to Mannheim, a clarification of these categories is important and indispensable for any deeper analysis (Mannheim, 1952/1928: 308).

A generation is, according to Mannheim, a temporal unit consisting of individuals born at the same time, and therefore they have a 'generation location' in history. This means that more important than a common year of birth is the individuals' *co-existence* in history. Since individuals born in the same time are contemporaries, they constitute a generation, just because they are subjects of common influences. They experience the same intellectual, social and political influences 'both in the early, formative, and in their later years', and therefore they get specific experiences differing from other generations. A generation then represents, according to Mannheim, a unique type of structural and temporal location based on the dynamic interplay between being born in a particular year and the social and political events that occur while a birth cohort ages.

This however also presupposes a 'community of location', referring to the participation in the same historical and social circumstances. In this respect, Mannheim exemplifies, among others, contemporaries in China and Germany, for whom this community of location is lacking. Because of this they do not have shared experiences of the social world, and consequently they do not constitute a generation together. A generation thus consists of a group of individuals born during the same time period, who are united by similar life experiences and a coherent cultural background. A generation could then be said to represent a common location, not only in time but also in space, resulting in a common cultural background.

'Generation location', 'co-existence', and 'community of location' are the conditions that together contain the potentialities necessary for developing collective bonds, or a special mentality, between contemporary individuals, which give the foundation to a 'generation as actuality'. In order to constitute a generation as actuality, a shared feeling of 'participation in the common destiny' is required, meaning a consciousness among the members of a certain generation of their shared history and common social experiences of society. Referring to this, later interpreters of Mannheim use the term 'generation consciousness', although he himself did not use it. In the following, however, I will use this term, mostly because it is well known, and also because it fits rather well with Mannheim's analogy between the concepts of generation and social class.

Mannheim drew an explicit analogy between generation and social class, not only in the essay *The Problem of Generations*, but also in his essay *The Problem of the Intelligentsia* (1956). His position is that class position is an objective fact, whether the individual in question knows his class position or not, and whether he acknowledges it or not. He states that 'generation location' is an objective fact similar to that of class position. As all individuals belong to a particular generation within a given society, generation membership is permanent throughout the life course. In this respect generations are distinguished from age groups. Belonging to the same class, or belonging to the same generation, has, according to Mannheim, the perception of a shared location in the social and historical process in common. This gives the individuals a specific range of potential experiences, predisposing them for certain modes of thought and historically relevant actions. Class-consciousness does not necessarily accompany a class position, and correspondingly generation consciousness does not automatically follow a shared generation location; the generation location only contains the potentialities for contemporary individuals to become an actual generation.

Hence, a 'generation as actuality' could be considered as being determined by the generation members' consciousness of their shared history and subjective feelings of belonging together. In order to develop shared feelings of belonging together because of participation in a common destiny, a shared experience of a significant historical event is presumed. In this respect, Mannheim emphasized rather the importance of rapidity in social change, especially a process of dynamic de-stabilization, during the formative period early in life. Examples of such events mentioned by Mannheim are wars, revolutions, economic crises, and the like.

All individuals with a shared 'generation location' are, however, not equally influenced by their common historical experiences and exposures, nor do they have common life course experiences. Because of this, all of them do not develop the same 'generation consciousness', or the same mentalities. According to this, Mannheim means that it is possible to identify different and even polar forms of responses to the experiences made by contemporaries. Within the same actual generation there can thus exist a number of subgroups and subdivisions, which can even be antagonistic to each other. Dealing with these kinds of groups, Mannheim used the term 'generation unit', and within any generation there can exist a number of differentiated, antagonistic generation units with a generation consciousness of their own. However, together they constitute an actual generation.

Mannheim's concepts of 'generation units' and the differentiated 'generation consciousness' form the basis for explaining social change. The prerequisites for this are the continuous flow of generations, with the emergence of new participants, and the withdrawal of others. Because of a constant interaction between old and young generations, there is a transmission of the cultural heritage from generation to generation. A society is made up of a composite mentality of mutually antagonistic ideas and impulses, and only some of these can be dominant at any given time. According to Mannheim, those ideas that are dominating have their seat in groups that at a particular point in time acquire special significance, but the dominating ideas do not always pervade the whole society. Other generations, or 'generation units', may have opposite ideas.

When dominating ideas and mentalities change into others, it is not due to a new generation emerging which happens to have quite opposite ideas. What happens, according to Mannheim, is that the social situation changes, and it becomes possible for the other section of the actual generation, i.e. another 'generation unit', to reconstitute the tradition. The point is that the circumstances of a certain time period favour the formation of a new generation mentality at one or the other pole – a mentality already upheld by a minority among older generations. Emphasized by Mannheim is that the differentiation and polarization are always already present in society, among certain older and younger 'generation units'. Social change is thus due to the co-existing generation units, and the interaction between older and younger generations. In a time of rapid change, or dynamic de-stabilization, the ideas of a dominant generation unit might be replaced by the ideas of another generation unit, because they are better adapted to the new situation. For Mannheim, the basis for social change is an awareness of the possibility for collective action to alter existing social situations.

In later theoretical discussions, Mannheim's concept of 'generation consciousness' has been an inspiring source, and also forms the basis for research on the formation of generation life-styles, and elaboration on the construct of generation identity. The concept 'generation unit' is however quite ignored in earlier research, in spite of the fact that Mannheim himself linked the two concepts to each other.

Recent Perspectives on the Generation Construct

Present-day analyses of generations take a somewhat wider perspective than that of Mannheim, since influences from later scholars are also incorporated. These elaborations mostly focus on generation identity. For example, about 50 years ago Eisenstadt tried in his work *From Generation to Generation* (1951) to determine the relationship between structural conditions and the formation of age homogeneous groups, and the significance it had on their identity. Mainly interested in youth movements, he pointed out social expectations as especially important for developing an age homogeneous identity. 'The expectations, which are directed towards individuals with respect to their age, constitute one of the strongest, most essential links between the personality system of individuals and the social system in which they participate' (Eisenstadt, 1951: 32).

Eisenstadt's exact meaning is, however, not quite clear. As I understand him he is talking about generation identity formed by structural conditions in society because of certain expectations on age-related behaviour. He could instead, however, be talking about age identity, which I see as an analytically different kind of identity. To me, whereas age identity refers to common experiences of belonging to a certain age group, for example being a 75-year-old retiree in 2000, generation identity refers to the shared history of the generation members, such as, for example, having grown up during the Depression in the 1930s. It is possible, however, that Eisenstadt referred to both age and generation identity, which would correspond with Mannheim's idea of a generation encompassing historical and individual biographical time simultaneously. Although we can talk about an analytical distinction between generation and age identity, it might be hard, or perhaps impossible, to identify this difference empirically.

In later years we can also see the influences from the French sociologist Pierre Bourdieu, among others. As individuals born in the same period have a shared history, as well as a common biography, they might be said to have, according to Bourdieu (1984/1979), collective memories which are 'carved' into their bodies and minds. The structure of the society is thus reflected in the minds of people, and a generation represents 'embodied' history. Therefore, generations personify different life styles with an identity of their own.

Partly inspired by Mannheim and by the adoption of Bourdieu's sociology of culture and his related notions of habitus and hexis, Eyerman and Turner (1998), as cultural sociologists, are interested in the cultural dimensions of generation membership, and how generations maintain their identity over time and space. They even suggest that along with the postmodernization of culture, there may be a greater fluidity in generation identity and memory than has been the case so far. This view is more or less in accordance with Hazelrigg (1997: 117), who is of the opinion that the likelihood that a group identity will coalesce across the heterogeneity of 30 years, or even 20 years,[3] sharply diminishes because of the increasing individualization. His opinion is due to the presupposition that 'the tempo of social and cultural change' has greatly accelerated.[4]

Eyerman and Turner (1998: 93) also take up another angle in Mannheim's works, by seeing generations as organized in terms of social closure to maximize access to resources to their members, just like social classes in Weberian sociology. They even foresee generation as a more significant structural variable than class in the future, because '... generation can provide a useful dimension for the analysis of changing life cycles in modern society, especially in terms of intergenerational conflicts over scarce resources' (Eyerman and Turner, 1998: 104).

The authors search further and see generation, class, gender, and ethnicity as scales of differentiation in connection with structural and historical change, as all these factors can be thought of as different dimensions of a force field with varying degrees of significance at different historical moments (Eyerman and Turner, 1998: 90). In arguing for the usefulness of the construct of generation, McMullin carries this discussion even further and suggests that generation, class, gender, and ethnicity ought to be conceptualized as sets of social relations characterized by power, as being fundamental structures and organizing features of social life (McMullin, 2000: 525).

In that case, class, gender, and generation could be treated as more comparable analytical categories. Elaborating this idea does however also require a conceptualization of the class and gender constructs which is beyond the theme of this article, but it could be a challenging task in future research.

Summarizing the overview of the generation construct so far:

- A generation as a birth cohort is based on the historical and chronological time dimensions, of which the latter is an indicator of life course experiences. This generation construct is to be seen as a bridge between individual life course experiences and historical changes during lifetime.
- A generation location includes the characteristics of the generation construct above, but is also based on co-existence among the contemporaries, not only in time but also in space, which form a common cultural background. This generation construct is thus multidimensional in its character.
- A generation as actuality, or a cultural generation, is characterized not only by a specific historical setting and common biographical characteristics, but also by generation consciousness, based on shared feelings of participation in a common destiny. Later researchers emphasize generation identity, shared value orientations, and a common life style. The demarcation line for being a generation as actuality is 'a sense of before and after' a specific historical event.

When researchers refer to Mannheim and his generation construct, it is often noted that Mannheim emphasized social change during the formative period early in life as crucial for developing a generation consciousness. Mannheim's theoretical assumptions of the significance of the effects on young people have to be viewed in light of the theories of human development at that time, i.e. about 80 years ago. Since then, modern life span developmental perspectives emphasize the continuous development of the ageing process. This means that the formative period early in life does not need to have the significance it was previously presumed to have.

Family Generations and Other Life Course Generations

The characteristics of family generations are quite distinct from those of generations as birth cohorts and generations as actualities. The term family generation is a genealogical term and refers to the position of the vertical lineage within families, such as grandparents, parents, and children. When determining what constitutes a family generation, family position during the life course is given priority to chronological age. This does not imply that chronological age and historical time are of no significance when studying family generations. On the contrary, family generations in a vertical lineage also form some kind of age generations, or birth cohorts, formed in a special historical setting. As families have their own combinations of life stages and historical anchoring, it is of special theoretical interest to study family generations in relation to chronological age, and the interplay between the specific family time and historical time. For example, what has a 40-year-old mother to a new-born baby in a two-generation family in common with a 20-year-old mother, or with another 40-year-old woman being a grandmother in a family of four or five generations?

Family generations might be seen as special kinds of life course generations, for which I have argued earlier (Hammarström, 1986). When departing from life course position, like family position, instead of chronological age, it is also possible to determine other kinds of life course generations besides family generations. Examples of such life course generations could be educational generations, referring to individuals who start a certain education at the same time, irrespective of their chronological age, or academic generations which Bourdieu has studied (1988).

Although both family generations and other life course generations are determined by life course positions in a certain system at the expense of chronological age, they are not yet completely comparable. Most important is that an individual can have several family positions at the same time, for example being a child, and a parent, and sometimes even a grandparent, and the probability for this is increasing with higher chronological age. Further, the temporal distance between parent and child generations generally represents a time frame of about 20–30 years, and sometimes even longer. In comparison, the same individual can almost always only be a member of one educational generation within a specific educational system. The temporal distance between the life course generations often covers much shorter periods of time, for example four, five or ten years when talking about generations of doctoral students – depending on how the dividing lines between them are defined.

In spite of the similarities in determining the generation membership out of life course positions, family generations are of a different character than other life course generations. When considering the criteria for generation membership in the sense that Mannheim gave it, it could however be questioned if life course generations, other than family generations, really are to be defined as generations, or if they are to be seen as cohorts. This is a question I will return to, when discussing the cohort construct in relation to the construct of generation.

The main characteristics of family generations and life course generations are thus as follows:

- A family generation is determined by family position during the life course.
- A life course generation is based on life course position within a certain social system, other than families.

The Cohort Construct

As mentioned in the introduction, the term cohort is originally a purely demographic term, referring to an aggregate of individuals born during a specific time period, that is a birth cohort. From a sociological point of view, the cohort construct in this meaning, defined by historical calendar time, could be claimed to be quite atheoretical. Whether the construct of cohort is atheoretical or not is, however, rather dependent upon the research problem and what is to be studied than by the definition itself.[5] Cohorts determined by year of birth can certainly be of sociological interest, depending on how the theoretical research problem is formulated.

When Norman Ryder in his article *The Cohort as a Concept in the Study of Social Change* (1965), written about 40 years after Mannheim's essay, developed the construct of cohort, the significance of common experiences was added to the original definition. A cohort is, according to him, defined as an aggregate of individuals who experience the same events within the same time interval, and are ageing together (Ryder, 1965: 845). Referring to this definition, Ryder viewed the concept of cohort as a sharper analytical tool than the concept of generation, as the term generation according to him signified all those within a broad and unspecified age span during a particular epoch. Furthermore, Ryder had the opinion that the term generation should be used solely in its original and unambiguous meaning as the temporal unit of kinship structure. As mentioned above, this opinion is also held in American handbooks of ageing.

Ryder emphasized the historical connection of the cohort construct. Because the historical location reflected the cohort's unique origin and history, he meant that each cohort was differentiated from all others. This does not, however, signify that a cohort is homogeneous in other characteristics. On the contrary, the meaning of sharing a common historical location was, according to Ryder, modified by other characteristics, such as education, working life experiences etc. This results in different subsets of a cohort with different time patterns of development, and Ryder thus rather emphasized intercohort variability.

Ryder also considered the impact of historical events on the life experiences of a specific cohort, and pointed out the significance of traumatic events, such as wars, revolutions, immigration, urbanization, and the like. Such events might have an impact on the crystallization of the mentality of a cohort, which in turn might provide the opportunity for social change. In this respect, Ryder emphasized, in accordance with Mannheim, that new cohorts 'do not cause change; they permit it' (Ryder, 1965: 846).

As Ryder pointed out, life course experiences are significant characteristics of a cohort. Besides the common historical location, a cohort could thus be determined as an aggregate of individuals, who are born in the same time interval, and/or having experienced the same event within the same time interval. In accordance with this wider definition, a cohort could also be determined by time of marriage, parenthood, education etc. This means that birth cohorts are only a special case of cohort. Defining cohorts out of life course positions is also suggested by Neugarten et al. (1965), among others. Consequently, we can also talk about social cohorts, such as family cohorts, educational cohorts etc., that is, constructs more or less equivalent with the above mentioned life course generations.

Similar to Mannheim and his analogy between generation and social class Ryder viewed the cohort as a structural category with the same kind of analytical utility as social class. Since they both serve as 'surrogate indices' for the common experiences of many persons in each category they have, as such, explanatory power. His opinion was however that the cohort conceptually most closely resembled the ethnic group, since membership is determined at birth, and this implies that the cohort is not an organized group.

The influences from Mannheim on Ryder's work are evident. However, even if Ryder was influenced by Mannheim, there are some obvious differences between Mannheim's conceptualization of a generation and Ryder's conceptualization of a cohort. The most important one is that Ryder did not consider the distinction between 'generation location' and 'generation as actuality'. Rather, he doubted the possibility of a transformation from location into actualities, meaning that the cohort would acquire the organized characteristics of some kind of temporal community. In this respect, Ryder seems to have misunderstood Mannheim's conceptualization of generation, as Mannheim emphasized that generations are not to be seen as communities, nor associations, nor groups. The analogy he made was with social class. Further, in Ryder's view cohorts can be involved in social change without prescribing a special self-consciousness. His opinion was rather that the cohort identity will be blurred in later years, as age progressively becomes less precise. Instead Ryder emphasized the similarity of social exposure among the individuals of a certain cohort.

Cohorts in Relation to Age Strata: The Age Stratification Perspective

The influences of Mannheim and Ryder are as obvious in the age stratification perspective, developed by Riley and her colleagues (Riley et al., 1972) and later evolved into the ageing and society perspective (Riley, 1988, 1994: 438). The age stratification perspective is based on the view that societies as a whole are structured on the grounds of age, as well as members of society being stratified on the ground of age. Age is thus seen as a central organizing principle in society, as outlined by Linton (1942) and Parsons (1942).

In this perspective, the central concepts are both age strata and cohorts. Age strata, or age groups, are formed by aggregates of similarly aged individuals such as 20-year-old people, or 65-year-old people, and refer to a certain point in the individual's life course. Age strata are thus ordered in time, and mobility from one age stratum to another during the life course is universal and irreversible (Riley et al., 1972: 23). Departing from Ryder's definition, a cohort, defined by year of birth or by social stage of life, refers to people who are ageing together along both individual biographical time and historical time. The membership is permanent, and for any given cohort the pattern of ageing will reflect the unique historical background of the cohort (Riley et al., 1972: 11; Riley, 1985: 374). The cohort is thus seen as the link between the life course of individuals and the sweep of history (Riley, 1971: 80; Riley et al., 1972: 21).

Cohort ageing, on the other hand, is a term that refers to the continuous advancement of a cohort from one age category to another over its life span. At given historical periods, people of different ages in the existing cohorts pass through age-related structures, and thereby encounter the associated role opportunities and norms. The influence of these encounters is two-directional. In one direction, lives of cohort members are influenced by such structures and their historical changes; in the other direction, the collective lives of cohort members also exert influence on these structures (Uhlenberg and Riley, 1996).

Various age strata differ not only in age, but also in the cohorts to which they belong and the associated historical experiences. By combining analysis of age strata with analysis of cohorts, the age stratification perspective is thought to encompass both changes in life and changes in structures. Because of the interrelationships between membership in age strata, cohorts, and historical period, the age stratification perspective strives to understand the interdependence between age cohorts, social structures, and individual ageing processes. The analytical model of this perspective further provides a way to empirically explore differences related to ageing effects, cohort effects and period effects (Riley et al., 1972; Riley, 1996). According to Bengtson et al. (1997: S82), this approach provides valuable links between individual development and historical change, and has a crucial role in disentangling the effects of cross-sectional age stratification from longitudinal life course ageing. The age stratification perspective presupposes, however, longitudinal studies of individuals as well as of cohorts in order to be used to its full advantage.

The age stratification perspective has its intellectual roots in role theory and the sociology of Talcott Parsons. It was developed in order to parallel class stratification in certain respects (Riley et al., 1972: xiv), and age stratification is itself a metaphorical concept based on an analogy with class stratification. Differing from Ryder (1965), Riley et al. compare age strata, and not cohorts, with social class, and this comparison reveals some of their differences. The most important, according to Riley et al. (1972: 23) is that whereas an individual's social class tends to be more or less permanent over time, membership in different age strata is a fluid process because of the nature of ageing.

The influences from Mannheim on Riley et al.'s conceptualization of cohort could imply that cohorts are synonymous with generations. This has not, however, been the intention of Riley et al. Nevertheless, it could have been the case if the construct of cohort also was characterized as an age category linked by 'life style, value patterns, or collective trauma', as Harris (1988) suggests. In Riley et al.'s conceptualizations of cohorts, cohort consciousness, common life-styles, value patterns, etc. are not even mentioned.

Because of the analytical distinction between historical and chronological time and the life course, we can differentiate between three kinds of cohorts:

- Birth cohorts, who have a common historical location; that is, the demographic construct of cohort.
- Birth cohorts, who have a common historical location and share certain life course experiences because of a common chronological age. That is, a sociologically developed construct based on the demographic construct. The distinction between this kind of cohort and the demographic construct is however mainly of theoretical rather than of analytical interest.
- Social cohorts or life course cohorts, which are determined by social life stage, such as family position, or educational position etc., at certain points in time.

The construct of cohort is thus a uni-dimensional construct based only on the historical time dimension. As I see it, the cohort construct has its greatest advantages when combined with age strata in the analytical model of the age stratification perspective developed by Riley and colleagues (Riley et al., 1972; Riley, 1988, 1994: 438). This is because of the possibility of analyzing ageing effects separately from historical change, as mentioned above.

Cohorts in Comparison with Generations

When comparing the cohort constructs with the various generation constructs elaborated by Mannheim, we can identify some similarities, but also some differences.

It is quite evident that Mannheim's concept of generation, whatever its meaning, is theoretically distinct from the construct of cohort in its demographic sense, as the latter is defined exclusively by historical calendar time. Furthermore, the sociological construct of cohort, meaning a birth cohort with a common historical location and shared social experiences in the life course, in the capacity of being a unidimensional construct, includes only part of Mannheim's construct of 'generation location'.

Social cohorts, on the other hand, are special kinds of cohorts without correspondence in Mannheim's writings. Instead they show theoretical similarities with family generations and other life course generations, based on life course position, as mentioned above. As the term cohort most often leads to associations with birth cohorts, the term generation is sometimes preferable to cohort. The use of the term 'generation' presuppose that this kind of generation also meets the criteria of being a generation in Mannheim's meaning, at least 'generation location'.

'Generation location' refers not only to a common historical location and shared social experiences in the life course, but also to a common location in space resulting in a shared cultural background. The multi-dimensionality of the construct is evident.

Finally, the construct of 'generation as actuality' is mainly determined by a set of cohort-related characteristics acquired as a result of the impact of rapidity in social change. A 'generation as actuality' is characterized by generation consciousness, or a special mentality related to a shared feeling of participation in a common destiny. A 'generation as actuality' may further consist of a number of distinct generation units. Accordingly, this construct has theoretical qualities of another kind than all the above mentioned constructs of cohort.

As I understand the generation construct in Mannheim's meaning, it encompasses both life course dynamics and socio-structural change, simultaneously. In spite of the fact that a cohort is also seen to be a link between the life course of individuals and the sweep of history (Riley et al., 1972: 21), a cohort is not quite comparable with the generation construct. The most significant reason is that the cultural aspect of belonging to a certain cohort is lacking in the latter conceptualization.

According to Harrison C. White, the distinction between cohorts and generations is that the former refers to year of birth, whereas a generation is a 'joint interpretative construction which insists upon and builds among tangible cohorts in defining a style recognized from outside and from within' (White, 1992: 32). He views a generation as a contingent construct, which emerges as an identity expressed across social networks. Crucial to the emergence of a generation is enough space being afforded them by predecessor cohorts (White, 1992: 44).

A reasonable conclusion from this discussion is that the generation construct in Mannheim's meaning is quite distinct from the cohort construct. When deciding which construct is preferable it is however not only a matter of theoretical conceptualizations, but is also related to the theoretical research problem. The Dutch sociologist Henck Becker has given the following advice, when deciding which construct is the more proper from a theoretical point of view:

> In the case where the research hypothesis is that cohort-related characteristics during the life course are acquired in the formative period, or later in life as a result of the impact of major events, the generation construct is preferable. On the other hand, if the research hypothesis is that cohort-related characteristics during the life course are acquired as a result of other impacts than of major events, the concept of cohort is to prefer. (Becker, 1993: 838)

As we can see, Becker here refers to Mannheim's construct of 'generation as actuality'. Even if his guideline seems theoretically reasonable, at least in positivist oriented research; it is of rather limited practical use when empirically determining what constitutes a generation.

How to Determine Cohorts and Generations in Empirical Research

One of the empirical implications of the theoretical constructs of cohort and generations is how they are to be operationalized and empirically determined. Although the two constructs have the relation to historical time in common, there are yet some differences between defining a cohort and determining what constitutes a generation in Mannheim's meaning.

The discussion about how to define *cohorts* in empirical research mainly concerns whether cohorts are to be determined by year of birth or by social stage of life. In demographic studies, year of birth or a specific time interval quite logically defines a cohort. In sociological studies too, cohorts are usually defined operationally by year of birth, that is historical calendar time. As Schaie (1996) states, this is sometimes considered to be problematic, because the cohorts are often determined by an arbitrary definition of a point in time without reference to a theoretical point of departure. This critical point of view could be understood as a recommendation to avoid year of birth as a dividing line between cohorts in favour of life course position. As I understand Schaie, his critical point of view is to advise that the dividing line between the cohorts should be determined by the theoretical research problem in order to avoid the arbitrary division between the cohorts. Depending on the aim of the study, the dividing line could then be either year of birth or life course position. Crucial, is the relation to the historical calendar time.

To determine a cohort by year of birth or a specific time interval, instead of by social stage of life, could also be seen as a particular benefit, because temporal data are easily measured. According to the American sociologist Duan Alwin, the term 'birth cohort' is preferable to the term 'generation' because it is operationally more precise, and because it specifies an exact linkage to history (Alwin, 1992: 8, note 2).

However, in the case where social stages of life are the main objects of the study, the cohorts should of course be determined by life course position, that is, a common social location during a specific historical time period. As mentioned earlier, examples of such social stages of life, not determined by year of birth or chronological age, are historical calendar time for marriage, or starting a special kind of education. This of course applies to so-called 'life course generations', in which case this term is preferable. Even if the research problem departs from social stage of life, or life course position, the consideration of the historical time dimension is of significance. In certain cases, the chronological time dimension could also be considered, as chronological age is sometimes, as a social marker for locating individuals in social space, and not as an 'empty container' (Maddox and Campbell, 1985; Green, 1993).

Even if it is quite clear how to determine *family generations* from family positions in empirical studies, the significance of historical calendar time and chronological age is also of concern to studies on family generations. When determining family generations from family positions, the chronological age of the people in those positions can differ widely. The chronological distance between family generations differs from family to family. In a study of three family generations carried out by myself, the age span between the 423 grandmothers varied between 65 and 97 years of age (Hammarström, 1986, 1993a, 1993b).

Compared with the cohort construct, a weakness with Mannheim's construct of *generation*, is its difficulty in empirically defining what constitutes a generation. This means an actual generation, as well as generation location, because of the multi-dimensionality of the constructs. What might be quite clear from the discussion above is that grouping individuals only on the basis of year of birth does not make a generation in Mannheim's meaning. This also concerns 'generation location', or 'generation as actuality', that is, a generation characterized by generation consciousness – or generation identity, shared value orientations and a common life style. Do the Swedish baby-boomers, born 1940-1949,[6] for example, form a generation, as is sometimes suggested? Is the so-called 'Protest Generation'[7] a generation, or rather a 'generation unit'?

How to define generations in empirical research is solved in slightly varying ways in different empirical studies, mainly dependent on whether the research approach is quantitatively or qualitatively oriented. Influenced by German historicism, Mannheim himself however, emphasized the qualitatively oriented approach to the quantitative one, or rather to French positivist oriented studies, but he did not give any guidelines for determining generations empirically. Research carried out in Europe has mostly departed from the experiences of World War II as a dividing line between generations. Experiences of World War II meet rather well the criteria of a trauma, supposed to have had an impact on individuals in their formative years rather than on people in later years. There are also studies on generations using school education as a dividing line, which seems quite reasonable since the education system has been changing over time. This is also in line with Ryder's (1965) view, as he saw education as a significant 'cohort creator'.

We can identify two main ways to determine generations in empirical studies. One of them is to tentatively delimit generations in relation to historical periods based on the theoretical research problem, and the dividing lines might be confirmed – or not – in the later analysis. This approach is more positivist oriented and most often used in quantitative research. For example, in Ronald Inglehart's well-known study on social change, *The Silent Revolution* (1977) based on quantitative data, he identified two generations. In the empirical study he separated between cohorts born before the end of World War II and cohorts born thereafter. In the analysis, it was shown that each of the two groups of cohorts had certain values in common but differing from each other. The original operational definition of the two generations, determined by year of birth related to a specific historical event, also connected with economic and socio-political change, was then justified afterwards through the empirical results. Inspired by Inglehart's studies, a similar approach was used by Henck Becker (1992) in a quantitative study in the Netherlands of values and political attitudes.

The other way to determine what constitutes a generation is to identify generation membership in the analytical process, that is, during or after the empirical data is gathered. This more qualitative approach usually aims to determine generations on the basis of their generation identity in relation to specific historical periods. This approach was used by the Finnish sociologist J.P. Roos (1985). From a study on autobiographies, he identified four generations of Finns, based on their generation identity connected with their shared experiences of the different wars in Finland during the 1900s. In another Finnish study on a younger sample, three educational generations, similar to Roos' three younger generations, were identified out of a typology of life stories (Antikainen et al., 1996). In both these qualitatively oriented studies, the generations were identified in the analytical process after the empirical study was carried out.

Resulting from the assumption that generation location determines certain ways of experiencing and thinking Roos (1985: 182) suggests social changes connected with rapid industrialization, urbanization, and the development of the welfare state as dividing lines between generations in future research. He considers these structural changes as the very dramatic periods, which represent boundaries between generations born during the 1900s, and which may give rise to similarities in experiences in Finland. According to Roos, structural changes as these might more or less be the same in other nations, even if the time structure is not identical. This makes some sense, at least in Western European countries, where for example, Becker's study in the Netherlands (mentioned above) shows a similar generation pattern as Roos' Finnish study, even though the studies are carried out in different ways, and in different countries.

According to Alasutari (1995), there are countless surveys where the population of Finland has been divided into four generations in line with the classification suggested by Roos (1985), and based on his qualitative analysis of life-stories. This suggests that the heuristic theory developed by Roos has subsequently been proven correct at the level of the total population. However, this does not mean that the dividing lines between different generations run exactly where they are supposed to according to the theory (Alasutari 1995: 144).

Independent of whether the studies mentioned above are based on quantitative or qualitative data, they have in common that the final determination of what constitutes a generation is made in the course of the analytical process. This seems to be the most advisable way to determine whether cohort-related characteristics are acquired as a result of the impact of major events, or refer to impacts other than those of major events. This is also in accordance with Becker's (1993) guideline for deciding which of the two constructs, cohort or generation, is preferable. As mentioned above, this seems to be the only way to identify a specific generation identity, or generation consciousness, if the study is aiming at that. The implication of this is that it is mainly an analytical task to determine what empirically constitutes a generation, a generation location or an actual generation.

Thus the general conclusion I want to draw is that to determine what empirically constitutes a cohort, either a birth cohort or a social cohort, is mainly a theoretical task, and dependent on the theoretical research problem of the study. It is central however, that a cohort is empirically measurable. To determine what constitutes a generation in empirical research is an analytical task, and of course dependent on the theoretical research problem. This might also concern the question of how to determine generation units. The constructs of generations, and generation units, could then be seen as analytical instruments.

Concluding Discussion

Returning to the question in the former section as to whether the baby-boomers form a generation in Mannheim's meaning we find different opinions about that in the literature. Among researchers in the United States, it is argued that the baby-boomers do not form a generation, because of a too great individual heterogeneity (for example, Cornman and Kingson, 1996). In the Netherlands on the other hand, the baby-boomers seem to form a generation according to Becker (1992). In Sweden, people born during the 1940s are more or less designated as a generation distinct from other birth cohorts, brought about by the fact that they are the first cohorts to grow up during the expansion of the Swedish Welfare State and with increasing educational opportunities. They are sometimes called the first 'welfare-state generation', but also the selfish generation, for having had the opportunity to take advantage of the benefits of the welfare state for their own sake more than preceding and subsequent age groups. It could be claimed that the fact of being pointed out as a special generation has led to generation identification.

However, it has also been argued that only the part of the group born during the 1940s, called the 'Protest Generation', meet the criteria of being a generation in the sense of having a shared history, life style and value patterns. Swedish studies have also delineated people born during the 1970s as a generation, and as being representatives for the 'welfare-crisis' period. They not only have more individualistic values and attitudes than older people (Andersson et al., 1993), they have attitudes differing from older people concerning welfare policy and priorities between public and private home help provision, financing and care management for old people in need (Hammarström, 2000, 2001).

The differing views on the baby-boomers being a generation is not only a matter of how different researchers determine what constitutes a generation in empirical research. The varying views, or different empirical results, between researchers in the United States and Europe might also be explained in relation to Mannheim's construct of 'community of location'. Research in European countries carried out in rather small nation-states is probably characterized by such a community of location as being one basis for a common cultural background, a basis which might be lacking in a large nation-state such as the United States. As mentioned earlier, community of location is one of the prerequisites for constituting a generation, and also for becoming an actual generation because of the necessity of shared experiences. Co-existence is not enough.

Departing further from Mannheim, another reason for the different views could be that Mannheim's theoretical construct of 'generation units' has been neglected in earlier research. The baby-boomers could thus theoretically constitute an actual generation, within which the so-called 'Protest Generation' form one generation unit, whereas the 'silent' baby-boomers may form another, or several others, with quite different and even antagonistic mentalities. This could also be viewed as intracohort heterogeneity, which could be more visible in a continent like the United States. The implications of Mannheim's elaboration could be that intracohort heterogeneity under certain conditions might be viewed as criteria of distinct generation units. For example, to the 'Protest Generation' is often ascribed a political orientation to the Left, other 'generation units' among the baby-boomers might be more conservatively oriented. This assumption allows for new approaches, even when studying social change and the changing welfare policy, or the changing ageing policy in Sweden.

From the discussion above, it seems as though previous research has mainly focused on the constructs of 'generation' and 'generation consciousness', while the construct of 'generation unit' has been neglected. Of significant interest is how the construct of 'generation unit' can contribute to future research, for example when studying ageing and social change.

Ideas for Future Research

Considering that generation units and the differentiated generation consciousness according to Mannheim form the basis for social change, it seems reasonable that the construct of 'generation unit' can shed light over policy changes. A suggested research object could be that of the Swedish welfare policy, including the ageing policy, which is transforming from more general solutions to more privatized and market-oriented ones. This is however an assumption to be investigated. An analytical task is then to identify generations, and separate 'generation units', related for example to economic change in society. Also, because of the presumptions of increasing individuality, fragmentation and heterogeneity in society, Mannheim's construct of 'generation units' could be one of the significant theoretical constructs when studying different generations and cohorts.

Of importance for the future, also pointed out in international gerontological research, is knowledge about relations between generations, including family generations, and between cohorts, and as well as their interactions, in the ageing society. One reason for this is that we cannot take for granted that 50 year old people of today, in the course of the next 30 years, will be and act like the 80 year old people of today. Important issues are also the different strategies adapted by ageing cohorts to cope, not only with deterioration and transitions of different kinds, but also with social change such as increasing automation and new technology, including information technology. Of interest is the illumination of differences between cohorts, and between family generations, and their interactions concerning how changes like these are influencing their views on the ageing process and what constitutes old age. Studies on relations between generations, and between cohorts, could focus on social integration and disintegration, and social inclusion and exclusion, as well as social conflicts and ageism.

The multicultural society also raises questions about the consequences for different cohorts, and generations, including family generations. This also lead to the ideas of Eyerman and Turner (1998) and McMullin (2000), mentioned earlier in this article, suggesting an elaboration of generation, class, gender, and ethnicity as comparable analytical categories. This then requires a conceptualization of all the four constructs in relation to each other. Related questions are how generations and cohort experiences differ across class, gender and ethnicity. Depending on the theoretical framework though, sociologists usually give priority to only one of these variables. Considering that high chronological age is mainly a female phenomenon in most Western countries, it seems reasonable to at least consider gender aspects of the concepts of age cohort, and generation. Quoting Riley: 'After 40 years of research … did we realize that a theory of age must include a theory of gender' (Riley, 1998: 31).

Notes

1 This is as obvious, when looking through *Abstracts in Social Gerontology*, 1990-2000.

2 In the literature on age and ageing, there is a multitude of time dimensions, for example, biological time and psychological time, and correspondingly biological and psychological age and ageing. These concepts are however not relevant for my further discussion of the constructs of cohorts and generations.

3 The waves of generations related to social change are sometimes imagined to be rhythmic and encompass about 30 years (Hazelrigg, 1997; Hardy and Waite, 1997).

4 A similar position was already taken about thirty years earlier by Ryder (1965).

5 Cohorts in the meaning of birth cohorts are further used to describe changes in the age structure of populations, which as such is a basic condition for the development of gerontology as a discipline.

6 The term baby-boomers refers to slightly different points in time in different countries, as it concerns the increase of the fertility rate. Therefore, in most Western countries the term refers to those born after World War II. Sweden is in this case an exception, because this increase of the fertility rate happened a few years earlier.

7 This term generally refers to those who were protesting against, amongst/above all, the Vietnam War.

References

Alasutari, P. (1995), *Researching Culture: Qualitative Method and Cultural Studies*, Sage Publ. Inc., London.

Alwin, D.F. (1992), 'Aging, Cohorts, and Social Change: An Examination of the Generational Replacement Model of Social Change', in H.A. Becker (ed.), *Dynamics of Cohort and Generations Research*, Thesis Publishers, Amsterdam, pp. 53-95.

Andersson, Å., Furth, T. and Holmberg, I. (1993), *70-talister: Om värderingar förr, nu och i framtiden* (The 70s: On Values in the Past, Present, and in the Future), Natur och Kultur, Stockholm.

Antikainen, A., Houtsonen, J., Houtelin, H. and Kauppila, J. (1996), *Living in a Learning Society: Life Histories, Identities and Education*, The Falmer Press, London.

Becker, H.A. (1992), 'A Pattern of Generations and its Consequences', in H.A. Becker (ed.), *Dynamics of Cohort and Generations Research*, Thesis Publishers, Amsterdam, pp. 319-248.

Becker, H.A. (1993), 'Epilogue', in H.A. Becker and P.L.J. Hermkens (eds.), *Solidarity of Generations: Demographic, Economic and Social Change, and its Consequences*, Thesis Publishers, Amsterdam, Vol. II, pp. 837-844.

Bengtson, V.L., Burgess, E.O. and Parrot, T.M. (1997), 'Theory, Explanation, and a Third Generation of Theoretical Development in Social Gerontology', *Journal of Gerontology: Social Sciences*, Vol. 52B (2), pp. S72-S88.

Berger, P.L. and Luckmann, T. (1967), *The Social Construction of Reality: A Treatise in the Sociology of Knowledge*, Anchor Books, Doubleday and Company, New York.

Bourdieu, P. (1984/1979), *Distinction: A Social Critique of the Judgement of Taste*, Routledge and Kegan Paul, London.

Bourdieu, P. (1988), *Homo Academicus*, University of Stanford Press, Stanford.

Cornman, J.M. and Kingson, E.R. (1996), 'Trends, Issues, Perspectives and Values for the Aging of the Baby Boom Cohorts', *The Gerontologist*, Vol. 36, pp. 15-26.

Dannefer, D. (1988), 'What's in a Name? An Account of the Neglect of Variability in the Study of Aging', in J.E. Birren and V.L. Bengtson (eds.), *Emergent Theories of Aging*, Springer Publ. Comp, New York, pp. 356-384.

Eisenstadt, S.N. (1951), *From Generation to Generation: Age Groups and Social Structure*, Routledge and Kegan Paul, Ltd, London.

Eyerman, R. and Turner, B.S. (1998), 'Outline of a Theory of Generations', *European Journal of Social Theory*, Vol. 1 (1), pp. 91-106.

Green, B.S. (1993), *Gerontology and the Construction of Old Age: A Study of Discourse Analysis*, Aldine de Gruyter, New York.

Hammarström, G. (1986), *Solidaritetsmönster mellan generationer* (Solidarity Between Generations), Projektet 'Äldre i samhället – förr, nu och i framtiden', Arbetsrapport 27, Sociologiska institutionen, Uppsala universitet.

Hammarström, G. (1993a), *Värdeförändring och kontinuitet i tre generationer* (Value Change and Continuity in Three Generations), Acta Universitatis Upsaliensis, Almqvist and Wiksell International, Stockholm.

Hammarström, G. (1993b), 'Solidarity and Values in Three Generations', in H.A. Becker and P.L.J. Hermkens (eds.), *Solidarity of Generations: Demographic, Economic and Social Change, and its Consequences*, Thesis Publishers, Amsterdam, Vol. II, pp. 683-709.

Hammarström, G. (2000), 'Visioner eller realiteter? Generationsskillnader i synen på att ta hand om äldre' (Visions or Realities? Generation Differences in Attitudes Towards Home Help Provision for Old People), in *I väntan på framtiden*, Försäkringskasseförbundet, Fakta nr 2, Stockholm, pp. 104-123.

Hammarström, G. (2001), *Changing Priorities of Public and Non-Public Home Help Provision for Elders in a Changing Society? The Case of Sweden*. Paper presented at the 17th International Congress in Gerontology, Vancouver, Canada, July, 1-6, 2001.

Hardy, M.A. (ed.) (1997), *Studying Aging and Social Change: Conceptual and Methodological Issues*, Sage Publ. Inc., London.

Hardy, M.A. and Waite, L. (1997), 'Doing Time: Reconciling Biography With History in the Study of Social Change', in M.A. Hardy (ed.), *Studying Aging and Social Change: Conceptual and Methodological Issues*, Sage Publ. Inc., London, pp. 1-21.

Harris, D. (1988), *Dictionary of Gerontology*, Greenwood, Westport, CT.

Hazelrigg, L. (1997), 'On the Importance of Age', in M.A. Hardy (ed.), *Studying Aging and Social Change: Conceptual and Methodological Issues*, Sage Publ. Inc., London, pp. 93-128.

Inglehart, R. (1977), *The Silent Revolution: Changing Values and Political Style among Western Publics*, Princeton University Press, Princeton, New Jersey.

Kohli, M. (1988), 'Ageing as a Challenge for Sociological Theory', *Ageing and Society*, Vol. 8 (4), pp. 367-394.

Laslett, P. (1992), 'Is There a Generational Contract?' in P. Laslett and J.S. Fishkin (eds.), *Justice between Age Groups and Generations*, Yale University Press, New Haven.

Linton, R. (1942), 'Age and Sex Categories', *American Sociological Review*, Vol. 7 (5), pp. 589-603.

Lynott, R.J. and Lynott, P.P. (1996), 'Tracing the Course of Theoretical Development in the Sociology of Aging', *The Gerontologist*, Vol. 36 (6), pp. 749-760.

Maddox, G.L. and Campbell, R.T. (1985), 'Scope, Concepts and Methods in the Study of Aging', in R.H. Binstock and E. Shanas (eds.), *Handbook of Aging and the Social Sciences*, Van Nostrand Reinhold, New York, pp. 3-31.

Mannheim, K. (1928/1952), 'The Problems of Generations', in P. Kecskemeti (ed.), *Essays in the Sociology of Knowledge*, Routledge and Kegan Paul, Ltd, London.

Mannheim, K. (1956), 'The Problem of the Intelligentsia: An Inquiry into its Past and Present Role', in E. Mannheim and P. Kecskmeti (eds.), *Essays on the Sociology of Culture*, Routledge and Kegan Paul, London.

McMullin, J.A. (2000), 'Diversity and the State of Sociological Aging Theory', *The Gerontologist*, Vol. 40 (5), pp. 517-530.

Mills, C.W. (1959), *The Sociological Imagination*, Grove Press, Inc, New York.

Minkler, M. and Estes, C.L. (eds.) (1999), *Critical Gerontology: Perspectives from Political and Moral Economy*, Baywood Publishing Company, Inc, Amityville.

Murphy, J.W. and Longino, C.F. (1997), 'Toward a Postmodern Understanding of Aging and Identity', *Journal of Ageing and Identity*, Vol. 2 (2), pp. 81-91.

Neugarten, B.L. and Datan, N. (1973), 'Sociological Perspectives on the Life Cycle', in. P.B. Baltes and K.W. Schaie (eds.), *Life-Span Developmental Psychology: Personality and Socialization*, Academic Press, New York.

Neugarten, B.L., Moore, J.W. and Lowe, J.C. (1965), 'Age Norms, Age Constraints, and Adult Socialization', *American Journal of Sociology*, Vol. 70, pp. 710-717.

Parsons, T. (1942), 'Age and Sex in the Social Structure of the United States', *American Sociological Review*, Vol. 7, pp. 604-616.

Rawls, J. (1971), *A Theory of Justice*, Harvard University Press, Cambridge.

Ray, R.E. (1966), 'A Postmodern Perspective on Feminist Gerontology', *The Gerontologist*, Vol. 36 (5), pp. 674-680.

Riley, M.W. (1971), 'Social Gerontology and the Age Stratification of Society', *The Gerontologist*, Vol. 11, pp. 79-97.

Riley, M.W. (1985), 'Age Strata in Social Systems', in R.H. Binstock and E. Shanas (eds.), *Handbook of Ageing and the Social Sciences*, Van Nostran Reinhold, New York, pp. 369-411.

Riley, M.W. (1988), 'On the Significance of Age in Society', in M.W. Riley, B.J. Huber and B.B. Hess (eds.), *Social Structures and Human Lives*, Sage, Newbury Park CA., pp. 24-45.

Riley, M.W. (1994), 'Aging and Society: Past, Present and the Future', *The Gerontologist*, Vol. 34 (4), pp. 436-446.

Riley, M.W. (1996), 'Age Stratification', in *Encyclopedia of Gerontology: Age, Aging, and the Aged*, Vol. I, A-K, Academic Press, San Diego, pp. 81-92.

Riley, M.W. (1998), 'A Life Course Perspective: Autobiographical Notes', in J. Giele, G. Elder (eds.), *Methods of Life Course Research: Qualitative and Quantitiative Approaches*, Sage Publ. Inc., Thousands Oaks.

Riley, M.W., Johnson, M. and Foner, A. (eds.) (1972), *Aging and Society: A Sociology of Age Stratification*, Vol. III, Russel Sage Foundation, New York.

Riley, M.W. and Riley, J.W. (1999), 'Sociological Research on Age: Legacy and Challenge', *Ageing and Society*, Vol. 19 (Part1), pp. 123-132.

Roos, J.P. (1985), 'Life Stories of Social Changes: Four Generations in Finland', *International Journal of Oral History*, no. 6, pp. 179-190.

Ryder, N.B. (1965), 'The Cohort as a Study in the Concept of Social Change', *American Sociological Review*, Vol. 30 (6), pp. 843-861.

Schaie, K.W. (1996), 'Generational Differences', in *Encyclopedia of Gerontology: Age, Aging, and the Aged*, Vol. I, A-K, Academic Press, San Diego, pp. 567-576.

Tornstam, L. (1992), 'The Quo Vadis of Gerontology: On the Gerontological Research Paradigm', *The Gerontologist*, Vol. 32 (3), pp. 18-326.

Uhlenberg, P. and Riley, M.W. (1996), 'Cohort Studies', in *Encyclopedia of Gerontology: Age, Aging, and the Aged*, Vol. I, A-K, Academic Press, San Diego, pp. 299-310.

Walker, A. (1990), 'The Economic Burden of Ageing and the Prospects of Intergenerational Conflict', *Ageing and Society*, Vol. 10 (4), pp. 377-396.

Walker, A. (1993), 'Intergenerational Relations and the Welfare Restructuring: The Social Construction of an Intergenerational Problem', in V.L. Bengtson and W.A. Achenbaum (eds.), *The Changing Contract Across Generations*, Aldine de Gruyter, New York.

White, H.C. (1992), 'Succession and Generations: Looking Back on Chains of Opportunity', in H.A. Becker (ed.), *Dynamics of Cohort and Generations Research*, Thesis Publishers, Amsterdam, pp. 31-51.

Chapter 4

Age, Ageing and the Life Course

Anna-Liisa Närvänen

> A major part of the attractiveness of studying ageing and the life course derives from its absorption of a variety of disciplinary interests and backgrounds. Thus, we have learned enough to know that the twists and turns of the life course are determined by the convergence of many different kinds of processes: historical, social structural, cultural, normative, and personality. To deal with ageing and the life course from the perspective of one of those processes is complex enough. But to see how they come together in giving shape and focus to people's lives through time is indeed a challenge to theoretical and methodological ingenuity. (Pearlin, 1982 p. 72)

The quotation is from a reading, *Aging and Life Course Transitions: An Interdisciplinary Perspective*, edited by Hareven and Adams and published in 1982. Several papers in the reading discussed the need for a changed view in research on ageing and older people, such as the need for multidisciplinary or interdisciplinary approaches, and for a life course perspective. Tornstam discussed this in relation to research on the processes of ageing, and Hareven in relation to research on the life course (1982). Tornstam argued for interdisciplinary research that enables the study of ageing at the micro and mezzo levels and in relation to structural factors at the macro level (1982). The arguments presented in the reading recur in current discussions of the subject area. Many now consider Hareven's work of the 1970s and 1980s on the life course perspective groundbreaking. Hareven stressed that the life course perspective is by nature interdisciplinary and historical. It combines sociological, psychological, demographic and economic concepts and methods. It is historical in that it puts individual time in relation to historical time and to intergenerational relations within the family: 'It attempts to follow the movement of individuals through different family configurations and roles and is concerned with the determinants of timing patterns that affect these transitions' (1982: 5). Age, ageing, generation, and life course are concepts inextricably bound up with time. In both the (family) generation perspective and the life course perspective, ageing refers to a life from birth until death. Perceptions of what it means to grow older, intergenerational relations, and the meaning of various phases in a life course, are issues that can only be approached by putting the individual life, i.e., the individual biography, in relation to other people and to its historical context.

Tornstam's (1982) discussion of the elderly as a heterogeneous rather than homogeneous group, and of how we should not regard older people solely as dependent, but must also acknowledge their inherent resources, recurs in research on older people conducted in the 1990s, particularly as criticism towards research that contributes to stereotypes of them as a social problem, and as a homogeneous group. Demand increased in the 1990s for studies showing the diversity of experiences of age and ageing, such as the effects of ethnicity, social class, generational affiliation, health, and gender (cf. Coleman and Bond, 1990; Fry, 1995; Ginn and Arber, 1995; Bury, 2000).

Interdisciplinary research on ageing and the life course is, thus, not a new discovery. But, even though the development of life course research, began in earnest in the 1980s, it is now considered a research perspective that is, in relation to ageing, in sore need of theoretical and empirical elaboration (Hareven, 1995; Bury, 2000). Hareven discusses this in relation to gerontological research claiming that very little has been done to integrate different gerontological approaches in research on ageing, or to interpret them from the life course perspective.

The growing body of literature about these perspectives is a sign that such perspectives have been gaining in acceptance since the 1980s. There are several approaches to research on ageing and the life course in the sociology, psychology, biology, history, and demographics of ageing that fall within the framework of the overall concept of the life course perspective (see Sörensen, Weinert and Sherrod, 1986). The main distinguishing characteristic to date has been quantitative studies, and cohort studies in particular. Qualitative studies on age and ageing comprise a less thoroughly explored approach to research on ageing and later life – though there is a considerable sociological literature on biography, life history and oral history. Biographical studies, such as life history research on family histories and autobiographies can explore these questions from a new perspective. Life history research is, for example, still relatively unusual in research on the elderly and ageing (Bornat, 2000). While research on the life course has become nearly a paradigm in gerontological research, it is based on premises, which are designed in such a way that almost no one has asked people about their beliefs and views on the life course (cf. Keith et al., 1994). There is a lack of qualitative studies in late adulthood and old age.

This chapter has the character of a review and one intent is to provide a theoretical discussion of pivotal concepts, i.e. ageing and life course, but it should be mentioned that the review is not exhaustive. The main aim is to contribute to a discussion of future research approaches as well as to further research issues, on the basis of the review.

Ageing in Gerontology

What is meant by age and ageing may seem obvious. The simplest approach is to think in terms of chronological time and the life of an individual within its span.

The word 'ageing' is used in the vernacular as a synonym for growing old. The ageing person, thus, is the one who is growing old. Conversely, different disciplines may provide different answers to the questions of what is meant by ageing and when it begins as a process. McPherson differentiates between different types of ageing, such as biological, chronological, psychological, and social ageing (1983). Ginn and Arber (1995) make a similar distinction between chronological, social, and physiological age.

Ageing has traditionally been considered a biological process, according to McPherson: 'For many years ageing was considered to be mainly a biological process that was inevitable, universal, and irreversible. The process begins at birth and is characterized by ten or twenty years of growth, followed by a plateau or decline in the size and efficiency of the organism' (1983: 4). Ageing can thus be defined as a process which contains both the life phase characterized by growing up and growing older. Ageing has traditionally been defined in terms of a process that involves the *decline* of cognitive, physiological and/or biological functions, and this view is still immanent in social gerontological definitions of ageing and age. Biological ageing refers to 'internal and external changes in the structure and functioning of the organism that influence behaviour and longevity' (McPherson, 1983: 7). Biological ageing results inevitably in age-based changes (senescence) in the organism, in the musculature, bones, etc. McPherson's discussion of biological age is very similar to that of Ginn and Arber, who discuss physiological ageing as that which 'relates to functional ability and the gradual decline in bone density, muscle tone and strength' (1995: 10). Biological/physiological ageing varies among individuals and groups and between the sexes. Psychological ageing is also defined in terms of senescence and refers to changes in personality, decline in cognitive ability, memory functions etc. (McPherson, 1983). These definitions then, clearly focus on the decline of an individual's capabilities.

Chronological ageing refers to an individual's chronological age and calendar time. Chronological age however, means more than simply the determination of an individual's age from birth, in years, months, and days. It is socially and culturally significant (McPherson, 1983; Ginn and Arber, 1995). Age in this sense places an individual in the social structure through status differentiation, which occurs for instance through age-graded laws that govern rights and obligations in society (e.g. age of majority, age of military conscription, age of retirement). Chronological age may also constitute grounds for the categorization of individuals and groups. Ginn and Arber assert that the definition of older people as a social problem, and as a homogeneous group based on chronological age, has obscured the differences between groups and individuals based on variations in health, gender, ethnicity, and social class (1995).

Social ageing may be seen as related to chronological age. Social ageing represents 'regular patterns of behaviour in individuals or groups as they interact with others within a specific social system' (McPherson, 1983: 8). According to Ginn and Arber, social ageing, or more accurately, social age, is socially constructed and 'refers to age norms as to appropriate attitudes and behaviour, subjective perceptions (how old one feels) and ascribed age (one's age as attributed by others)' (1995: 7). Ginn and Arber and McPherson thus stress age norms and their meaning and consequences in relation to behaviour, action, and interaction. In other words, age norms that define the activities considered acceptable for an individual or group of a particular age, and who are thus in a particular phase of life, influence how individuals act and how they are perceived by others. It follows that interaction with others is influenced by these norms, and therefor the individual's self-image.

Social ageing is, thus, also related to socially defined life phases and their meaning. Every society features socially defined and institutionalized life phases of age-based social positions and the associated norms, expectations, rights, and obligations (McPherson, 1983, cf. Närvänen, 1994). Childhood, youth, early and late middle age, and old age are examples of socially differentiated life phases, each bearing different meanings. Social schedules linked to a life phase define, for instance, when people are expected to marry and have children (marry here used in a wider sense i.e., to live in a close and usually permanent relation, not necessarily in in the legal sense of marriage). Failure to comply with socially defined expectations in various life phases is a normative breach that can engender negative social sanctions from others. The definitions of life phases and their normative importance varies among cultures, of course, with respect to number and meaning, as well as to the rites of passage that denote the transition from one life phase to another (cf. Närvänen, 1994). As discussed in particular by Ginn and Arber, age norms are not equal to all, in different life phases, but are also genderized. Socially defined schedules for marrying and starting a family may be different for men and women, as well as are those norms applicable to men and women in the sphere of working life (Ginn and Arber, 1995). The normative meanings immanent in life phases may also differ among cultures and subgroups in a society, for example those normative meanings associated with ethnicity and social class, as well as in time and space (cf. Fry, 1995).

Gerontological definitions of ageing in terms of chronological and social ageing do not inherently entail the delineation of certain age groups that can be studied in attempts to understand what ageing means. Definitions of social ageing, and social age in particular, may be seen as an attempt to gain understanding of ageing as a social and cultural phenomenon which applies to all age groups and life phases. However, when put in relation to definitions of ageing in terms of gradual cognitive, physiological, and biological decline, the concept of social ageing applies to older persons. Gerontology, as a discipline which has focused on the processes of ageing, defined in terms of a decline in functions, has thus concentrated on ageing among the middle-aged and the older persons, and on ageing populations (i.e., the demographic changes that result from postponed and lower fertility, and increasing longevity among the population and thus a generally older population).

The question is whether the traditional definition of ageing, used in social gerontology, based primarily on biological, physiological, and cognitive changes that cause impaired function, must necessarily be the point of departure for research on ageing and the life course. A consequence of a conceptualization of ageing in terms of biological/physiological decline may be that research on ageing becomes focused on ageing as a problem, in respect, for example, to health. Another consequence is that research issues central to understanding what age and ageing means, and how such meanings change over time and space for individuals and groups in different life phases, are not included in the field of research. I will therefore propose an alternative conceptualization with regard to age and ageing in terms of biographical and historical time.

Age, Ageing, and the Life Course in Terms of Biographical and Historical Time

Time and issues related to time are central to a holistic perspective on people's lives in relation to society and social changes over time, which is the core of a biographical perspective: 'Adopting a biographical perspective leads by definition to an overview of the whole life and hence to the historical events that have shaped a life' (Miller, 2000: 21). Biographical time and historical time are linked. Conceptualizing age and ageing in terms of biographical time and its relation to historical time is, in comparison to gerontological definitions, an alternative means of defining age and ageing, and may reveal perspectives and issues other than those of gerontology, not least because biographical time is not limited to ages that entail decline of cognitive or physiological function.

Bury discusses ageing in terms of biographical time and historical time (2000). Biographical time is an individual's life with all of its idiosyncrasies, and refers to various events and experiences in the individual's life such as schooling, working life, marriage, divorce, becoming chronically ill etc. However, Bury also points out that the individual life, and the events that seem unique from the individual perspective are also affected by the social contexts in which the individual lives, and by age-related structures in society like enforced age of retirement (2000). Biographical time is thus related to social structures and to the course of history, even if it may be regarded analytically as separate from historical time. Historical time refers first and foremost to cohort effects and period effects. Different individuals belong to different age cohorts, and therewith to different age groups that age in different historical contexts (Bury, 2000).

There is a substantive difference between Bury's conceptualization and the gerontological definitions outlined above. In Bury's conceptualization, biological and physiological processes do not stand out as separate from ageing as a social and cultural phenomenon, but rather are encompassed by the biographical time as a given part of an individual's experience of ageing. Ageing, then, refers primarily to 'the processes, experiences, and events that occur during a person's lifetime – that is, the *experiential* aspects of ageing' (Bury, 2000: 88, italics original). According to Bury, studies of ageing need not be restricted to studies of older persons.

Bury does not refer to Hareven in his arguments. None the less, there are similarities between Hareven's and Bury's thinking, albeit Hareven argues primarily from the life course perspective, rather than in relation to age and ageing as such. Hareven discusses the life course explicitly in terms of individual time and historical time. She emphasizes the importance of the individual's social network and the social role of the individual in various life phases in relation to various groups and individuals (1982). The notion of family makes the links between an individual's biography and (family) generational affiliation pronounced.

As conceptualized by Hareven, individual time refers to an individual's various careers over the life course, the changes in them, and in the roles associated with them. Individual time is thus intimately linked with the family, i.e., the careers and roles related to the family or families to which the individual belongs (1982). How people organize and plan their careers and the social roles connected to them over the life course are thus fundamental questions in this context. Hareven emphasizes the meaning of earlier life phases and changes in the individual's career over time – that to understand what the transition to 'old age' means demands an understanding of what happened in an individual's earlier years, and the individual's family networks and how they have changed over time. With this argument, Hareven sheds light on the meaning of social networks and family generational affiliation in research on age, ageing, and life course. Age in itself is not always the only or most important aspect to understanding changes in a life course. Changes in family status and roles may emerge as equally or more important (1982). In a similar fashion to Bury, Hareven discusses historical time, i.e., the need to relate changes in a life course to demographic, social, and economic factors (and changes) and to the individual's cultural background. Hareven puts particular emphasis on the importance of understanding an individual life course in light of local changes, which she claims have a more distinct effect on the life course than do macro-social changes (1982). This account of local changes thus highlights the importance of both time and place(s) with regard to life course and biography.

The common denominator found in the arguments of Bury and Hareven is that age, or ageing and the life course, are discussed in terms of time. They are, thus related, and are socially/historically embedded processes and experiences. Distinctions such as biological/physiological ageing, and psychological/cognitive ageing, versus social ageing, are not necessarily particularly interesting or valuable as analytical and theoretical tools for qualitative studies of ageing and the life course in the social sciences. Physiological and psychological ageing, the changes that take place in an individual's body, are instead here considered as an aspect of an individual's biography and life course, and as such, a part of the experiences of ageing to be examined. The social and cultural meanings ascribed to the various ages and life phases, and which affect the individual's self-image, careers, etc., defined as social ageing, are also part of an individual's biography, and captured in the relations between biographical time and historical time. Thus, the strength of the biographical approach to age and ageing is, that it implies all disciplinary aspects as experienced by the individuals.

Social Understanding of Ageing: Institutionalization of the Life Course and Individual Biography

The sociology of age as a new area of sociological research was introduced by Riley, one of the pioneers of sociological research on age (Riley, 1998, 1987). The fundamental idea for Riley and her colleagues was that ageing should be defined as a lifelong process, from birth to death. Riley attempted to introduce this perspective by asserting that research on ageing should also focus on children and people in middle age, rather than solely on older persons (Riley, 1998). The sociology of age was then described as a field that provides a theoretical framework for understanding the inter-relationship between the course of human life and social structures (cf. Riley, 1986, 1987). Riley's premise is that ageing over the life course and age as a structural characteristic in all societies is interrelated. Knowledge about social changes over time is then a condition for understanding ageing in a life course, perspective. Ageing and society are viewed from a process perspective focused on social change. From this perspective, other concepts related to time, such as age cohorts and generations, become central. It is however clear that the life course in Riley's research refers primarily to studies of age cohorts. This is shown by the statement of the purpose of this kind of life course analysis, which is to understand the dynamics of human ageing in successive cohorts: when they are born, grow up, age, and finally die and are replaced by other people on the one hand, and the dynamics of social changes when cohorts of people pass through social institutions organized according to age on the other (Riley, 1987).

Riley brings some key principles to light in life course research, in which the simultaneous influence of action on structure and the reverse become particularly distinct. The principle of differences in ageing between different cohorts means that when society changes, people in different cohorts age in different ways: people who belong to different cohorts differ from one another with respect to age, age criteria in relation to social roles, and with respect to the historical experiences to which the cohorts have been exposed.

Riley worked with Parsons and Merton, and her scholarly thinking was also deeply influenced by American sociology, which after the 1950s was strongly functionalist and oriented to quantitative studies (Riley, 1987). In Riley's studies, cohorts refer to birth cohorts, which is a common application of the term cohort, and is sometimes used as a synonym for generation (Kertzer, 1983). Riley, however, clearly distinguishes the concepts: 'To achieve a degree of clarification, we had to settle on an arbitrary nomenclature, such as "aging" to include the lifelong process from birth to death, and "cohort" for a set of people born at the same time (reserving "generation" for the kinship context)' (Riley, 1987: 2).

Life course research has developed markedly in the past twenty years. Sörensen, Weinert and Sherrod (1986) provide an overview of different perspectives on the life course in a reader that presents the biological, psychological, and sociological perspectives. There are distinct disciplinary differences between the perspectives. The psychological perspective on lifespan is based theoretically on developmental psychology and focused on individual development and changes during various stages of life (Filipp and Olbrich, 1986). The focus of sociological (and historical) studies of the life course is not on individual personal development or stages of development, but rather, primarily, on socially defined, institutionalized life phases and their meanings, as well as issues related to how historical changes, with respect to structural factors, change people's lives (see Meyer, 1986; Sörensen, 1986). The difference between the psychological and sociological perspectives on the life course is fundamental, as Hockey and James stated: 'By situating our discussion of ageing within a life course, rather than a life cycle perspective it becomes possible to emphasize the variations and continuities in social status and position which people experience as they mature' (1993:14). However, there is also life course research based on approaches where theories of developmental psychology are integrated with sociological (structural functionalist) theories (Giele and Elder, 1998).

Several authors have advocated a life course perspective on research on age and ageing as the perspective that is most promising for the study of individual lives, i.e., biographical time in relation to historical time and structural factors (cf. Hareven, 1982; Kohli, 1988; Hockey and James, 1993; Bury, 2000). In her early discussion of life course research, Hareven emphasizes the importance of studying how life phases in a life course are defined historically, and how these definitions have changed and are changing over time (1982). Childhood, for instance, began to emerge as a separate life phase in the 19th century, as a result of the interplay of changing values related to motherhood and the family in middle-class families, particularly in cities, the separation of the home and the workplace, and the demographic changes that came with lower child mortality rates. Childhood came to be regarded as a separate life phase, a concept which was also spread in popular literature and non-fiction, and resulted in special laws, for example against child labour. As Hareven says, this does not mean that people prior to the change could not have been aware of age-related life phases like childhood, but rather, and mainly, that a life phase became institutionalized in a society by means of various processes. On the subject of processes that have contributed to the emergence and institutionalization of old age as a separate life phase, Hareven refers to the growing body of gerontological literature, negative stereotypes of the elderly, and the pension system. Hareven's argument does not however entail focus on isolated life phases. On the contrary, Hareven also emphasizes the importance of understanding experiences of a life phase and its changes in light of other life phases and experiences, meaning that interest must be focused on the life course as a whole rather than on separate life phases, and that the individual biography should be understood contextually and in relation to historical changes (Hareven, 1982, 1995, cf. Imhof, 1986). Even Riley finds a life course perspective necessary to studying how social change processes and age structures affect each other: 'These studies must describe in detail how differences in ageing patterns are not only caused by social variations and changes but, in turn, cause further social changes, resulting in still further alterations in ageing patterns' (1986: 172).

The distinguishing characteristic of the sociological perspective on the life course is the interest on institutionalization. The life course refers to institutionalized beliefs about life from birth to death; while socially organized, defined, and institutionalized life phases are sequences in the life course (see Meyer, 1986; Kohli, 1986). However, this does not mean that theories about, and empirical studies of, the life course should be limited to structural factors alone. According to Kohli, life course theory is predicated on a structural and a constructivist perspective (1986). According to Kohli, a life course

> is an "institution" in the sense of a set of regulations of a specific dimension of life, namely, its temporal extension. It socializes in two ways: It regulates the movement of individuals through their life in terms of career pathways and age strata, and it regulates their biographically relevant actions by structuring their perspectives for movement through life. It has thus a double impact: on the social positions in their sequential organization, as well as on the symbolic horizons within which individuals conceive of themselves (and of others) and plan their actions. (1986: 272)

The difficulties involved in formulating relations between structure and action are also reflected in theoretical discussions of structure and biography within the framework of various sociological life course perspectives. Bertaux, however, questions the structural perspective and claims that life course approaches must be formulated in terms of processes (diachrony rather than synchrony), rather than in terms of structures (1982, cf. Hareven, 1982).

The relationships between biography, history, structural factors, and local contexts are thus brought forward as key dimensions in life course studies. Life course research has a strong theoretical bias towards a structural perspective and quantitative studies at the aggregated level, but is also characterized by theoretical vagueness: 'More theoretically informed research is needed (including qualitative studies of particular localities) which examines the constraints in later life (especially those of class and gender) and the individual and collective strategies people devise to deal with them.' (Bury, 1995: 29.) Issues of the life course must also be studied in the context of a comparative study of culture. The life course as an age-related institution is the hallmark primarily of industrialized and post-industrial societies. How the life course is defined and understood in cultures with other kinds of economic systems, with other relationships to work, and with other histories, is not self-evident (see Fry, 1995). One may also ask what the transition to the late modern or postmodern society and globalization may entail in relation to socially defined life phases and ageing as well as the related issues of deinstitutionalization and destandardization of the life course. According to Bury, theories on the postmodern society paint an overly romantic picture of ageing and the life course, yet are not particularly well-founded empirically, which calls for empirical studies of how people define their lives and their opportunities in life (2000).

Some Final Reflections

In the following text, I will be discussing research on ageing and the life course with two partially divergent focuses. First, I will present a more overarching discussion about approaches to and perspectives on research in this field. Thereafter, the discussion is intended to discuss some specific research issues in the field, focusing on issues of identity, time and space.

The Diversity of Ageing

A question posed in this chapter is whether research on age and ageing should be limited to studies of middle-aged and older persons, and whether an interdisciplinary research field on ageing and the life course should, as its point of departure, adopt the traditional gerontological definition of ageing. The traditional gerontological definition of research on ageing, and what ageing as a process should imply, has gained a firm foothold in the field of research. Attempts to introduce other definitions of ageing have not been notably successful. Riley and her colleagues, for instance, tried to originate a new definition of the verb 'ageing' to encompass the entire life course, i.e., ageing from birth to death, in the same way that the noun 'age' refers to all ages (1998). Riley and her colleagues also conducted research within the field of the sociology of ageing on various age groups, and emphasized the life course perspective (1998). However, they did not successfully introduce a new definition of ageing in terms of the entire life course.

I have argued that understanding ageing in a society should be based on looking at ageing in a wider context. Hockey and James emphasize in particular how ideas about individualism, gender, personal status, and the life course are embedded in cultures and social contexts (1993). Accordingly, ageing must also be understood contextually.

According to Fry (1995), gerontology has as a discipline begun to grow from a narrow perspective focused on old age, to a discipline with a broader perspective on questions of age and ageing, as well as on how age is defined and used in different cultures and societies. Fry also argues for studies of the social significance of age, as well as how age is used to create social order. These issues cannot be answered by the exclusive study of older people in a society or a culture. Studies of ageing and age should thus also examine questions of how different social groups organize interdependencies between people of different ages (Fry, 1995).

Research with focus on specific age categories has contributed to the understanding of age-specific groups, but has also created scientific problems (Pearlin, 1982). Specific concepts and theoretical arguments tend to be developed in relation to particular age groups, which has impeded the development of theoretical ideas meant to be relevant to the entire life course. As a result, Pearlin asserts that we need to study specific age groups in relation to others, and emphasizes the importance of comparisons between and within age groups, in order to enable research on the processes of ageing, as well as different kinds of life courses to be carried out.

Hareven, in her discussion of life course research, also highlights the need to relate different life phases to one another and to historical and cultural contexts:

> The social conditions of children and adolescents in a given society are related to the way in which adulthood is perceived in that society. Conversely, the role and position of adults and the aged are related to the treatment of children and youths. The formidable task of investigating the synchronization of individual development with social change requires an approach that would take into account the entire life course and various historical and cultural conditions, rather than simply concentrating on a specific age group. (1995: 121)

The premise I am proposing here for studies of thelife course and of ageing, conceptualized in terms of biographical and historical time, is to look at ageing as a lifelong process. This vitalizes questions that touch upon different life phases and life courses, as well as questions having to do with relations between and within different generations. As a deliberate premise for studies of ageing and its meaning, this approach is promising in the sense that it is still uncommon in theoretical and empirical studies of age and ageing. As evident above, several authors have emphasized the connections between structure and action (agency), i.e., structural factors and individual action (agency), as well as the links between biographical and historical time, or structure and biography, as significant to research on ageing and the life course. The question is then from which perspective the point of departure is taken. A structural perspective calls for demographic studies, cohort studies, or research on political or economic systems and structures, while a point of departure from biographical time is based on individual lives, relations between individuals and groups, and various perceptions and experiences of ageing.

That research on ageing and the life course has primarily been conducted from a structural perspective, i.e. through demographic studies, cohort studies, or studies of political and economic systems, while qualitative studies based on individuals and groups have not been especially common, naturally speaks in favour of the latter. For example, Kohli (1988), who advocates a biographical perspective, argues that structural factors and questions, such as economic and political factors, inequality and cultural aspects, can be studied from a biographical perspective. Neither cultural codes nor social classes can be considered static structural factors, but should rather be conceptualized within the framework of a biographical perspective on studies of ageing.

Qualitative studies on the issues of diversity of experiences of ageing, age and power, or social hierarchies and identities, as well as how they change in times of social changes, are then proposed here as important, along with fundamental theoretical work within the framework of this research (cf. Fry, 1995; Bury, 1995, 2000; Moen, 1996). Furthermore, ethnicity, class affiliation, and gender are also interesting in this context, as are the differences and similarities between and within life phases.

Time, Space, and Identities

As discussed above, theoretical and empirical work is needed – qualitative studies in particular – on ageing and the life course. The discussion of issues for further research has been carried out to a certain extent in the light of gaps in earlier research, and in part in the light of the issues concerning social change. Demographic changes lead to a change in the age structure. More people are growing old, and a greater number older persons are staying in relatively good physical health later in life, which can mean changes in lifestyles (cf. Laslett, 1991). In tandem with this, society is changing in other respects. According to theories on the late modern, or postmodern, society, social development is characterized by changed conditions of production, changes in the organization of work towards more flexible forms of employment, accelerating globalization, and a weakened welfare state (cf. Giddens, 1991; Hazan and Raz, 1997; Phillipson, 1998). The relationship between identities and social change is regarded as fundamental in this discussion. Identities and life courses, which in the past could to a greater extent seem institutionalized, taken for granted, and therefore self-evident, are no longer so in the postmodern society, according to this thinking. Living in a postmodern society means rather, living in a society where traditions and institutions (e.g., family and work) that used to be meaningful to an individual's self-image and the creation of identity, lose their value and identity thus becoming fragmented. Institutionalized and socially defined life phases and their normative meanings are, according to these theories, changing and differentiating, which causes a fragmentation of age-based identities (Hazan and Raz, 1997; Blaikie, 1997).

These theories postulate that the postmodern society places new demands on the individual, not least the requirement to create and negotiate one's way towards new lifestyles and identities. Collective identities, such as class identities, are presumed to be losing their meaning. In their place, pluralized, individualized, and fluid forms of day-by-day identities are said to flourish (Kumar, 1995; Hazan and Raz, 1997). The meanings of time(s) and space(s) are changing:

> It is a world in which social interaction can no longer rely on the intimacy of personal relationships, where territorial boundaries are meaningless unless charged with symbolic facades, where time is fragmented and what we call "he self" is a fluid, multiple identity asserted in specific performative context. (Hazan and Raz, 1997: 270)

Identities are not regarded here as individual stages of psychological development. Identities are displayed in a sort of 'performances', which means that the performing individual ought to have resources, arenas, and audiences for the performance. It is said that the postmodern society is characterized by a culture of consumption that is becoming ever more important to the creation of identity, since identities are to a great extent shaped through the consumption of goods and services, or – the consumption of lifestyles (see Featherstone and Hepworth, 1989, 1991; Chaney, 1995; Hazan and Raz, 1997). Consumption may then be seen as a resource for a performance. The postmodern society, with its pronounced culture of consumption can, according to Featherstone and Hepworth, bring about positive changes for older people, particularly because more youthful and positive images of older people are being developed (1989).

These theoretical outlines should, however, not be taken for granted. Thinking about social changes in the late modern society then actualizes research issues that focus on time, space, and identities in different life phases and ages, as in intergenerational relationship. Some of these questions are: What do biographical experiences and individual interpretations of the past, present, and future mean to one's opportunities, and one's definition of self? How do spatial differences influence the creation of identities in various life phases, such as living in the urban areas or in the country, or working in different institutional contexts? What performance arenas and contexts are used in different life phases to express identities? Are these arenas different in terms of both time and space for different age groups? How are they socially differentiated based on gender or social background?

In summary, it may be said that both theoretical ideas about social change in postmodern society and the research on ageing that is lacking today, actualizes questions with regard to temporality, as well as to spatiality and their meaning on the creation and expression of identities in various life phases.

Conclusions

As discussed in the chapter, there is a need for both theoretical work and qualitative empirical studies on the issues of the social meanings of age, ageing and life course. I have proposed a perspective that should discuss the issues of age and ageing from a life course perspective, with biographical time as the point of departure. Consequently, ageing as a social phenomenon then should be defined in terms of the lifetime, from birth to death. Such a perspective is necessary for the social understanding of these issues. The life course perspective implies that different ages and the different life phases within a life course should be studied in terms of how they are interrelated, thus defining each other and the social meanings of the ages and life phases. Understanding this interrelatedness is a necessary condition for understanding the separate ages or life phases. This calls for theoretical and empirical studies on the interrelatedness of the social meanings of age(s) and life phases over time, as well as the issues of age and life phase related identities in the changing society.

References

Bertaux, D. (1982), 'The Life Course Approach as a Challenge to the Social Sciences', in T.K. Hareven and K.J. Adams (eds.), *Aging and Life Course Transitions: An Interdisciplinary Perspective*, The Guilford Press, New York, pp. 127-150.

Blaikie, A. (1997), 'Age Consciousness and Modernity. The Social Reconstruction of Retirement', *Self, Agency & Society*, Vol. 1 (1), pp. 9-26.

Bornat, J., Dimmock, B., Jones, D. and Peace, S. (2000), 'Researching the Implications of Family Change for Older People: the Contribution of a Life-History Approach', in P. Chamberlayne, J. Bornat and T. Wengraf (eds.), *The Turn to Biographical Methods in Social Science. Comparative Issues and Examples*, Routledge, London, pp. 244-260.

Bury, M. (1995), 'Ageing, Gender and Sociological Theory', in S. Arber and J. Ginn (eds.), *Connecting Gender and Ageing*, Open University Press, Buckingham, pp. 15-29.

Bury, M. (2000), 'Health, Ageing and the Life Course, in Health, Medicine and Society', in S.J. Williams, J. Gabe and M. Calnan (eds.), *Key Theories, Future Agendas*, Routledge, London, pp. 87-105.

Chaney, D. (1995), 'Creating Memories. Some Images of Aging in Mass Tourism', in M. Featherstone and A. Wernick (eds.), *Images of Aging. Cultural Representations of Later Life*, Routledge, London, pp. 209-224.

Coleman, P. and Bond, J. (1990), 'Ageing in the Twentieth Century', in J. Bond and P. Coleman (eds.), *Ageing in Society: An Introduction to Social Gerontology*, Sage Publications, London, pp. 1-16.

Featherstone, M. and Hepworth, M. (1989), 'Ageing and Old Age: Reflections on the Postmodern Life Course', in B. Bytheway (ed.), *Becoming and Being Old: Sociological Approaches to Later Life*, Sage Publications, London.

Featherstone, M. and Hepworth, M. (1991), 'The Mask of Ageing and the Postmodern Life Course', in M. Featherstone, M. Hepworth and B.S. Turner (eds.), *The Body: Social Process and Cultural Theory*, Sage Publications, London.

Filipp, S-H. and Olbrich, E. (1986), 'Human Development Across the Life-Span: Overview and Highlights of the Psychological Perspective', in A.B. Sörensen, F.E. Weinert and L.R. Sherrod (eds.), *Human Development and the Life Course: Multidisciplinary Perspectives*, Hillsdale, New Jersey, pp. 343-376.

Fry, C.L. (1995), 'Age, Aging and Culture', in R.H. Binstock and L.K. George (eds.), *Handbook of Aging and the Social Sciences*, Academic Press, San Diego, pp. 118-136.

Giddens, A. (1991), *Modernity and Self-Identity: Self and Society in the Late Modern Age*, Polity Press, Cambridge.

Giele, J.Z. and Elder, G.H. Jr. (1998), 'Life Course Research: Development of a Field', in J.Z. Giele and G.H. Elder Jr. (eds.), *Methods of Life Course Research. Qualitative and Quantitative Approaches*, Sage Publications, Thousand Oaks, pp. 5-27.

Ginn, J. and Arber, S. (1995), '"Only Connect": Gender Relations and Ageing', in S. Arber and J. Ginn (eds.), *Connecting Gender and Ageing*, Open University Press, Buckingham, pp. 1-14.

Hareven, T.K. (1982), 'The Life Course and Aging in Historical Perspective', in T.K. Hareven and K.J. Adams (eds.), *Aging and Life Course Transitions: An Interdisciplinary Perspective*, The Guilford Press, New York, pp. 1-26.

Hareven, T.K. (1995), Changing Images of Aging and the Social Construction of the Life Course, in M. Featherstone and A. Wernick (eds.), *Images of Aging. Cultural Representations of Later Life*, Routledge, London, pp. 119-134.

Hareven, T.K. and Adams, K.J. (1982), *Aging and Life Course Transitions: An Interdisciplinary Perspective*, The Guilford Press, New York.

Hazan, H. and Raz, A.E. (1997), 'The Authorized Self: How Middle Age Defines Old Age in the Postmodern', *Semiotica*, Vol. 113 (3/4), pp. 257-276.

Hockey, J. and James, A. (1993), *Growing Up and Growing Old. Ageing and the Life Course*, Sage Publications, London.

Imhof, A.E. (1986), 'Life Course Patterns of Women and Their Husbands: 16th to 20th Century', in A.B. Sörensen, F.E. Weinert, and L.R. Sherrod, (eds.), *Human Development and the Life Course: Multidisciplinary Perspectives*, Hillsdale, New Jersey, pp. 247-270.

Keith, J., Fry, C.L., Glascock, A.P., Ikels, C., Dickerson-Putman, J., Harpending, H.C. and Draper, P. (1994), *The Aging Experience. Diversity and Commonality Across Cultures*, Sage Publications, Thousand Oaks.

Kertzer, D.I. (1983), 'Generation as a Sociological Problem', *American Review of Sociology*, Vol. 9, pp. 125-149.

Kohli, M. (1986), 'Social Organization and Subjective Construction of the Life Course', in A.B. Sörensen, F.E.Weinert, and L.R. Sherrod, (eds.), *Human Development and the Life Course: Multidisciplinary Perspectives*, Hillsdale, New Jersey, pp. 271-292.

Kohli, M. (1988), 'Ageing as a Challenge for Sociological Theory', *Ageing and Society*, Vol. 8, pp. 367-394.

Kumar, K. (1995), *From Post-Industrial to Postmodern Society: New Theories of the Contemporary World*, Blackwell, Oxford.

Laslett, P. (1991), *A Fresh Map of Life. The Emergence of the Third Age*, Harvard University Press, Harvard.

McPherson, B.D. (1983), *Aging as a Social Process. An Introduction to Individual and Population Aging*, Butterworths, Toronto.

Meyer, J.W. (1986), 'The Self and The Life Course: Institutionalization and Its Effects', in A.B. Sörensen, F.E. Weinert, and L.R. Sherrod, (eds.) *Human Development and the Life Course: Multidisciplinary Perspectives*, Hillsdale, New Jersey, pp. 199-216.

Miller, R.L. (2000), *Researching Life Stories and Family Histories*, Sage Publications, London.

Moen, P. (1996), 'Gender, Age, and the Life Course', in R.H. Binstock and L.K. George (eds.), *Handbook of Aging and the Social Sciences*, Academic Press, San Diego, pp. 171-187.

Närvänen, A-L. (1994), *Temporalitet och social ordning*, (Temporality and Social Order), (Diss.), Linköping University, Linköping.

Pearlin, L.I. (1982), 'Discontinuities in the Study of Aging', in T.K. Hareven and K.J. Adams (eds.), *Aging and Life Course Transitions: An Interdisciplinary Perspective*, The Guilford Press, New York, pp. 55-74.

Phillipson, C. (1998), *Reconstructing Old Age. New Agendas in Social Theory and Practice*, Sage Publications, London.

Riley, M.W. (1986), 'Overview and Highlights of a Sociological Perspective', in A.B. Sörensen, F.E. Weinert and L.R. Sherrod (eds.), *Human Development and the Life Course: Multidisciplinary Perspectives*, Hillsdale, New Jersey, pp. 153-175.

Riley, M.W. (1987), 'On the Significance of Age in Sociology', *American Sociological Review*, Vol. 52, pp. 1-14.

Riley, M.W. (1998), 'A Life Course Approach: Autobiographical Notes', in J.Z. Giele and G.H. Elder Jr. (eds.), *Methods of Life Course Research Qualitative and Quantitative Approaches*, Sage Publications, Thousand Oaks, pp. 28-51.

Sörensen, A.B. (1986), 'Social Structure and Mechanisms of Life Course Processes', in A.B. Sörensen, F.E. Weinert and L.R. Sherrod (eds.), *Human Development and the Life Course: Multidisciplinary Perspectives*, Hillsdale, New Jersey, pp. 177-197.

Sörensen, A.B., Weinert, F.E. and Sherrod, L.R. (1986), *Human Development and the Life Course: Multidisciplinary Perspectives*, Hillsdale, New Jersey.

Tornstam, L. (1982), 'Gerontology in a Dynamic Society', in T.K. Hareven and K.J. Adams (eds.), *Aging and Life Course Transitions: An Interdisciplinary Perspective*, The Guilford Press, New York, pp. 183-220.

Chapter 5

Old Women's Ailments in the Light of History

Birgitta Odén

The Bible teaches us that old age, two or three thousand years ago, meant ailments. Ecclesiastes – four or five centuries before Christ – speaks of the evil days that approach with old age: when the sound of the mill fades, when the chirping of the sparrow grows faint and the songbirds fall silent; when people are afraid of a steep place and the street is full of terrors.

In these texts old age is governed by the ailments that precede the moment when 'the silver cord is snapped and the golden bowl is broken… the dust returns to the earth as it began'.

Throughout Hebrew legislation, children are enjoined to take care of their aged parents when they need it. Paul repeats this in his first epistle to Timothy: 'And if anyone does not make provision for his relations, and especially for members of his own household, he has denied the faith and is worse than an unbeliever.'

Ailments and care needs are thus linked together in a normative form.

Yet the care of the aged can be taken back much further than the centuries around the birth of Christ.

Two years ago a remarkable fossil was found in south-east France, in the area long since identified by palaeontologists as the territory of the Neanderthals. The find consisted of a well-preserved jaw that belonged to an elderly individual. The wear on the teeth allowed osteologists to determine the age. Even more remarkably, they were also able to show that this person had not been capable of procuring and chewing food in later life. He or she must have been *cared for*. The Franco-American team that conducted the analysis of the 200,000-year-old jaw spoke of 'les premiers pas de la solidarité'.[1]

The care of old individuals with bone injuries and other infirmities can be followed through the millennia up to our own historical times, thanks to osteological estimates of age at death and the degree of healing in skeletal injuries. There are relatively few finds so far, but osteology is advancing rapidly. The most interesting find for my topic comes from the excavation of a Viking Age cemetery at Fjälkinge near Lund in southern Sweden, where 25 per cent of the dead proved to be elderly, mostly women – who thus outlived many men, younger women, and small children.[2]

Against the background of this extremely long historical perspective on care, we are justified in asking: *what ailments* afflicted old people, and *what care* was given to them?

1.

The historian of ideas Roger Qvarsell, in his *Vårdens idéhistoria* (1991) has given us an invaluable textbook for understanding and systematizing the history of care. He began by asserting that care and nursing were originally tasks for women and that the work was done in the home. This work has 'therefore *not been visible* when historians try to describe these societies' (p. 21, my italics).

A similar conclusion was recently drawn by Lotta Holme and Ingrid Olsson (2000) as regards the history of caring for the disabled in the home, outside the institutions: home care is a black hole in the absence of sources.[3] They wrote:

> On the other hand, there seems to have been absolutely no research on the presumably very large field concerning all the functionally disabled people who never even came into contact with any institution, and who lived more or less integrated in the community and in the home.

These historians of medical thought have thereby pointed out that there may be a serious lack of sources when it comes to analyzing old people's infirmities and the care of them in bygone times. Old people's illnesses were rarely registered in the records of the public health system. The modern history of medical care, as we know, is usually based on material from the hospitals. Hospitals were originally founded to rehabilitate people who would be capable of working again. Old people could be brought into hospitals in an emergency, it is true, but they were often sent home again quickly to be cared for in the home. That is why we know so little about the ailments of old age and how they were looked after.

The aim of this chapter is to try to fill the gaps in the source material by making spot checks in various types of sources other than those left by the public care system, to see whether it might be possible in the future to fill the vacuum, after systematic studies have been carried out to supplement these spot checks.

The study concentrates on old women, although it is obvious that the gaps in the source material also affect the study of old men and make it difficult to investigate any differences in care forms between men and women. The reason for the choice of women is that recent historical research has been able to show that less is known about the living conditions of women than of men. In his study of old age in France, for example, Peter Stearns was able in 1977 to show that the conditions were different for old women than for men, and that much less research had been done on them.[4] In Sweden, women's work and ageing were therefore considered by Christina Carlsson Wetterberg in the project 'The Elderly in Society – Past, Present, and Future'.[5] My own work on medical history in recent years has been inspired by historical and literary scholars in Lund who have focused on women. Attention has been drawn to the need to increase the supply of source material about home care.

2.

It is a truism to point out that old women are afflicted by ailments. Modern geriatrics teaches us that osteoporosis can affect women after the menopause. Uterine prolapse and incontinence are becoming increasingly common in earlier years. Impairments in vision and hearing are almost inevitable for both men and women. Dental status deteriorates. The short-term memory gets weaker. Osteoarthritis in the major joints becomes common. A need arises for care and nursing when the activities of daily living (ADL) can no longer be performed. These are physical ailments, which can affect people as a consequence of the ageing process – not always, not everyone, but often. To this we can add diseases that are not specifically age-related but which are a common cause of death among men and women: cardiovascular diseases, pulmonary diseases, and cancer. Two female doctors have registered about 80 diseases and ailments by interviewing twenty elderly women about their life stories.[6]

It is more difficult to ascertain the ailments suffered by old women in the past. In death registers the usual cause of death for elderly people is 'old age' or 'frailty'. Sometimes the cause of death is stated as 'dropsy', and in certain periods infectious diseases are recorded. Osteoarthritis can be identified in skeletal finds. In the clergy's lists of old and poor people from Skåne in 1696 I have found the following infirmities stated for living people over the age of sixty: blindness, deafness, dumbness, falling sickness, consumption, hernia. It is often stated that the sick people were bedridden or used crutches.[7]

There may however have been ailments that were never mentioned in public registers because they belonged to the 'shameful' sphere, such as uterine prolapse or incontinence. The English historian of medicine Valerie Fildes has studied the earlier part of the life course and found striking silences even in private sources when it comes to menstruation and pregnancies.[8] The Swedish historian of medicine Karin Johannisson made similar observations about the difficulty of finding evidence of menstruation problems in women's letters or autobiographies. This was concealed 'behind the strong walls of modesty and intimacy'.[9]

How were these problems handled in an age when nursing care was provided within the home – invisible to the historian's eye? And what ailments led to death? What was the terminal stage of an old woman's life like in the past?

3.

The first category of source material that I have consulted consists of the clergymen's registers of death and records of catechetical examinations in the home.

It is well known that most church records have very scant data on disease and the care of people who were sick and nursed at home. Sometimes, however, the priests become more communicative, more focused on biographical information. I shall therefore attempt to extract knowledge from a well-known published Danish source, *Levnedsløb i Sørbymagle og Kirkerup kirkebøger 1646-1731*. It was Christian IV, through his instruction of 11 May 1646, who ordered parish records to be kept, although he did not require the clergy to record life stories. Old people – those aged over 60 – account for 47 per cent of the deceased.[10]

It is well known that the occurrence of biographies in parish records depends on the personal initiative and interest of the individual priest. In the records from Sørbymagle it is chiefly Mads Prom, vicar 1646-1688, who gives detailed information about the lives of the dead. During the time that Mads Prom kept the records, 633 people were buried in Sørbymagle. Of these, 58 were old women with widely differing destinies, from Johanne Christofers, who died at the age of 94 and 'had lived well with the favour of many good people and a good reputation according to every good man', to the old woman beggar who died in a roadside ditch because no one had dared to give her shelter after the king had issued a decree prohibiting people from helping beggars.

When going through these old women's biographies one is struck by the wandering life they led, marrying young, remarrying several times, and having many children. Yet they had few children still alive when they reached their own terminal stage. Most of them did not have a surviving husband either.

The cause of death is rarely diagnosed, apart from the plague and other infectious diseases which the priests could easily identify and which society needed to control.

The most interesting feature of Prom's obituaries is the regular details of how long the old women had been 'weak' or 'sick' and how long they had been bedridden before they died. This frail state had often lasted one or two years, but they had only been bedridden for one or two weeks or just a few days. From these noticeable discrepancies one can draw the conclusion that old women, despite the frailty of old age, kept on their feet as long as they could, and it was only in the terminal stage that they received care in bed. They were prepared for death by means of holy communion.

Some of the 58 old women fell at a great age and broke their hips – still a typical old-age complaint today, especially among women. In one of these fractures we are told that the bone healed naturally and that no barber's hands needed to be used. The woman lived on 'but gradually overcome by age and destitution'. If her skeleton could be identified it would show precisely the signs that prehistoric skeletons sometimes show: a disabling injury but continued life through care.

Yet another observation can be made in the material. For the final period in bed the old women were often brought to the home of a son or daughter. This is what happened to Anna, the mother of Lauritz the tailor. The priest, however, added a note: 'In her last abode she received the treatment usually given by ungrateful children.'

To what extent are Mads Prom's obituaries unique? To test this I have looked at parish records in Skåne and Blekinge, where influence from the Danish tradition ought to have made itself felt. The result was meagre. Some records of deaths and burials, such as that from Loshult for 1781, contain details of the number of children and a short history of the illness, but we are rarely told the number of *surviving* children or where the deceased had been cared for during the terminal period. Among the elderly women in this register of deaths we find a widow who died at the age of 93. She had been bedridden with old age for twelve years and her conduct had been praiseworthy. She had borne eleven children, some of whom were still alive. The register does not state where she was cared for or by whom.

The most famous register of deaths with obituaries in Skåne was kept between 1724 and 1771 by Dean Severin Schlyter for the parish of Borgeby. Schlyter regularly records the number of children borne by the deceased, but he rarely states whether they were still alive or whether they nursed the old woman.

Schlyter's most detailed obituary concerns his own wife, who was taken ill with severe boils on her thighs, which made her unable to walk. She was carried around in sheets and a wheelchair was made for her, but she spent most of her time in bed. Finally she contracted pneumonia. At the same time she was pregnant. Both the mother and the child died after the delivery. Before this, she had in her 'wretched' state given birth to thirteen children, eight of whom were still alive.

To find so much information about home nursing seems to be unusual in the clergy's death registers; it may be ascribed to the emotional circumstances.

4.

The other category of source that deserves to be surveyed is *funeral sermons*. Most Swedish funeral sermons were for men, but the Lund historian Barbro Bergner has collected and analysed about a hundred examples concerning women from the seventeenth century, orations in which the disease, the care, and the death are reported in detail.

Funeral sermons are a very special cultural genre which were intended to describe the life of the deceased, to comfort the mourners and assure them that the deceased had led a Christian life and thus earned eternal life with God. The aim influences the contents: the purpose is to emphasize the subject's piety rather than the social circumstances.

It is in the nature of the genre that the printed sermons chiefly concerned the women of the bourgeoisie and the nobility. Most of them were women of fertile age who left a grieving husband and small children behind them. Twelve per cent of Bergner's sample nevertheless were women aged between 65 and 89 – always defined as senescent or aged.

Bergner finds that a typical feature for this group of old women is the great emphasis placed on whether they had left grandchildren behind them. This was perceived as a reward for a God-fearing life. In view of the pattern of mortality in the seventeenth century, it is understandable that having children and grandchildren was reckoned as 'the crown of old age'. An old woman, Brita Sittman, died in 1671 at the age of 85, and a few days before she died she gathered her children, grandchildren, and great-grandchildren around her – there were 79 'of the fruit of her bodily seed'.[11]

The old women's illnesses are often described as the weaknesses of old age, but sometimes acute causes of death occur, such as *skälvesot*, 'the shivers'. An old woman who was housekeeper on a farm got severe pains in her chest, which today would probably be diagnosed as a coronary thrombosis. She carried on working as long as she could and refused to take the folk cures that the maid wanted to give her. She finally asked to be put in her bed, where she died after a few hours.

Bergner's findings are as yet only available in a short article, but I hope that her continued work will give us further knowledge about the home care of dying women – from small children to nonagenarians. She has excerpted a large body of material that could shed light on terminal care in practice. Some excerpts give particularly detailed accounts of the entire course of the disease and of the various measures taken to relieve acute pain. The patient was often in a multimorbid state. Swollen legs, severe headaches, high fever, erysipelas on the face, and insomnia *simultaneously* for several weeks could make the death more arduous. Cupping was attempted, but it led to inflammation in the incision. Insomnia could be relieved by reading from Saint Augustine's book about the love of God. Dying was regularly combined with religious ritual. In one case the priest concluded that the woman's severe illness was not the worst thing but that 'the frailty of old age must have been her greatest torment and trouble'. The dying woman was 65 years old!

5.

A third genre, which ought to be able to yield some information about the form taken by home nursing, is *autobiographies*. It is striking, however, that autobiographies written by old women are uncommon in printed form. The literary historian Eva Hættner Aurelius (1996), who has written an important dissertation about female autobiographies, has no examples of any describing the ailments of old age in bygone times.

A change nevertheless occurred in the last quarter of the twentieth century. Life-story narratives have become a kind of therapy for ageing people. Peter Öberg (1997), a gerontologist in Uppsala, has described the origin of this modern genre. Gerontology has focused on ageing as a process, as a result of which written memoirs and oral interviews have become a major category of material. The source material is often archived, but it is rarely printed. I have gone through the material collected by the journalist Maj Ödman roughly twenty years ago, which is in the archives of the Swedish Broadcasting Corporation. It is my impression that this material could serve as source material for the ailments of old women and the form of home nursing. The task, however, is time-consuming, and an analysis would probably give very little material on the history of care. Most life-story narratives are concerned with work or relations, whereas diseases and ailments have been perceived as too private to be written down or revealed in interviews.

Things are different with *diaries*. They often speak bluntly about ailments and cures. Peasant diaries have attracted attention in recent years, now that historical research has taken a turn towards cultural and social history. The diaries that I know, however, were all written by men. The peasant diaries from Dalarna that the historian Anna Götlind (2001) has used are especially interesting. They also report the ailments suffered by the women in the family. The literary scholar Christina Sjöblad (1997) has analysed several diaries from the eighteenth century written by aristocratic women, which contain some data on diseases and home care.

Since Prime Minister Tage Erlander's diaries started to be published in 2001, we have been given a unique opportunity to compare the difference in content between the selection principles of a spontaneous diary and the deliberate sorting that takes place in memoir writing. When it comes to illness, ailments, and care, the difference is striking. Ailments were obviously not considered worthy subjects to make public. From this it follows that continued searching for new sources on old women's ailments should focus on diaries and not memoirs.

6.

Ethnological records should also be a good potential source of material of the 'oral history' kind. In our project 'The Elderly in Society – Past, Present, and Future' the ethnologist Gunilla Kjellman (1983, 1984) conducted a survey of old material already available in folklife archives. It turned out that details of home care were rarely collected in the past. Work, church attendance, and death are included in the questionnaires but rarely questions about care. And, as the proverb says: as the question, so the answer.

Kjellman therefore worked mainly with material from the database in Umeå, based on parish records, but she supplemented this material with her own questions in the field. Her research was chiefly geared to housing but it yielded certain results that are of interest for my topic – above all, that it was common in the nineteenth century that old parents who had moved to some sort of retreat returned to the main farmhouse when the children fell ill. This applied particularly to the old mother after she had been widowed. The pattern from Sørbymagle is repeated here.

When we seek to investigate the situation of old women in our own days, we find that the new ethnology has done outstanding work in describing the care of old women's – and men's – ailments by means of interviews. The theoretical framework has been developed in collaboration with anthropology and sociology. The databases that have been built up will provide an inexhaustible source of material for tomorrow's historians of care. The Lund ethnologist Finnur Magnússon has summed up the state of research in *Humanistisk hälsoforskning* (2000). Yet the rule still applies: as the question, so the answer. The questions are just as important as the answers and require special critical analysis.

7.

The source material in my own work that has proved most rewarding is the *letters*.

In the collection of articles *Jämmerdal och fröjdesal* (1997), Eva Österberg has shown that the letters written by Catharina Wallenstedt, the widow of a civil service nobleman, to her daughter Greta between 1672 and 1718 contain a large amount of information about her own ailments and those of relatives and friends. In view of women's caring role in the home, it is natural that the women swap their experiences and give advice from woman to woman.

Catharina Wallenstedt reached the age of 92, and in her last twenty years she underwent the usual fate of old women: losing her husband, brothers and sisters, children and grandchildren. When she herself died in 1719 the only surviving members of her once flourishing family were her daughter Greta and a single grandson. Her son Carl Philip had suffered from severe gout and foot injuries as a result of an accident. In his last letter to his mother he describes how he eases the pain and swelling with a poultice of parsnips boiled in milk and wrapped around the foot with linen. Within a year he was dead. There is probably more information of this kind to be found in the unpublished letters in the National Archives.

The significance of letters in studies of non-institutional care is also well illustrated by Johan Pontén's book about the healing skills of priests and his own family's private care of mentally ill people in Korsberga in Småland.

My own studies of old women's infirmities have chiefly been based on Selma Lagerlöf's letters to various women: to her friends from her time as a teacher in Landskrona, to her translators, to the author Sophie Elkan, to her sister Gerda, to the problematic Ida Bäckmann. Since Selma Lagerlöf wrote numerous letters and was a famous cultural personality, these letters have been preserved and frequently reprinted. In her autumn years she wrote regularly to Baroness Henriette Coyet at Torup in Skåne; in return she received answers and good advice. The letters – still privately owned – testify to the home nursing of the 1930s in the upper stratum of society.[12]

I have had the privilege of analysing the letters to and from Henriette Coyet together with a doctor, Henriette Coyet's granddaughter, Associate Professor Margareta Nyman, with many years' experience of old women's ailments from the 1940s until our own days. Thanks to her I have been able to diagnose the symptoms and assess the nursing methods in the light of modern medicine.

The literary scholar Lars Ulvenstam, in his dissertation *Den åldrande Selma Lagerlöf* (1955), observes that Selma Lagerlöf began to suffer the ailments of old age already in the 1920s, when she was in her sixties. She felt a great tiredness, food did not agree with her, and she felt that her ideas did not flow as copiously as they had done. She tried to cure herself at home by reading books about self-care. A book about yoga by the German psychologist of religion Hohlenberg had been translated into Swedish in 1917, and from it she learnt how to do Indian breathing exercises to reduce her fatigue. In 1926 a Swiss doctor sent her a journal about vegetarian diet as a cure for gastritis, and when she was to visit Henriette Coyet at Torup for the first time, she gave detailed instructions about her vegetarian diet: 'I prefer to eat potato purée and drink Ramlösa.'

It is possible that she suffered a senile depression as early as the 1920s. She wrote to Ida Bäckmann in 1927 that she had become 'indifferent to life with all its troubles' – a feeling that had started to seize her 'like most old people', she adds.

The purely chance encounter with Henriette Coyet at the celebrations for her seventieth birthday lifted the depression. In the first letters to Henriette Coyet she describes her earlier weariness of life and the growing zest she felt after meeting Henriette Coyet and starting to correspond with her. During the ten years that the correspondence lasted, Selma Lagerlöf often spoke of her ailments and her fatigue but less often about her depressive spells.

In this short presentation I shall not describe in detail her range of illnesses. Instead I shall concentrate on the three forms of care that emerge from the material.

To begin with, Selma Lagerlöf had constant problems with her airways; she herself diagnosed it as influenza, pulmonary catarrh, respiratory tract catarrh, bronchitis, and the like.

In the 1930s pneumonia was one of the most common causes of death among old women. This was ten years before the discovery of antibiotics. There was no medicine to treat the disease. It is therefore natural that any form of cold required attentive care. By 1900 the universal cure for all kinds of disease was to be confined to bed, according to Qvarsell (1991). And the letters confirm this. Selma Lagerlöf constantly took to her bed.

Both Selma Lagerlöf and Henriette Coyet were privileged in that they had large households to look after them. They stayed in bed even when it meant missing important events in life: Selma Lagerlöf could not attend the banquet when she herself received the Nobel Prize, and Henriette Coyet stayed in bed when the king visited Torup and a grand royal dinner was served.

In 1934 Selma Lagerlöf contracted inflammation of the bladder. That too was cured by weeks in bed. In the following year she reports on pulmonary catarrh and a suffusion from one eye – 'once again old age on the attack', she complains. She is finally admitted to the Sophiahemmet hospital in Stockholm. This cures her. 'If I hadn't come to Stockholm I suppose the germs would have finished me', she says in a letter to Torup. Her ailments increased in 1937. Selma Lagerlöf contracted shingles, her heart was giving trouble, and her whole household caught the flu. Selma called herself 'sick and fragile as glass'. She had to move to live with her sister to get care. The doctor diagnosed acute overstrain and ordered her to stay in bed in total isolation. In 1939 she received a vitamin injection at the Red Cross nursing home, yet she still felt dizzy and was afraid of a stroke – which Heidenstam had recently suffered. But Selma was cocky. She thought that she had looked after her mind better than Heidenstam had done. Yet she suffered a brain haemorrhage around Christmas 1939 and died after a few weeks in bed.

Let us now look at the medication. Selma Lagerlöf's consistent ailments were anaemia and heart trouble. To cure the anaemia the doctors prescribed iron medicine, but this did not help. She herself relied on 'Astra's Liver Wine', which could be bought without a prescription, and which helped her. She wrote to Henriette Coyet that this miracle cure made 'the muscles swell and grow bigger than they were before, one becomes lively and optimistic and just waits to get rid of the wrinkles and acquire dark hair'. When the liver wine ceased to have any effect, she felt much more poorly, with heart problems, breathlessness, and heart palpitations. Henriette Coyet obtained the assistance of a doctor in Lund for her, but to no avail.

Selma Lagerlöf preferred to inform herself of various 'household remedies' against her sick stomach and her rheumatism. She thought that these remedies helped but that the care of her body had affected her brain – 'it is lying fallow'. On another occasion she uses an English medicine, Aeriform Bacterol, which was sprayed in through the nose and was thought to stop suppuration in the nasal passage.

Selma Lagerlöf's description of home care for old women's ailments in the 1930s is in the border zone between folk medicine, alternative oriental cures, and advice from professional physicians.

A third treatment method was to visit a spa or a sanatorium. This too was typical of the times. Spas had grown up everywhere since the seventeenth century, partly to cure syphilis and tuberculosis among the lower classes, partly to allow paying guests from the upper classes to take the waters and bathe. Around 1900 new needs had been signalled, particularly among ageing people who could not be cured and who were therefore not admitted to the emergency hospitals. Official statistics for the 1930s show that there were twelve health spas in Sweden with 32,000 guests per year. Yet this form of care was declining. In 1940 there were five spas left with 16,000 patients.[13] The historian of ideas Elisabet Mansén has given us a detailed description of spa culture before 1880 in *Ett paradis på jorden* (2001), where she declares that people went to spas 'to steel themselves against the infirmities of old age'. Her source material consists of letters and diaries and of annual reports sent to the Board of Health.

In her later years Selma Lagerlöf spent long periods at Skodsborg, in Marstrand, at the Hultafors sanatorium, at the Ulricehamn winter sanatorium. These stays were 'tedious' but she took baths, massages, and walks. In addition, she was confined to bed at times. When any staff member took ill, she too was sent to a sanatorium.

The *mental ailment* that the ageing Selma Lagerlöf mainly suffered from was fatigue and lack of concentration. In 1928 the third part of the Löwenskiöld suite had appeared and Selma Lagerlöf had immediately begun to write the fourth and last part. Drafts and fragments are preserved, but the book was never completed. Instead she passionately embarked on *Memoirs of My Childhood*, clearly inspired by her new-found friendship with Henriette Coyet. The book was finished in 1930.

After that she planned a book about the economic upswing and decline in Värmland in the nineteenth century. An enthusiastic account of the contents is included in a letter to Henriette Coyet, but the book was never written. Instead a new part of her memoirs appeared, *Selma Lovisa Ottilia Lagerlöfs dagbok* (1932), but this was broken off when she got to the age of 14, never reaching the age of 17-18 as planned.

According to Lars Ulvenstam, who has studied the ageing Selma Lagerlöf's plans and the manuscripts she left at her death, she returned time and again to the fourth part of the Löwenskiöld suite without having the energy to finish it, despite many drafts and plans.

Instead she had the idea of writing a biography of her friend Sophie Elkan, who died in 1921. Yet this plan also fell through owing to her concentration problems. She was also constantly disturbed by requests to dramatize earlier novels, boldly struggling to meet these expectations. She herself felt that drama did not suit her temperament as an author. *Gösta Berling* at the Royal Dramatic Theatre was not a success.

Fatigue and lack of concentration are natural consequences of an old woman's ailments in combination with constant commitments to the cultural élite and the general public. She had been brought up to believe that letters were to be replied to, and every major birthday that she celebrated required writing countless pathetic letters of thanks.

Selma Lagerlöf was of course not the only ageing woman in her circle who suffered from ailments. Her sister Greta, her housekeeper Miss Lundgren, and her faithful friend and secretary Valborg Ohlander were also constantly afflicted by infirmities and confined to bed. Henriette Coyet, who was not in the habit of complaining about life, caught influenza with otitis as a consequence, which persisted for four years, despite perforation of the eardrum and an infra-red lamp. She ended up totally deaf in one ear. She started having difficulties remembering names, and her granddaughter remembers that the family began to suspect that she was slightly senile. She wrote to Selma Lagerlöf in December 1939 – at the age of 78 – that she felt 'strangely stagnant, as if she could never be herself again'.

The year after Selma Lagerlöf's death, Henriette Coyet fell and fractured the neck of the femur. Broken hips are a common ailment among elderly women with osteoporosis. In 1941 this was not repaired with a nail; instead, the leg was suspended in a traction frame. Henriette Coyet could not cope with this form of care, which made her confused and aggressive. She was returned to her home and nursed there for three months, growing weaker and wasting away. Curiously enough, she stopped speaking Swedish and communicated only in French – an example of language change in old age, which has not yet attracted much attention in gerontology.

8.

And so I approach – not without a certain hesitation – yet another group of sources: *literature*.[14] Can an author's fictitious world really function as a source for filling the black holes in home care? I believe that it can, even though the knowledge we acquire belongs to the author's experience and personal insight. This is particularly important because authors often belong to other classes and groups than those who write letters, diaries, and memoirs. This gives a broader basis for formulating hypotheses.

Let me begin my collection of examples with *Maja*, a novel by Anni Blomqvist from Åland (1970). The experience that is focused on here is the schooling of a very young woman in the care of dying people – a very trying experience that belongs to women's socialization into adult life. Ivar Lo-Johansson, in his *Only a Mother* (1939) and Vilhelm Moberg in *The Last Letter Home* (1959) have highlighted the worry of pregnancy late in life and death in childbirth, a significant topic for understanding the position of the menopause in the ageing process.

Anyone who wants to obtain an idea of the significance of literature as a source for the history of home care will benefit from reading Merete Mazzarella's *Hem från festen* (1992). I myself have learnt a great deal about the problems of ageing from John Bayley's *Iris: A Memoir of Iris Murdoch* (1998), Sven Fagerbring's *Pelagius* (1998), and Emmy Gut's book about the experience of ageing, *Ålderdomen som erfarenhet* (1998). All these works are on the boundary between fiction and memoir, but they concern old people's infirmities in today's world of care, and the black hole that I have tried to fill.

9.

I have tried to shed empirical light on my thesis that the black hole in the history of medical care – home care – could be filled with the systematic use of untraditional source material, chiefly funeral sermons and letter collections.

The collections of letters that I have used ends in 1940, when the Second World War had broken out. The end of the war saw the start of a new era in the history of eldercare. Hospitals were opened to old people and were quickly filled with long-stay cases. This has given us access to public source material for the study of old people's illness and care. Geriatrics has evolved into an independent discipline.[15] The demands for municipal home care give us a new body of bureaucratic source material created by care personnel about nursing in the home. New, more reliable source material is now available.

Modern research is developing medicines and technology that are revolutionizing the care of old people's ailments. Confinement to bed has been replaced by exercise and motion. Antibiotics and vaccines postpone death. Terminal care has been developed through palliative care and the hospice movement.[16]

The bill recently put before the Swedish parliament – *Death Concerns Us All* (2000) – entails a certain return to terminal care in the home, the terminal care which we had for centuries, but which historians have hitherto found difficult to document. Filling the gap – and this is my message in this article – requires extensive and systematic collection of data and an interest in individual destinies in various historical contexts. Historical experience can be used both to issue warnings and to hold up good examples concerning today's attempts to solve tomorrow's problems: the many very old, multimorbid, weak people, those who, according to the forecasts, will be mainly women, often without any relatives to give them family care and the love that over the centuries has chiefly been the responsibility of women in the home.[17]

Notes

1 Lebel et al., 2001; *Science et vie*, 2001.
2 Arcini, 1999, pp. 66, 157 (citing B. Helgesson's report, 1990).
3 Holme and Olsson, 2000, p. 233.
4 Stearns, 1977.
5 Carlsson Wetterberg, 1988; Odén, 1990a.
6 Carlstedt and Forssén, 1999.
7 Lund Cathedral Chapter Archives E III a, list of beggars pursuant to the Royal Decree of 17 December 1695.
8 Fildes, 1986, p. 188.
9 Johannisson, 1994, p. 113.
10 Arcini, 1999, pp. 66f.
11 Bergner, 1997, p. 83.
12 Odén, 2000, p. 386.
13 SOS:K.
14 See the critical discussion of literature and historical research in *Historisk Tidskrift*, 2001:3, 2002: l.
15 Odén, 1990b.
16 Beck-Friis and Strang, 1995.
17 *Riv ålderstrappan*, 2002.

References

Unpublished sources

Lund Cathedral Chapter Archives E III a, list of beggars pursuant to the Royal Decree of 17 December 1695. Provincial Archives in Lund.

Published sources

Arcini, C. (1999), *Health and Disease in Early Lund*, Archaeologia Lundensia 8, Lund.

Beck-Friis, B. and Strang, P. (1995), *Palliativ medicin*, Stockholm.

Bergner, B. (1997), 'Dygden som levnadskonst: Kvinnliga dygdeideal under stormaktstiden', in E. Österberg (ed.), *Jämmerdal och fröjdesal: Kvinnor i stormaktstidens Sverige*, Atlantis, Stockholm.

Carlsson Wetterberg, C. (1988) 'Kvinnor, arbete och åldrande.' *Scandia*, Vol. 54 (2), pp. 235-250.

Carlstedt, G. and Forssén, A. (1999), *Mellan ansvar och makt*, Luleå Tekniska Universitet, Luleå.

Erlander, S. (ed.) (2001), *Tage Erlander: Dagböcker 1945-1949*, Gidlund, Hedemora.

Fildes, V. (1986), *Breasts, Bottles and Babies: A History of Infant Feeding*, Edinburgh University Press, Edinburgh.

Götlind, A. (2001), *Att åldras i Backåkers*, Dalarnas Forskningsråd, Falun.

Hættner Aurelius, E. (1996), *Inför lagen: Kvinnliga självbiografier från Agneta Horn till Fredrika Bremer*, Lund University Press, Lund.

Helgesson, B. (1965), *Rapport. Arkeologisk undersökning 1990. Fjälkinge 35:60*, Länsmuseets rapportserie 5.

Højrup, O. and Jensen, S. (1963), *Levnedsløb i Sørbymagle og Kirkerup kirkebøger 1646-1731*, Udvalget, Copenhagen.

Holme, L. and Olsson, I. (2000), 'Handikapphistorisk forskning', in R. Qvarsell and U. Torell (eds.), *Humanistisk hälsoforskning*, Tema Hälsa Universitetet, Linköping.

Johannisson, K. (1994), *Den mörka kontinenten: Kvinnan, medicinen och fin-de-siècle*, Norstedt, Stockholm.

Kjellman, G. (1983), *Åldringskultur i urbana miljöer. En etnologisk studie av boendemönster och livsformer bland äldre*, De äldre i samhället, Arbetsrapport 28, Lund.

Kjellman, G. (1984), *Kultur och åldrande: En etnologisk studie av boendemönster och livsformer bland äldre på svensk landsbygd*, De äldre i samhället, Arbetsrapport 17, Sociologiska institutionen, Uppsala universitet, Uppsala.

Kommittén om vård i livets slutskede (2000), 'Döden angår oss alla', Statens offentliga utredningar, SOU 2000:6, Fritzes, Stockholm.

Lebel, S. et al. (2001), 'Comparative Morphology and Paleobiology of Middle Pleistocene Human Remains from the Ban de l'Aubesier, Vaucluse, France' *Proceedings of the National Academy of Sciences*, Vol. 98, p. 20.

Mansén, E. (2001), *Ett paradis på jorden: Om den svenska kurortskulturen 1680-1880*, Atlantis, Stockholm.

Mazzarella, M. (1992), *Hem från festen*, Söderström, Helsinki.

Öberg, P. (1997), *Livet som berättelse: Om biografi och åldrande*, Almqvist & Wiksell International, Uppsala.

Odén, B. (1990a), 'Att studera de äldre i samhället', in K. Härnqvist and N-E. Svensson (eds.), *Forskning i ett föränderligt samhälle: Stiftelsen Riksbankens jubileumsfond 1965-1990*, Gidlund, Hedemora.

Odén, B. (1990b), 'Disciplinbildning mellan universitet och samhälle', in *Liberala perspektiv: Till Jörgen Weibull*, Wiken, Höganäs.

Odén, B. 'Gamla kvinnors vishet', in A. Jönsson and A. Piltz (eds.) (2000), *Språkets speglingar: Festskrift till Birger Bergh*, Lund.

Österberg, E. (1997), 'På samhällsstegens högsta topp: Drottning eller husfru' in E. Österberg (ed.), *Jämmerdal och fröjdesal: Kvinnor i stormaktstidens Sverige*, Atlantis, Stockholm.

Qvarsell, R. (1991), *Vårdens idéhistoria*, Carlsson, Stockholm.

Qvarsell, R. (1997), 'Mental hygien och psykisk hälsovård', in B.E. Eriksson and R. Qvarsell (eds.), *Hur skall själen läkas?*, Stockholm.

Science et vie, (2001), 1010, November.

Senior 2005 (2002), 'Riv ålderstrappan: Livslopp i förändring', Statens offentliga utredningar, SOU 2002:29, Fritzes, Stockholm.

Sjöblad, C. (1997), *Min vandring dag för dag: Kvinnors dagböcker från 1700-talet*, Carlsson, Stockholm.

Stearns, P. (1977), *Old Age in European Society: The Case of France*, Croom Helm, London.

Sveriges officiella statistik Allmän hälso- och sjukvård (1930, 1940).

The Revised English Bible with the Apocrypha, (1996), Cambridge.

Ulvenstam, L. (1955), *Den åldrande Selma Lagerlöf*, Stockholm.

Chapter 6

Researching Home Help Services for the Elderly in Japan and Sweden: How Cultural Concepts Affect the Research Design

Els-Marie Anbäcken

Ageing happens in a cultural context (Fry, 2000)

In qualitative research there is a more or less tacit agreement that the researcher her/himself is a tool, an interpreter of the field being studied. Little has been done which examines the 'hidden' preconceptions of researchers, the importance of being aware of them, and using them in to conduct the research. This is what I attempt to do by presenting and discussing one aspect of an ongoing research project on elderly persons utilizing home help services in Japan and Sweden. The way in which the elderly individual is seen in Japan and in Sweden respectively, I have used as a key to open the door to a discussion on this theme.[1]

The Comparative Research Project on Frail Elderly Individuals with Home Help Services around the Clock

In 1998 a research group at Kwansei Gakuin University, Nishinomiya, Japan, approached us[2] concerning collaboration in a comparative study on frail elderly persons with around the clock home help services. Since the 1970s home help services have been common in Sweden and have been utilized by many elderly individuals, but there has been a change in policy during the last ten years, and home help services have become restricted to those with greater care needs. Further, there is now in Sweden more emphasis on care than on household services (Szebehely, 2000). With the so-called Gold Plan of 1989-1999 in Japan, home help services have become part of national policy. Home services and institutional services are the two main concepts comprising this policy to develop care for the elderly. In the summer of 1997 the government passed a bill on national care insurance, and this was implemented in April 2000. Prior to this, it had taken three intensive years to prepare and formalize a system comprising economic issues, assessment, providers of care, education and staffing, among many other factors, on both national and municipal levels. The media have eagerly followed every move, and have continuously kept the general public informed.

The study briefly presented here began during this preparatory period, and the initial part was published shortly before implementation of the care insurance.[3] The aim of the study was to examine the quality of the home help services from the user's point of view, as well as from the perspective of family members.

What then motivates comparative studies with a theme such as this? Hannerz (1983) discusses comparisons in social anthropology in terms of a continuous process of contrasting, by which the specifics of each culture or society become clearer. He makes a remark which rhymes well with my own view: 'other societies are useful to think with' (1983:33, my translation). This has obviously been the path chosen by the Japanese, as they have studied almost every step taken in Swedish policies on the care of the elderly. There are numerous books, articles and TV programmes on Sweden as 'the number one welfare state' – but critical voices have also been heard, and publications on those 'cold Swedes' who do not care about their elderly parents can also be found. For the past ten years I have studied and followed the way in which the Japanese social welfare system for the elderly functions from a socio-cultural perspective. I have noted how the systems being developed have been influenced by Sweden, but I have also seen how differently they have been developed. However, although Japan and Sweden are socio-culturally different in many ways, they do share one thing: the large proportion of persons aged 65 and over comprise around 17 per cent of the population, and both countries have nearly the same average life expectancy, Japanese women being two years ahead, 84, in 1999 (Kono, 2000), as compared to 82 in Sweden in 2000 (Svenska Kommunförbundet, 2001). Life expectancy for men in Japan and Sweden is roughly the same i.e., around 77 years of age.

Our original plan was to undertake an entirely qualitative study. However, the survey that was being designed by the Japanese group was quantitative, a standardized questionnaire. The intention was for home helper staff to use it in interviews with the elderly and with primary caregivers. Here we encountered the first communication obstacle, because we had never planned for a quantitative survey in Sweden. As we had limited resources in the Swedish research group, we could not carry out a large number of interviews. However, to accommodate those conducting the Japanese study we performed a strategic sampling of 20 cases for this survey (with one loss).[4] In Japan, 151 surveys were carried out (Kono, 2000:141). My personal thinking on this difference in preferred methods is that it reflects the fact that qualitative methods are rather uncommon and untried in Japan. In fact I often hear that the research which is requested, and which is therefore easier to get funding for, is quantitative.

The first part of the comparative study was not reported in the joint paper.[5] For the second part of the project we decided to work together right from the start. We agreed to do a qualitative study based on an interview guide covering specific areas.[6] Yet, the Japanese group trod another path as they concentrated on interviewing the family caregivers, while the Swedish researchers stuck to the original plan of having three perspectives.[7] These were the elderly person's own experience and evaluation of home help services, the home helper's conception of the client's daily life and about how satisfactory the home help services were, and thirdly, the family member's (spouse or child) view concerning home help services for the elderly individual.

This ongoing process of communication between the two research groups confirmed that the home situation for the elderly differed in many ways. The majority of those interviewed in Japan were elderly persons living with their child or spouse. Our data from Sweden showed that in nearly 200 cases of older persons using home help services, none lived with a child. There were married couples, however, and in those cases the spouse was seen as the primary caregiver regardless of whether or not he/she provided most of the care.

Thus, we knew right from the beginning that interviewing directed at the primary caregiver would be problematic. In Japan, someone in the family, often a daughter-in-law or a daughter, but increasingly also the spouse, is seen as the primary caregiver. In Sweden it is usually the home helper or the spouse. Moreover, even though the spouse is considered the caregiver in a moral sense, the more direct care such as assistance in going to the toilet and showering is performed by the home helper. As the study progressed we also discovered that in Japan the primary caregiver (the family member) was chosen for this interview, not the old person herself/himself.

Another difference emerged in how we defined around-the-clock home help services. In Japan this means that the services are given at scheduled intervals around the clock. In Sweden basically all home help is on a 24-hour basis if the utilizer of home help is connected to the home help station through an alarm system, which the majority are. However, those visited regularly around the clock are relatively few in number (in our study, seven out of 19). Thus, simply using the same term '24-hour home help', without reflecting on what this entails can be misleading.[8]

The interview guides were formulated through a process involving e-mail communication and several of face-to-face meetings. We had to translate from Japanese to English and from English to Japanese – and later also into Swedish, as some Swedish students were going to do some of the interviewing. This process required some compromising, and both sides had to accept the fact that some questions were inapt. On the one hand, thanks to the model chosen, i.e., an interview guide, the interview situation could be conducted so as to fit each context. On the other hand, this freedom also meant that our preconceptions guided our interviewing. In analysing the material, this aspect needs to be studied as part of the research design.

The one big difference here was that the Japanese researchers told us that the elderly persons could not be asked these questions[9] directly; some had dementia, and others were too frail. I did not participate in any of the Japanese interviews, but with my own experience in conducting interviews in Japan in mind, I believe it would have been possible to do some interviews directly. However, had the Japanese interviewers done so they would have had to waive certain tacit socio-cultural rules. Moreover, the family caregivers – the primary caregivers – would probably not want this, since they are the experts on the elderly persons, and they would therefore answer for them. Of course, this could also be the case in Sweden if the person receiving care is very frail or is disabled because of dementia.

What I find most startling, from my Swedish perspective, is the view expressed by the Japanese researchers when they presented a model for analysing the qualitative interviews. According to their perspective, the main users of home help services are the family caregivers. It became clear that this was the 'taken-for-granted' presupposition with which they had worked throughout the study. Herein lies a marked difference. In Sweden, even if it is clearly recognized that home help services are a great help and support for the family caregiver (usually the spouse), the elderly person who is the subject of the care is the user of home help services and is thus the subject, not the object, of the whole process (cf. Szebehely, 1998: 75). This is of course our preconception!

This difference is now creating a challenging problem for us in the analysis phase of the study. The categories that the researchers in Japan have found and formulated from the interviews are based on the assumption that the users of home help services are the primary caregivers, thus the family caregiver. In Sweden, on the other hand, we have assumed that the elderly person himself/herself is the user.[10] Thus, the focus in Japan is on the primary caregiver's opinions and feelings concerning what is good care, while in Sweden the elderly persons are considered to be in charge of their own lives, even if they are frail and disabled. In Japan they are dependent on their children or spouse; they are reduced to a 'patient status' and have to rely on others. Their identity could be described as being rooted in the dependent condition in which they find themselves, not in the individual persons they are. Another way of describing this would be to say that frail, elderly Japanese people enjoy being taken care of by their children. Their 'patient status' is a way for them to cope with, and perhaps accept, their weakened physical (and possibly mental) condition.

After years of studying the Japanese care system for the elderly from a socio-cultural point of view, taking the point of departure in culture defined as norms, traditions and patterns of behaviour, this should not have surprised me. What was startling, however, was the realization that although we communicated closely with our Japanese co-researchers (with whom we had discussed the study from exactly this point of view and emphasized the differences between Japan and Sweden in terms of filial duty), we none the less ended up with different perspectives as we were about to analyse our material.

It is precisely this difference, which is also the main focal point in this chapter, and that I regard as one of the most interesting results of our study (at least so far), since it reveals the depth of norms and traditions held not only by those being studied, but also by those doing the research. If we take the position, as I do, that in qualitative research the researcher is a research instrument (Spradley 1980:57), this can have implications about which we need to be more aware. This became obvious when analysis of the data from this cross-cultural comparative research was begun.

We will now take a closer look at the other aspect of the research project that was mentioned initially. I will begin with some brief background material.

During nearly ten years of research in this field, my special interest has been, and continues to be, in the different ways of thinking and feeling concerning what should constitute the ideal life and care for the elderly – although almost the same words tend to be used to describe this in both Japan and Sweden.[11] For example, people would probably give similar answers if asked what meant most to them: security and safety, children and grandchildren (if there are children), and health. But if they were questioned in more detail as to what was meant, the answers would vary.[12] Swedish answers would probably deal more with economic security and socializing with children and grandchildren, while those from the Japanese would be more about security in relation to children, and expectations (or the lack thereof) directed toward their children in times of need. To a Swede, health would probably be an important factor with respect to being able to live independently, and to being able to remain living at home. A Japanese, on the other hand, would probably think about avoiding a move to a nursing home for the aged, but also about not becoming a nuisance or a burden to his/her children, who would be doing the primary caregiving.[13] With this rather rough comparison in mind, we will take a look at some deeply rooted views both on what is considered to be a good life in one's old age, as well as on how the elderly and the ageing process are perceived. Throughout, we will relate these to our preconceptions, and how we may include them by means of exploring them.

Views on Life in Old Age – and Hidden Preconceptions on the Part of Researchers

> What is defined as a good life for older people, and by older people, in different social and cultural settings? What features of these settings influence these definitions and how?
> How are the influences of these social characteristics mediated by cultural norms and values, such as filial piety, individual independence, peer bonds, domestic arrangements, and family responsibilities?
> How are the implications of health or functionality shaped by attributes of the social and cultural context, such as definitions of full functionality of care and attitudes toward giving and receiving it? (Keith et al., 1994:xvii)

These questions, taken from the introduction to *The ageing experience* ... (ibid.) summarize the views harboured by many in socio-cultural studies on ageing and the care of the elderly. They are indeed central, but not only regarding our views about those we study. We also need to include ourselves and the cultural setting in which we are raised in order to be able to study and compare these considerations.

With this in mind, we will take a look at some Japanese and Swedish factors concerning old age and family relations. I base my statements on the results of my Ph.D. thesis (1997) as well as on the continuous follow-up of how this field is developing in Japan.[14] I have perceived the 'main stream' feeling in contemporary Japanese society, regardless of whether the relationship is seen as good, warm, easy-going or tense, as being that it is the duty of children to take care of their parents when they grow old and need help, especially when one of the parents is alone after his/her spouse's death (Anbäcken, 1997). To be left alone is commonly seen as an impossible state of affairs, since the elderly are classified as dependent, and a dependent person must depend on someone. There are signs indicating a tendency towards change here. An increasing number of older persons choose to live more independently than the older generation of only ten years ago. However, the roots of tradition are strong, and in many ways one can describe Japan as a society where culture is nurtured, and where old ideals are recreated into new patterns. In Japan, the old person was traditionally described in terms of a return to childhood (Formanek, 1992:251). The aged person and the infant were thus in a somewhat parallel situation. The term 'aged' did not necessarily mean a person of pensionable age, but rather a person who had reached the so-called 'old-old' age of 80, or a person needing some kind of support. This view can still be discerned in the way elderly, frail people are treated, i.e. more or less as infants who need constant 'motherly' care. However, surveys conducted in Japan show that people increasingly accept and prefer formal care in combination with informal care, and our comparative study of 24-hour home help confirms this: home help services are to a large extent a complement to the care provided by the family.

On the other hand, a deep-rooted conception in the Swedish mind concerning parent-child relations is that parents do not want to be transformed into their children's infants (Odén, 1992:54). Various reports clearly indicate that older people in Sweden (and the Nordic countries) continue to prefer care from the formal social care system, rather than informal care (cf. Andersson, 2000:26).

In this context it should be mentioned that in Japan there are two basic views concerning old age, one is biological and emphasizes the physical decline; a view which the European 'Lebenstreppe' mirrors as well (Schenda, cited in Formanek, 1992:245). The other is based on Confucian concepts, and stresses the mental strength and wisdom of the elderly, who thus are to be respected (ibid:253). Palmore has emphasized this respectful view of the elderly in his research, which is vividly mirrored in the title of his book *The Honorable Elders* (Palmore, 1975).[15] Moreover, this is the common image in the West, including Sweden, when discussing old age in Japan. Koyano (and others) however, criticize Palmore's view as being superficial and not reflecting reality (Koyano, 1989:335). It is nonetheless interesting to draw parallels between this view and the theory of gerotranscendence that sociologist Lars Tornstam has developed (1998:264-285). Gerotranscendence emphasizes that in their old age, as they draw closer to the end of life, people become more thoughtful, reflecting on their life, accepting it as it has been, and looking back on life and seeing it all fit together. This image is close to traditional

Asian images of the elderly as being the wise ones in the society – and thus worthy of honour.

Filial Duty in Japan and Sweden

Anyone studying the care of the elderly in Japan from a socio-cultural point of view is confronted with the norm of filial duty. When I began my fieldwork in the autumn of 1992, I was aware of the concept of filial duty (*oyakôkô*). However, it was not until I interviewed people in private homes, in institutions, and at the Division of Social Welfare for the elderly at city halls; and met with many elderly individuals as well as their children, caregivers, receivers of care, staff members, family members, researchers and students, that the importance of filial duty really came to the fore.

In Sweden, the role of family caregivers has only recently become highlighted. In the spring of 2000 I found the term filial duty (or responsibility)[16] treated at length in Sweden by Dr Marianne Winqvist at Uppsala University in her book on the ageing family (Winqvist, 1999). Winqvist applied a life form analysis based on her interviews with adult children, concerning their relationship to their elderly parents who needed help of different kinds. I find the results valuable with respect to cross-cultural comparative studies on care for the elderly, since a rather substantial amount of research has been done internationally on elderly persons, their families and care (especially in East Asian cultures), where filial duty has been one of the key concepts used in interpreting and analysing data. Of course studies conducted in Sweden, for example Lennart Johansson's dissertation, *Caring for the next of kin ...* (1991), have also revealed the large share of the care that families provide for elderly relatives in Sweden. However, Winqvist was first to specifically focus on and analyse adult children in relation to their ageing parents with care needs.

The scope of this chapter does not allow an in-depth discussion of Winqvist's results, but her work has inspired me to continue comparing the role of the family in Japan and Sweden with respect to older persons. During the past few years there has been a new focus in the official policy concerning family carers in Sweden, and as a result of the 1997/1998 National Plan of Action, quite a number of projects have been launched under the heading of 'Anhörig (Relative) 300'.

What are the differences and similarities in filial duty? How can the concept of filial duty be identified and analysed when this is an almost unknown concept in Sweden, while in Japan it is still part of everyday language? Looking more closely at this issue has made me aware of the impact of Judeo-Christian ethics on our society, and on the very foundations of democracy. The Lutheran heritage of Swedish culture and society, and the Biblical commandment about honouring one's parents,[17] combined with an emphasis on the husband-wife relationship inherent in both the Jewish and the Christian tradition, can be seen in how we view and act when it comes to caring for our next of kin. The historian Birgitta Odén touches upon this theme in her discussion on attitudes towards the elderly in Swedish society (Odén, 1993:66-67; 85). I have also related this to the roles of husband and wife (spouses), since in Sweden the main responsibility lies with the spouse, while in Japan the children occupy this role in the first place.

This has inspired me to compare the different consequences attached to two similar moral codes concerning the role of children towards their parents: honouring one's parents according to the Bible, and showing filial duty as dictated in Confucianism. In Sweden as well as in Japan, caring for aged parents is an unquestioned norm. The differences in meaning vary, however, and this is precisely the point I would like to make when comparing Sweden and Japan in terms of values and patterns of behaviour connected with caring for elderly parents. In addition, such norms also have implications regarding how older persons themselves are viewed and treated in the care system, be it formal or informal. As a consequence, their daily life is affected, because whether the person is treated as a 'dependent person' (the old person is the object of care), or as a person who needs supportive help (the old person is the subject of care) makes a difference. However, the experience of being an object or a subject may differ in the two countries.

This way of analysing concepts, the 'whats and whys' of them is, I argue, fruitful in comparative socio-cultural research designs, as it can both help researchers become aware of their culturally coloured 'glasses', and provide tools with which to work with the empirical material.

Independence, Autonomy and Dependence

In Sweden, independence is nearly seen as a necessary quality for a close relationship between grown children and parents. As independent persons in a close relationship, people can show that they care, but not to the point of breaking through the walls of independence manifested most concretely in the separate homes of the older and younger generations.

When Japanese elderly people live together with a child, they have a close relationship – that cuts both ways. At the same time, however, according to Rosenmayr (1982:62) there is very little contact with the other children who live elsewhere, something which was also confirmed in my own research. Geographical distance does not seem to play as important a role in Sweden as it does in Japan, since people can feel close to each other even if they do not meet very often ('intimacy at a distance', a definition coined by Rosenmayr and explained and developed in Formanek and Linhart, 1997:27). The desired distance, according to Sundström, is neither too far away nor too close to one another. More than half of the elderly people in Sweden live within 15 km of their nearest child (Sundström, 1987:52-55). More recent studies also confirm this (for example in Socialstyrelsen, 2000:11).

Independence and self-determination are emphasized in the Swedish National Plan of Action for Policies Concerning the Elderly (1997/1998), which has some of the following goals: The elderly should:

be able to grow old with a feeling of security and with maintained independence
be able to live an active life and be able to influence society and their own daily life
be treated with respect
have access to good care. (my translation)

I found the following statement in the 1992 annual Japanese white paper on health and welfare:

> In particular, concern is great for those 75 years and over, categorized as late-stage-elderly, since the ability to take care of these aged has been weakened due to shrinking family sizes and the growing number of females working outside home. In response to these circumstances, better welfare services must be provided at home so that the elderly can live with their families and communicate with neighbors even when they need care. (MWH: 1992, p. 48)

The emphasis differs in the Swedish and Japanese official policies for elderly people.[18] In my interpretation, the Japanese policy considers the family as something that is taken for granted, and indirectly this implies dependency. The Swedish policy takes for granted that the old person should be treated as a subject who is guaranteed support in order to be able to continue with his/her daily life.

The theory of '*Amae*' – sometimes referred to in terms of a 'Japanese kind of dependency', to be indulged, has been introduced by the Japanese psychiatrist Takeo Doi, whose book on this subject has become something of a classic in, as well as on, Japan. It provides arguments particularly to those who emphasise the uniqueness of the Japanese people, while Doi actually points to general human behaviour. Based on 20 years of living in Japan, I find his conclusions applicable – but not only to Japan. Much of it is general, though I agree that the need for *amae* is stronger, and is moulded into the very structures of Japanese society. Doi translates *amae* into the terminology of Western society in terms of 'the psychological desire to belong' (Doi, 1974:141). Swedner, a sociologist with a special interest in Japan, describes freedom in Japan as the right to *amae* (1994:31), which I interpret as the emotional freedom to depend on others rather than the freedom of independence. I argued in my doctoral thesis (1997:122) that 'in a deeper sense this relationship characterized by amae – belonging and dependency – helps to cement the mutual expectations between parents and children concerning dependency from childhood to old age…'.

Perhaps *amae* could be described as a kind of 'collective consciousness', which Odén refers to when explaining that fundamental values must be found when analysing the norms which guide human actions (Odén, 1993:64). However, I find that the concept of filial duty, as it appears in the Japanese (and other East Asian countries with a Confucian value orientation), fits better into such a description. To my way of thinking, *amae* is rather to be seen as one aspect of the filial duty concept. Again, the point here is to see that a concept with (in this case) a Japanese origin can have relevance in the Swedish (or that of some other nation) context.

Moreover, it is when we compare and analyse on this level that we become aware of our preconceptions and can use them to inform and improve our research design.

Does Honouring Mean Co-living?

In Japan, co-living with one's children has been, and continues to be, the traditional family pattern for aged persons, although this is decreasing. Various sources indicate the same tendency towards a continuous decline in the number of people aged 65 and over who live with their children. There has been approximately a one per cent decrease per year since the 1960s.

The Nation-wide Survey about Life and Care for the Elderly followed tendencies concerning care and parent-child relationships on a ten-year-basis, conducting surveys on the same items in 1981, 1987 and 1992, in two age groups: those between 60 and 70, and those between 30 and 40. The co-living of elderly individuals with their children has changed as follows. In 1981 the figure was 63.9 per cent, in 1987 it had decreased to 58.9 per cent, and in 1992 to 53.9 per cent, or about a one per cent decrease per year.[19] The survey further shows that the decline is higher in urban areas than in the countryside, where co-living is more common.[20] When asked about co-living when elderly parents become physically weaker or lose their spouse, between 70 and 80 per cent of both age groups answered in 1992 that co-living was to be preferred (*The Survey on Life and Care for the Elderly*, 1992). Today, statistics tell that even though the three-generation family households have continued to decline in proportion, still 49 per cent of those aged 60 years and over co-live with their children. Furthermore, the share is larger, the older people become (Kono, 2000:41).

The element of self-sacrifice in terms of fulfilling this duty irrespective of the demands on oneself is also clear. A Japanese woman of around 75 years, who lived with her mother who was in her 90s, and a daughter, daughter-in-law, and grandchildren said, 'Until now we have been doing this as a personal sacrifice, but the next generation will not do it at the expense of themselves'. This comment well mirrors one of the ideas often expressed these days in Japan. This needs be linked to the current development of both institutional and home care services for the elderly – and their families. Home-help services in particular, which were expanded according to plan during the 1990s, have resulted in a 'normalization' of this service – which in the early days, and also at the beginning of my research in 1992, was considered as almost improper for those elderly individuals who lived with their children. This service has traditionally been the duty of the daughter-in-law or daughter, but has now become accepted as a service to which the elderly and their co-living next of kin are also entitled. The interviews in our ongoing study also indicate this. Looking at historical developments in Sweden, the same can be said; as people get used to new services, much of the stigma attached to new solutions such as the taking over of family matters by institutions, disappears (cf. Odén, 1993:68).

In Sweden, co-living is rare, but when looking back some 50 years Sundström found that 27 per cent of Swedish people aged 65 and over lived with one of their children, although in most cases this was an unmarried child. Of those aged 30-49 in 1987, only two per cent lived with parents. Often these were unmarried children (Sundström, 1987:54-55).

Thus, separate living is the normal situation, and the relationship between elderly parents and their children depend on other matters such as personalities, in-laws, geographical proximity, work, and grandchildren. Winqvist also suggests that the life forms[21] of both parents and children also play an important part regarding the relationship (Winqvist, 1999). Living independently cannot be seen as equivalent to having cut off the relationship with one's kin. In what is generally portrayed as ideal cases, the elderly and their children communicate regularly. And such ideal cases probably illustrate the average situation in Swedish society. Those older people who rarely or never see their children are fewer and fewer in number – in 1987 they accounted for roughly one per cent (Sundström, 1987:56). Sundström argues that the welfare society has strengthened the family, thus going against the common assumption that traditional loyalties and family ties are undermined as a consequence of advanced social welfare systems (ibid. 58). Perhaps we need to be a bit more observant here, since the cutbacks in the services for elderly persons in the 1990s have led to a clear recognition of the role of the family in elderly care. If family members feel too much pressure, this could result in negative developments, a risk which both Johansson (1998:101) and Szebehely stress (1998:85-87). If family caregiving becomes compulsory instead of being a free choice, there is a risk that this will turn into a negative experience.

Familism?

Familism bears resemblance to filial duty, but has a wider definition and lacks the direct links to a specific religion or world-view, something which, on the other hand I find characteristic for filial duty at least in the Confucian context. Familism is commonly linked to the strength of family bonds, the idea that the well-being of the whole family, the group, is more important than the well-being of the individual, and the individual must submit to what is best for the whole. This has implications regarding the care of the elderly, since the family is responsible for the well-being and welfare of its members. I find the concept of familism interesting because of the problems the usage of the term suggests, as displayed by Isela Luna and Young Mi Lim (1996), who discuss familism in a cross-cultural study of family caregiving among Mexican American and Anglo-American families. The authors point to the inconsistencies in familism literature. I quote:

> Of all inconsistencies in the literature, however, the most profound involves beliefs about whether familism is a phenomenon characteristic of all cultural groups, to varying degrees, or a phenomenon unique to only certain cultural groups. This inconsistency

> presents a unique dilemma to the underlying structure of a comparative framework of this phenomenon. As originally conceived, familism was not viewed as specifically descriptive of cultural groups; it was a phenomenon characteristic of families. (ibid.)

In my prior research I have used the definition of Japan as a familial society, referring to the work of the sociologist Tadashi Fukutake (1989) who defines familism as 'the pattern of behaviour and social relations, and the value system which characterize such a society' (ibid. 6). Perhaps I have used this concept somewhat uncritically, without explicitly discussing the term cross-cultural, although I did discuss it to some extent (1997:48-49) when probing deeper into at the role of the family system (*ie-seido*). In the comparative research on older people and their daily lives in the local welfare community context in Japan and Sweden, I find reason to scrutinize the concepts of family, family system and familism in the light of the arguments cited above. In other words, I need to check my cultural glasses. In both societies, the family is important for the elderly. However, the way families relate to their members, and the expectations they have regarding one another, differ. In this respect I suggest that the term familism can come in handy, especially when we look at social structures and legislation. In the welfare state of Sweden, there is hardly any family policy; rather, there is a policy based on the individual, where the individuals of the family are recognized. Still, much discussion centres around how the family should best be supported so that each of its individual members benefit – in other words, this would imply familism in the meaning presented in the above quotation. In the welfare society of Japan, the family is the basic unit in society in a way that differs from that found in Sweden – one could probably discuss this in terms of gender equality, or rather inequality, since Japanese Civil Law supports the family as a unit in different ways, with one a supporter, and the other (usually the woman) in a dependent position. The keeping of the household register system is also a preserving factor (Sugimoto, 1997:136-138).

Luna and Lim aimed at developing 'a measure of familism that could be used for between-group comparisons' (1996). This is what I have been looking for when comparing the similar yet different meanings of the family in the Japanese and Swedish contexts in general, and in the field of elderly care in particular. In this respect it would be interesting to determine what familism would mean in Swedish society. It is one thing, I argue, to make sweeping cross-cultural comparisons using terms like familism in order to make distinctions, for example, between East Asian and Northern European societies. It is another thing to analyse what familism, or family, stands for in the contexts to be studied. To ignore this can lead to mis-communication between scholars and in relation to those we study, as we use the same word (family) but perhaps imply different aspects of what 'family' represents. Moreover, in the case of Japan we need to link familism to filial duty, which means the duty of the children, especially the eldest son, to take care of the older generation (when they retire – the eldest son is then the head of the household). Even if this mainly concerns paperwork (official records) and decreasingly reflects the way families usually live, i.e. as nuclear families, the cultural image or 'cultural memory', as Lebra defines it (1979:338), is strong. In everyday language the traditional view is maintained, filial duty is still there, reshaped, recreated, 'modernized'. This can easily be seen in the many Japanese 'soap-operas' focusing on family relations.

What can be seen in this respect in Swedish 'soap-operas'?

This example of how to treat a concept that is central to the research project serves as an illustration of the problems of this chapter. The conclusion is that researchers are also moulded in their cultural setting. Even if we make efforts to free ourselves from this in our analysis, it may be more difficult to do so consistently throughout all the phases of a research project. This is why I believe that cross-cultural research is most reliable when researchers from participating countries are involved in each part of one another's study design on all levels, and especially in how the direct empirical fieldwork is conducted.

Filial Duty, Honour Your Father and Mother, and the Marriage Vow

When we talk about family caregiving related to the frail elderly in Sweden, we usually mean care given by the spouse and by the children – in that order. In Japan it is the other way round, by children and by the spouse. In conclusion I would like to offer some more thinking on this subject by focusing on the roots of these moral codes and social rules.[22]

'Honour your father and your mother … so that you may live long and that it may go well with you …' (Deuteronomy 5:16). Without probing the cultural setting of the biblical time, it suffices to say that the family and the honoured status of parents and older citizens were emphasized.

In Japan, where Confucianism is recognized as having left many marks on behaviour and moral conduct, the idea of honouring and obeying one's parents has become combined with Buddhism, and is linked to the religious rite of worshipping one's deceased parents (and ancestors), who in death, according to Buddhism have become gods. According to Wen-hui Tsai, offering sacrifices to deceased parents is listed among the duties of filial piety (1997:275).[23] This tenet implies a difference between the Old Testament commandment about honouring ones parents, and the Confucian rule of filial duty, in that the latter shades into worship. In the Biblical commandment and the texts connected with it, there is nothing about ancestor worship, rather the opposite: 'You shall have no other gods besides me' (Deuteronomy 5:7). Based on the research with which I have been involved, I do not think that filial duty necessarily should be seen as associated with ancestor worship, since the primary meaning of the concept involves taking care of ones old parents – traditionally, co-living with them has been included. However, it is not far-fetched to say that the presence of rituals connected with the family altar ('*butsudan*') in many Japanese homes, adds weight to expectations of filial duty.

The second example from the Bible is from Genesis 2:24: 'a man will leave his father and mother and be united to his wife, and they will become one flesh'. My argument, and here I quote myself, 'is that this separation between the parents and their married children has been an important element in shaping a family pattern that separates the nuclear family from the extended family, despite the fact that the extended family as well as the household type of family is well represented in the Old as well as the New Testament, and in many Western societies, well into modern times' (Anbäcken, 1997:261).[24]

Based on the ongoing studies as well as my previous research, I argue that the marriage vows in Swedish tradition, have helped to strengthen the strong sense of duty between husband and wife, while in Japan, the traditional view, that the woman enters her husband's family upon marriage, is supporting a family system where filial duty is central.[25]

In Sweden the relationship between parents and children has developed with an emphasis on individual integrity as an ideal, while in Japan the (stem-) family pattern of three-generation households, which has only recently begun to break-up, has fostered an awareness of the individual's role within the family (ibid.).[26] There may be objections to a discussion like this one. For example, one could argue that since 1947 there has been a 'new' civil code abolishing the old family pattern of paternalistic authoritarianism, and introducing the conjugal family as the family unit. However, the purpose of drawing attention to the fundamentals here, is to examine the roots of the values expressed in the two outlooks on life, Judaism/Christianity and Confucianism, and to see how crucial they have been in shaping the view towards as well as the role of the family (ibid. 263), irrespective of the civil code of 1947 (christened by the allied American post-war administration). This kind of 'digging after roots' is not to be practised only on the other but also on ourselves, the cultural soil we are planted in, and also the cultural setting of our academic environment.

'Ageing happens in a cultural context', were the opening words of this chapter, and I would like to add, that research on ageing and the elderly happens in a cultural context. We would do well to realize that research and researchers are part of the cultural context, and not simply those who are being researched. From the ongoing research on home-help for aged and frail persons in Japan and Sweden, I am thus learning lessons which will hopefully be useful not only in bringing the research project to a close,[27] but also for future studies.

Finally, to conclude my thoughts I will ponder a few seconds on 'reflexivity', as it emerges as another concluding concept in this study. Anthony Giddens has elaborated on reflexivity in terms of 'The reflexivity of modernity' (1990:36 ff) and I perceive here a certain linkage to what this chapter has brought to the fore. Comparative research involves in a distinct and unique way, a process where the communication between the two parties (whether nations, societies, or any phenomena labelled as culture) is absolutely crucial. When Giddens talks about the 'reflexive monitoring of action' to describe reflexivity he obviously wants to draw attention to 'the chronic character of the processes involved' (ibid. 36). Indeed, comparative research involves a chronic element of reflexivity, I would argue, both in terms of the contrasting and the reciprocal mirroring that takes place and is being communicated all the way, both when conducting the study and when analyzing the results of it.

Notes

1 I would like to express my deepfelt thanks to Dr. Ulla Wagner, former director of the Ethnographic Museum in Stockholm, for her very salient and supportive comments on this chapter. Any errors in this chapter rest solely with me.

2 'Us' refers to Owe Anbäcken, Associate Professor of Sociology, and Els-Marie Anbäcken, Assistant Professor of Social Care focusing on the elderly, both at Linköping University. The Japanese group consists of Hitsohi Asano, Professor of Sociology, Kwansei Gakuin University, Eisuke Okunishi, Assistant Professor, Osaka University of Human Sciences, Linda Sun, Assistant Professor, Osaka University of Human Sciences, and Kayoko Minemoto, Assistant Professor, Osaka University of Human Sciences.

3 Published as Kwansei Gakuin University, Sociology Department Studies no. 85, March 15, 2000.

4 This was the number of interviews upon which we had previously agreed.

5 The Japanese group presented their results in Japan. They made reference to our study but no comparisons were made. We had done a firsthand analysis of the Swedish results and added statistics from the home help areas from which our small sample was taken. In that way we could make some basic comparisons. We thus had information on total number of cases, gender, civil status, average amount of care, and what the care activities included (morning help, evening help, help to the toilet, showering, laundry, etc). Even though our survey was limited, the Swedish data could nevertheless be used in a comparative perspective.

6 We decided to interview 12 elderly persons from the sample in the first survey, one home helper for each case, and one family member if that relative was either the primary caregiver or regularly looked in on and helped his/her parent. The Japanese group managed to carry out this number of interviews while we in Sweden came to a close after finishing the 11th interview.

7 While the Swedish group decided to use the three interview guides, the Japanese group did not use the guide directed to the home helpers, although they considered including it. Moreover, the interview with the users blended into one in Japan as the family caregivers were the main interviewees.

8 The assessment system is also different; the Japanese use a system with certain levels based on the amount of care needed. In Sweden the prevailing view is holistic and takes medical, mental and social aspects into account. It could perhaps be said that the main assessment instrument involves asking the following question: what help does this person need in order to be able to continue to live independently in his/her own home with an acceptable quality of life?

9 The questions formulated in the interview guide turned out to be rather detailed, so in the Swedish part of the study we emphasized to the interviewers that these should be used as a guide in the interviews. All five interviewers were persons who encounter elderly persons in their work, and they felt confident about the interview situation. Thus far I have read only one of the Japanese interviews. From what I can see, the interviewer there

used the interview guide with the same kind of approach as the Swedish interviewers, i.e. with the freedom that an interview guide ought to be used , motivated mainly by respect for the interviewees.

10 There is one exception among our cases, a person who could only give yes or no responses or utter sounds which could be understood by the spouse and, to some extent, the main home helper. In this interview the spouse was present and answered the questions for her, but continually included her in the conversation. In another interview, where the spouse was considered as the primary caregiver, the interviews with them were not done separately, but together. It seemed the most natural way to do it. Could this also be a result of the researcher's cultural glasses? Husband and wife are seen as one …

11 My focus in the empirical study has been on those older individuals who need assistance, and on the role of their families, but the overall perspective involves what constitutes a good life in one's old age, regardless of one's physical condition.

12 Of course the answers would also vary inter-culturally.

13 The fear of senile dementia and of becoming bedridden is often mentioned.

14 As for developments in Sweden, I have studied these but not done any research on my own except that presented here. However, the first steps of a comparative study on older people in the local welfare society in Japan and Sweden, were underway at the time of the presentation of this chapter in February 2000, together with Håkan Karp, Ph.D. candidate and junior lecturer in Social Care Sciences at Mälardalen University College. Since then, the research group has a new member, Ingrid Johansson, Ph.D. and senior lecturer, at the same University in Sweden. We have visited Rikyo University in Tokyo and have established a research network with Professor Yasuhito Kinoshita for this project. Preparation in terms of a lot of discussions and the gathering of background material has been followed by the first steps of the field studies during 2002. One of the doctoral students at ISAL, Linköping University Janicke Andersson is also participating in one of the sub-studies of this project.

15 Christie Kiefer's and Yasuhito Kinoshita's book title *Refuge of the Honored, Social Organization in a Japanese Retirement Community* conveys the same message (1992).

16 The Swedish term she uses is 'filial förpliktelse' (1999:56).

17 The notion of honouring one's parents can be found in other traditions, here I focus on the combination of duties to old parents and duties to one's spouse, which I find differs profoundly when comparing the Japanese and Swedish cultural heritage.

18 The 1995-1996 white paper shows a noteworthy change in policy, as if the government realized it had to accept the fact that changes had occurred. The increasingly diversified family lifestyles are being acknowledged, as is also a more 'Western' view on the role of the family: 'In an affluent society with an improved living standard, it is emotional support which is emphasized more than the function of sustaining daily living' (1997:7). Still, it is too early to talk about a shift – I maintain what I concluded in 1997, that a Japanese way of combining the 'diversified family' with the traditions of filial duty is probable. The fact is that even with a large expansion of the care services for frail and disabled elderly persons, this will not suffice, so the Government will keep on supporting the families to 'help one another (support function) when a member becomes sick, too old to work, or in need of long-term care' (MHW, 1997:7). In Sweden, on the other hand, the important role of family caregivers has recently become officially acknowledged (see page 46). Still, as far as I can see, this is not contradictory to the basic value expressed in the action plan.

19 According to the 1995-1996 white paper the figure was 55.3 per cent in 1994.

20 In this respect the Tokyo metropolitan area naturally differs from rural municipalities.
21 'Life form', according to Winqvist, is the definition of the pattern of life we have been socialized into since childhood, and there are 'at least two determining levels, the ideological and the material' (1999:80, my translation). In her work she makes use of three life forms: the self-employed, the wage earner and the 'careerist' (ibid. 83).
22 To me there is no contradiction paralleling these two concepts: moral codes and social rules. While I basically think that social rules are a result of moral codes, I also think there is a reciprocity, a mutual influence similar to what the theory of cultural lag attempts to explain (Ogburn, 1964).
23 Filial piety (which Wen-hui Tsai uses) and filial duty are used to convey the same meaning: I would say that piety has a more religious, or symbolic, nuance (cf. Anbäcken, 1997:5). Tsai refers to the classical Confucianism (Book 11:5) in which is said: '... offer sacrifices to them according to the rites.' (ibid. 275).
24 In Sweden the definition of family includes cohabiting couples, especially when they have children.
25 The question 'Who would you save, your wife or your mother', was posed by an acquaintance of mine in China, to his colleagues. Westerners among his colleagues answered: 'my wife' while the Chinese answered 'my mother' – without hesitation. I found a parallel to this in a study on inter-generational relationships among Chinese, Japanese, and Korean Americans (Ishii-Kuntz, 1997).
26 For a fuller discussion on this I refer to my Ph.D. thesis.
27 The research project was presented as a paper in progress at the Nordic Congress of Gerontology in Aarhus, Denmark 25-28 May 2002.

Bibliography

Anbäcken, E-M. (1997), *Who Cares? Culture, Structure, and Agency in Caring for the Elderly in Japan*, Department of Japanese Studies, Stockholm University, Stockholm.

Andersson, L. (2000), 'Äldrebarometern fångar europeiska attityder' (The Elderly Barometer Catches European Attitudes), *Äldre i Centrum* (Elderly in the Center), Vol. 14 (3), pp. 25-27.

Asano, H., Okunishi, E., Sun, L. and Minemoto, K. (2000), *Nijûyojikan taiyô ((junkaigata) hômuherupusâbisu no genjô to kadai* (To Cope with 24 Hours (Around the Clock) Home Help Services – the Present Condition and the Awaiting Tasks), Sociology Department Studies no 85, Kwansei Gakuin University, Japan.

'Deuteronomy', (1978), in *The Holy Bible*, New International Version, The Zondervan Corporation, Michigan, Grand Rapids.

Doi, T. (1974), *The Anatomy of Dependence*, Kodanska International Ltd., Tokyo.

Formanek, S. (1992), 'Normative Perceptions on Old Age in Japanese History. A Study Based on Literary Sources of the Nara and Heian Periods', in S. Formanek and S. Linhart (eds.), *Japanese Biographies; Life Histories, Life Cycles, Life Stages*, Verlag Der Österreichischen Akademie Der Wissenschaften, Vienna, pp. 9-32.

Formanek, S. and Linhart, S. (1997), ' Problems and Opportunities of the Study of Old Age in Asian Cultures', in S. Formanek and S. Linhart (eds.), *Ageing, Asian Experiences Past and Present*, Verlag Der Österreichischen Akademie Der Wissenschaften, Vienna, pp. 274-295.

Fry, C.L. (2000), 'Culture, Age, and Subjective Well-Being', *Journal of Family Issues*, Vol. 21 (6), pp. 751-777.

Fukutake, T. (1989), *The Japanese Social Structure. Its Evolution in the Modern Century*, 2nd ed., University of Tokyo Press, Tokyo.

'Genesis', (1978), in *The Holy Bible* New International Version, The Zondervan Corporation, Michigan, Grand Rapids.

Giddens, A. (1990), *The Consequences of Modernity*, Polity Press, Stanford, USA.

Hannerz, U. (1983), *Över gränser, Studier i dagens socialantropologi* (Transcending Borders, Studies in Social Anthropology of Today), Liber Förlag, Lund.

Ishii-Kuntz, M. (1997), 'Intergenerational Relationships Among Chinese, Japanese, and Korean American', *Family Relations*, Vol. 46 (1), pp. 23-32.

Johansson, L. (1991), *Caring for the Next of Kin, On Informal Care in Sweden* (Diss.), Uppsala University, Almqvist & Wiksell International, Stockholm.

Johansson, L. (1998), 'Anhöriga som omsorgsgivare och omsorgstagare' (Relatives as Caregivers and Recipients of Care), in *Äldreomsorgens vardag* (Care of the Elderly in Every Day Life), Socialvetenskapliga forskningsrådet (Swedish Council for Social Research), Wasa Grafiska, Stockholm.

Keith, J., Fry, C.L., Glascock, A.P., Ikels, C., Deickerson-Putman, J., Harpending, H.C. and Draper, P. (1994), *The Ageing Experience, Diversity and Commonality Across Cultures*, Sage publications, Thousand Oaks, California.

Kinoshita, Y. and Kiefer, W.C. (1992), *Refuge of the Honored, Social Organization in a Japanese Retirement Community*, University of California Press, Berkeley.

Kono, S. (2000), 'Demographic Aspects of Population Ageing in Japan', in *Aging in Japan 2000*, JARC, Japan Ageing Research Center.

Koyano, W. (1989), 'Japanese Attitudes Toward the Elderly. A Review of Research Findings', *Journal of Cross-Cultural Gerontology*, Vol. 4, pp. 335-345.

Lebra, T.S. (1979), 'The Dilemma and Strategies of Ageing Among Contemporary Japanese Women', *Ethnology, An International Journal of Cultural and Social Anthropology*, Vol. 18, pp. 337-354.

Luna, I. and Lim, Y.M. (1996), 'The Relevance of Familism in Cross-Cultural Studies of Family Caregiving', *Western Journal of Nursing Research*, Vol. 18 (3), pp. 267-284.

Odén, B. (1992), 'Kritisk professor varnar: Våra gamla vill inte bli vårdade av sina barn' (Critical Professor Warns: Our Elderly Do Not Want To Be Taken Care of by Their Children), *Svenska Journalen*, No 18, pp. 32-33, 54.

Odén, B., Svanborg A. and Tornstam, L. (1993), *Att åldras i Sverige* (Growing Old in Sweden), Natur och kultur, Stockholm.

Ogburn, W.F. (1964), *Social Change with Respect to Culture and Original Nature*, Peter Smith, Gloucester.

Palmore, E.B. (1975), *The Honorable Elders: Cross-cultural Analysis of Ageing in Japan*, Duke University Press, Durham, N. C.

Rosenmayr, L. (1982), 'Is the Japanese Family Really Different?', *Shakai Ronengaku*, (Social Gerontology), Vol. 16, pp. 61-70.

Spradley, J.P. (1980), *Participant Observation*, Holt, Rinehart and Winston, Orlando.

Sugimoto, Y. (1997), An Introduction to Japanese Society, Cambridge University Press, Cambridge.

Sundström, G. (1987), *Old Age Care in Sweden Yesterday, Today... Tomorrow?*, The Swedish Institute, Stockholm.

Svenska Kommunförbundet (2001), *Aktuellt om äldreomsorgen* (The Current Situation Within Elderly Care in Sweden), Svenska kommunförbundet, Stockholm.

Swedner, H. (1994), *Välfärdsarbete i Japan* (Welfare Working in Japan), Liber Utbildning, Stockholm.

Szebehely, M. (1998), 'Hustruns hjälp eller hemtjänstens?' (Help from the Wife or from the Home Helper?), in *Äldreomsorgens vardag* (Care of the Elderly in Every Day Life), Socialvetenskapliga forskningsrådet (Swedish Council for Social Research), Wasa Grafiska, Stockholm, pp. 73-88.

Szebehely, M. (2000), *Välfärd, vård och omsorg.* Antologi från Kommittén Välfärdsbokslutet, Socialdepartementet (Welfare and Care. Anthology from the Committee on the Welfare Balance Sheet. The National Board of Health and Welfare), Norstedts, Stockholm.

Tornstam, L. (1998), *Åldrandets socialpsykologi* (The Social Psychology of Ageing), 6th rev. ed., Rabén Prisma, Stockholm.

Tsai Wen-Hui (1997), 'Oriental Filial Piety and Modern Chinese Society in Taiwan', in S. Formanek and S. Linhart (eds.), *Ageing, Asian Experiences Past and Present*, Verlag Der Österreichischen Akademie Der Wissenschaaften, Vienna, pp. 274-295.

Winqvist, M. (1999), *Den åldrande familjen. Om vuxna barn och deras hjälpbehövande föräldrar* (The Aging Family. On Adult Children and Their Parents Who Require Assistance), Studentlitteratur, Lund.

Official reports

MHW Ministry of Health and Welfare (1992), *Annual Report on Health and Welfare*, JICWELS (Japan International Corportation of Welfare Services), Tokyo.

MHW Ministry of Health and Welfare (1997), *Annual Report on Health and Welfare, 1995-1996*, JICWELS (Japan International Corportation of Welfare Services), Tokyo.

Nationell handlingsplan för äldrepolitiken (National Plan of Action for Policies Concerning the Elderly) (1997/1998), No 113, SoU (White Paper), Riksdagens tryckeriexpedition, Stockholm.

Rôjin no seikatsu to kaigo ni kansuru chôsakekka no gaiyô (Summary of the Results of the Survey on Life and Care for the Elderly) (1992), Sômuchokan kambô rôjin taisakushitsu, Tokyo, Sept.

Socialstyrelsen (2000) (National Board of Health and Welfare) 'Bo hemma på äldre da'r' (Live at home in one's old age), *Äldreuppdraget* 2000:11, Socialstyrelsen, Stockholm.

Chapter 7

The Sense of Self in Alzheimer's Disease: The Person's Perspective[1]

Phyllis Braudy Harris

Sometimes I'm me, and sometimes I don't know who I am.
I don't know, it comes and it goes; I never know. You're not YOU;
you've got someone else kind of in back of you.
A 76-year-old woman with early stage Alzheimer's disease

Alzheimer's disease (AD) is a progressive, irreversible dementia that currently affects four million individuals in the United States. The prevalence rate of AD is estimated to double every five years beyond the age of 65, and the cost of caring for people with AD is estimated to be $100 billion dollars a year (Ernst et al., 1997; National Institute on Aging [NIA] , 2001). Thus, with the elderly being the fastest growing segment of the population, this disease is of significant and mounting concern to older adults and their families.

AD has devastating effects on diagnosed individuals in all areas of their daily lives: it affects memory, communication and social skills, and cognitive and functional abilities. One area in particular that is affected by AD is one's sense of self and self-esteem. All quality-of-life measures of AD and multi-dimensional constructs that assess the subjective experience of dementia include an appraisal of psychological well-being or emotional health (Albert and Logsdon, 2000; Birren and Diekmann, 1991; Brod et al., 1999; Lawton, 1991; Logsdon et al., 1999; Logsdon, 2002). This study delves into this psychological domain of the self in order to gain a better understanding of how AD affects selfhood from the perspective of the person with the disease.

Until recently, most information about the experience of dementia has been second-hand, from interviews with, and observations and surveys of caregivers, the

1 Author's Note: An earlier version of this manuscript appeared as Harris, P.B. and Sterin, G. J. (1999) 'The Insider's Perspective: Defining and Preserving the Self of Dementia', *Journal of Mental Health and Aging* 5(3): 241-257. This chapter is adapted with permission of Springer Publishing Company, Inc., New York 10012.

people involved in the daily activities of caring for a family member with dementia (Aneshensel et. al., 1995). It was not until the middle of the last decade that the voices of the people with dementia began to be heard, and the primary assumption that people with dementia could not communicate in meaningful ways was called into question (Woods, 1999; Woods, 2001; Whitlatch, 2001). It is this new approach within the field of dementia studies, that acknowledges the person *as the expert*, one whose views add a new, richer and different dimension to our understanding of what it is like *to live and cope* with a dementing illness, a perspective that has been missing from the literature. Listening to, and accepting the voices of the people with dementia makes them equal partners in this search for knowledge, and no longer helpless victims, thus empowering them and acknowledging their remaining strengths and abilities. This study presents these voices.

The Person with Dementia

Current research has moved beyond the medical model that defined the condition primarily as disease entity, neglecting the social-psychological factors involved in the definition and experience of the illness (Froggatt, 1988; Lyman, 1989), towards recognizing and *valueing* the subjective experiences of those with dementia. This paradigm shift places the concerns, needs and interests of those individuals with dementia, as defined by them verbally and non-verbally, in the centre of the research and dementia care arenas. Tom Kitwood and the Bradford Dementia Group have led this movement in dementia care (Kitwood, 1990, 1993a, 1993b, 1997; Kitwood and Benson, 1995). Kitwood discussed the ethical, social-psychological, and neurological significance of dementia – a view that encompasses the whole person instead of defining a person experiencing dementia solely by his/her neurological impairment. He proposed a framework, which emphasizes the social-psychological experience of the diagnosed individual that interacts with the neurological. Kitwood also believed that the social-psychological milieu of the dementia experience has been largely overlooked, and could have a detrimental or 'malignant social-psychological' impact on a person with dementia, greatly affecting her/his feeling of self-worth and sense of self.

Downs (1997), in her review of the literature on the emergence of the person in dementia research, outlines three major facets in this line of study that are now being examined as an outgrowth of this paradigm shift: the perspectives of individuals with dementia, the person's rights, and the individual's sense of self. Recent books in the area of dementia care such as Lisa Snyder's *Speaking Our Minds* (1999), and Phyllis Braudy Harris's *The Person with Alzheimer's Disease: Pathways to Understanding the Experience* (2002), exemplify the first two areas. Snyder describes, with a rich use of quotations, the lives of seven people in early stage AD whom she met in her role as a social worker. Her goal is to have us see and hear them as people struggling with a disease, rather than to view them, as they most often are, by the label, 'AD victims'. Harris's edited volume provides the first comprehensive overview of the subjective experience of living with progressive memory loss from the time of assessment to the nursing home placement, and brings together cutting-edge research from the United States and the United Kingdom. The emphasis on the right of the person with AD to be treated with dignity and respect is the underlying theme of the book. The present study, based on interviews with 22 people with AD and their caregivers, seeks to add to the discourse by expanding the perspective of persons with AD by specifically focusing on the third area outlined by Downs, the sense of self.

Sense of Self and Alzheimer's Disease

The diagnosed person's sense of self, its development, and aids for its preservation has been examined by Kitwood and the researchers from the Bradford Dementia Group (Kitwood, 1990, 1993a, 1993b, 1997; Kitwood and Bredin, 1992; Kitwood and Benson, 1995). Their research, based upon his theoretical framework, centers mainly on the impact of the social-psychological milieu on the diagnosed individual and her or his concept of personhood. Discussing the self in dementia, Kitwood focuses on the parts of self beyond memory, what he calls 'personhood', that includes feelings, emotions, reactions, and social abilities that are influenced by the interactions with others. He outlines in detail aspects of the caregiver relationship, which can demean and diminish the personhood of a person with AD (Kitwood, 1993b; Kitwood, 1997; Kitwood and Benson, 1995; Kitwood and Bredin, 1992).

Sabat and Harre (1992) further discuss the concept of self, dividing it into self (personal identity) and selves, somewhat analogous to the concept described by Erving Goffmann (1963) in his classic work, *The Presentation of Self in Everyday Life.* Sabat and Harre explain that people react to the selves we present, but in turn their reactions can impact upon our held concept of self, thereby creating, when negative, what Kitwood would term a malignant social psychology.

Sabat (1994) tested Kitwood's concept of 'malignant social psychology'. He demonstrated through a case study that by being present in either a 'malignant social-psychological' or a benign milieu, a person with AD can change his or her behavior, attitude and sense of self. In his latest work, Sabat (2001) delves deeper into the self and AD. He demonstrates that the excess disabilities of people with AD: disabilities not due to the neurological damage, but which result from demeaning treatment, a 'malignant social psychology' can be ameliorated, revealing intact aspects of selfhood in people even with moderate to severe AD.

Post (1995), with his coining of the term, 'hypercognitive culture' draws our attention to how much value our society places on cognitive abilities as the defining characteristic of a person's identity. He argues that people with AD have many abilities that remain, and that we need to listen more closely in order to understand who they are, and what they have to say (Post, 2001).

Our study, in adding to the discourse on self and AD, builds on the approach advocated by Post. It focuses on the person's own perceptions and definitions of self in early stage AD. This is a new area of research. It seeks to gain a more sensitive understanding of how a person defines her/his sense of self or personal identity. And in this process, some of our findings also point to the excess disability and malignant social psychology discussed by Sabat and Kitwood. The study seeks answers to three specific questions: 1) What happens to one's concept of self in early stage AD? 2) How do people with AD define their sense of self? 3) What affects the concept of self?

Study Design

In order to gain an in-depth understanding of the concept of self of a person with AD, a qualitative study based upon in-depth personal interviews and participant observations of early stage support groups was designed. The majority of the data for this presentation are from the interviews. Through contacts with a local chapter of the Alzheimer's Association, 22 people with early stage AD were interviewed. The researchers did not administer the Mini-Mental State Examination (MMSE) themselves. Diagnosis was made by the geriatric assessment units of local hospitals, and then individuals and their families were referred to the Association's early stage programs. All of the people were diagnosed with probable AD and had been diagnosed on average two years prior to the study. For 19 of these individuals, their caregivers were also interviewed; the remaining three interviewees were living independently, two with no local caregivers.

The demographic profile of the people with AD is as follows. Fifteen of the 22 people with dementia interviewed were female; 2 males and 2 females were African-American, and the rest were Caucasian. The average age was 71 years; however, the ages ranged from 54 to 84 years. The occupations were quite varied, from factory workers and housewives to lawyers and professors. As indicated by the occupations, educational level also varied greatly.

Seventeen of the interviews were conducted in the participants' homes by two researchers, one of whom had been recently diagnosed with AD. All the interviewees were made aware of this, and all were eager to discuss their experiences with this researcher. The last five interviews were done with a clinician, as the researcher with AD felt she was no longer able to handle the rigour of the interview process. Separate informed consent forms were designed for the persons with dementia and the caregivers. At the beginning of the interviews, the consent forms were discussed, the overall purpose of the project explained, and any questions answered.

The interviews took approximately two hours, broken into three consecutive sessions. In the first session, the two interviewers, the person with AD, and the caregivers (except as noted above) met together for an hour and a half. Then the researcher with AD or the clinician met alone with the person with AD, and the caregivers and the other researcher met together. With one of the researchers being diagnosed with probable AD, there is a strong possibility of researcher bias in that she could overly identify with the issues being discussed or steer the conversations. Nevertheless, since this study examines the subjective experience of living with dementia, the assets she brings to the interviewing process, because of her in-depth understanding of this experience and her research background, help to offset the bias. However, the other researcher was aware of this possible bias and was cognizant of it during the interviews, taking charge of the interviews to direct them back on target if this should happen. This was one of the reasons why all the interviews were taped and transcribed, and then compared with field notes.

An interview guide approach was used during the first interview. This approach used a set of predetermined topics (impact of living with progressive memory loss, concept of self, coping strategies and behaviours, used to live with AD, and marital and family relationships), developed from the research questions. For the purpose of this chapter, I will be focusing mainly on the sections of the interviews that covered the impact of living with AD and the concept of self.

Using the analytical strategy suggested by Glaser and Strauss (1967), the transcripts were read to develop substantive codes for each interview. The codes were then grouped into themes that emerged from the narratives and issues that were identified through the interview guide. The purpose of this methodology is to present a more in-depth, diverse and complex picture of a phenomenon that has been previously reported, and identify possible variables that need to be tested and confirmed in larger representative studies.

Findings

This section is divided into three parts, corresponding to the three research questions addressed above. Part One describes common themes relating to the impact of the AD experience on the concept of self, which emerged from the interviews and issues identified through the interview schedule. It also identifies a typology of different reaction patterns to the diagnosis, as people struggled to maintain their personal identity. The second section suggests concepts emerging from the narratives, describing the distinctive sets of core values that people with AD discussed in defining their sense of self. The last section examines the social-psychological milieu, as related through the narratives. Examples are given of social-psychological interactions that affirm an individual's concept of self, as well as of interactions that undermine it.

1. The Impact of AD on the Concept of Self

As demonstrated above, the 22 individuals we interviewed had widely varied lives prior to the diagnoses; but they shared many similar experiences in their common struggle to live with this disease and maintain their sense of self. The shared experiences involved a changing sense of self, losses, emotional reactions, development of coping strategies and awareness of the reactions of others (to be discussed in the third part of the findings section). A typology of different reaction patterns – to the diagnosis per se, as well as increasing deficits, also arose from the narratives.

Common themes

Changing sense of self (N=17) Seventeen individuals discussed a changing sense of self. For them, the self is not lost with the diagnosis of AD, but the sense of 'who one is', is often in a state of flux, as evidenced by the three quotes below. A 76-year-old woman expressed her experience this way: 'Sometimes I'm me, and sometimes I don't know who I am. I don't know, it comes and it goes; I never know. You're not *you*; you've got someone else kind of in back of you.' Another woman more poignantly lamented, 'I hate myself and the world ... who I am now, and what purpose is left in my life? Well, I guess only *I* can provide the answers to those questions, and strangely I have things that I still want to do, and say and *be*'. A 75-year-old man felt this experience very deeply when he exclaimed in anguish, 'I have no self-worth. I don't feel I have a reason for living. I'm no longer human'.

Five individuals did not have this experience of losing their sense of personal identity, but their sense of competency was badly shaken. As one 84-year-old woman explained, 'The disease has not affected *who I am*, but *what I can do*'.

Losses (N=18) Losses were on multiple levels, such as loss of meaningful roles, loss of independence, loss of self-worth and respect, loss of a sense of competency, loss of memory and loss of relationships that have been changed by the disease or ended because of it. These multiple losses were difficult to cope with, and they often could not be replaced. One 70-year-old woman lamented about the changed relationship and roles with her husband. She said: 'We used to be on equal footing with each other, a marriage of two accomplished people. Now, he is a *caregiver* and I am a *caregiven*. There must be a fine line between sensible adjustment to an essential level of dependence on others and on their memories, as compared to a total surrender of all independent thought and action'. Loss of independence and self-worth were major issues over which many of the individuals were grieving. Perhaps a 77-year-old woman expressed it most clearly when she stated: 'I get very frustrated, resentful and despondent. Don't forget, I ran the show, when you take that away from me, what have I got left?' These losses affected their personal identities.

Emotional reactions linked to efforts to maintain sense of self (N=20) The emotions most commonly expressed were: frustration, embarrassment/humiliation, anger and despondency. Others were fear, disempowerment and uselessness.

Some individuals expressed extreme frustration with trying to accomplish tasks, forgetting people, places or things, or over the treatment of others. One 70-year-old woman exclaimed: 'I get so frustrated at this disease. I have had lots of successes in my life until this disease hit ... Now, I do well at nothing. I get so frustrated, it comes out as steam at the people around me'. Another woman, 61 years old, discussed her frustration with her memory. 'I'll remember something today then I won't remember it tomorrow, and tomorrow is when I have to do it. I mean you can have plans to do something, and you make arrangements to do it and then the day comes, and it's gone. You are going to sit home. You feel so foolish.' Frustration was the most common reaction. The next was anger, displaced or intentionally focused on others who were perceived as trying to take away their independence, and embarrassment/humiliation at their forgetfulness and constant repetition. One man was extremely angry about the driving restrictions placed on him. He was 74 years old and had served as a pilot in the Royal Canadian Air Force during World War II. He exclaimed: 'I'm told I can't do this and I can't do that, and they don't know if you can or you can't, because they don't give you a chance to try. This is the thing that annoys me the most. I feel like a prisoner in my own home'. Another diagnosed individual admitted, 'I am angry at my dependence, and I make life miserable for my husband because I am so angry at how disabled I feel by what's happened to me'.

Coping strategies Multiple coping strategies were used by these individuals to maintain their sense of self and some control over their lives. The most effective and frequently-used strategies were: maintaining a daily routine, making lists, keeping a calendar, obtaining support from family members, attending support groups, retaining a sense of humour, and preserving their faith. These strategies are well known. However, a few individuals also developed unique strategies, based upon their skills that helped them cope. One woman, a writer and sociologist, kept a computer file that she called 'her crying room'. She would pour her heart and soul into this file, and after writing, she would feel better. It was her release, her 'therapy sessions'. A man who had been a very active community volunteer, continued in this role and became a spokesperson for the Alzheimer's Association; he spoke at various workshops and conferences. Another woman, a machinist who had worked in a computerized plant, found an affordable hand held computer through the Internet that assisted her in organizing her day. She wrote all her notes on the computer; that way she did not have notes scattered all over her bungalow. She stored the dates of all her appointments, and the computer was programmed to start ringing an hour before the appointment, so she would not forget it. She took her interest and experience with computers, and used it to maintain control in her life. Each of these three individuals found unique ways to maintain their self-identity through continuity with their past experiences and skills.

A typology of different reaction patterns A typology of five types emerged from the interviews that explained how these 22 individuals reacted to and approached the daunting challenge of living with a dementing illness while trying to maintain a sense of who they were. Each of the reaction patterns shared some of the common experiences described above, but had also unique characteristics and behaviours. The five types were named: 1) I'll live until I die, 2) I accept what I have, 3) There is nothing wrong with me, 4) I'm just struggling to get through the day, and 5) I'm giving up.

I'll live until I die (N=6) This first group, that reacted in accordance with the pattern, 'I'll live until I die', could be defined as the fighters, people actively involved in *living* with the disease. The group consisted of five women and one man from various socio-economic, ethnic and educational backgrounds. One woman had a Ph.D., and one woman never went beyond eighth grade; however, they shared a common perspective in that they were going to take control of this disease and their lives, as best they could. They were very independent people and their approach preserved that sense of who they were. Their words describe their approach. The 74-year-old woman with a Ph.D. discussed her experiences with AD, stating: 'I no longer have distaste for this disease; I can make it edible. I can make it better, if I am in a good mood, if I remember to, and if I have enough emotional stamina to *do* it'. A 61-year-old retired factory worker explained: 'You need to live today like it's your only day. This was the hand you were dealt with. My brain is dying. I know, but you learn tricks to cope. Don't be frightened to live your life, look it in the face for what it is'. A 71-year-old African-American man, a retired community activist, related his thoughts on his experience with AD:

> I know what I am headed for and I am not panicked about it. Somewhere in life I became what I call a realist, a pragmatist. It sort of goes back to my childhood. There was kind of cool guy in my neighborhood; he was a philosopher. He used to say all the time, "Always deal with the reality as what is, not what could have been, or should've been, but what it *is*". Now that stuck with me. I mean, I've got this problem, it ain't going away. I don't agonize over it. I gotta fault. I recognize that, and I cope with it. It ain't what happens to you that really matters, it's what you decide to do about it.

This group of individuals were actively involved in discovering ways to keep control of their lives. They continued to engage in activities that defined who they were.

I accept what I have (N=6) This group of four women and two men were upset and surprised when they received the diagnosis of AD, but acquiesced to the diagnosis without much of a struggle. Two of them have found some enjoyment and relief in living with AD. They could give up their responsibilities without feeling guilty. An 85-year-old retired social worker stated: 'I have never fought against it from the moment I heard what I had. It shocked me, but I didn't put up a fight. I'm facing the facts; I'm not doing anything about them, but I am facing them.' A 56-year-old retired businessman explained his reactions: 'If you've got it, you're going to have to live with it. It is important for me to understand it. So face it, enjoy the attention. I never really had a successful career, and now it's like I have a full-time job again – to be a good patient.'

This group of people accepted the diagnosis and were adjusting their new lives to it. They were able to fit their personal identities into their new roles without harming their sense of self.

There is nothing wrong with me (N=4) The dominant characteristic of this group's approach is denial of their situation. They could not accept the diagnosis of AD; it was too devastating to their sense of self. The denial often is expressed as anger toward the way people are treating them for 'no foreseeable reason', or by denying that they have many symptoms. One 78-year-old man, a retired chemist who evidenced many memory problems, stated numerous times throughout his interview: 'I'm strongly inclined to go back into business to some extent. My memory is not a big problem. It's good enough. I believe in the slogan, "if you don't use it you lose it"'. An 82-year-old housewife asserted: 'I don't notice too many changes'. When asked if she was still cooking or baking, her response was: 'Well I could do those things if I want to, but I don't want to. It's a lot of work'. For this type, their denial was necessary to maintain their sense of self.

I'm just struggling to get through the day (N=4) The struggle of living with AD is overwhelming to this type of diagnosed individual, and it is not a battle with which they are having many successes. Often they were trying to hide their diagnosis from business associates, friends and children. While all the individuals we interviewed were struggling to live with this condition, this group evidenced the effects the most acutely. The one man in this group was still trying to run his law practice and maintain his other community responsibilities. He was president of a large non-profit organization, and he talked about his dread of running the meetings. He admitted: 'On the way in, when I'm driving down, I'm rehearsing the names of the people and where they usually sit. I know all these men very well, but I don't want to walk in and say, "Hi, John", and it's Bill. I would be so embarrassed. It bothers me to think I have to be so careful in everything I do'. A 59-year-old housewife explained: 'I get angry with myself because things are not the same. I wonder where I am going to go, who I am and what I am going to do with the rest of my life. I think more of that than anything. You just have to every day try to make something out of that particular day. Some days I wake up and I say I do not want to do this, but I have to do this. I struggle sometimes to get through the day'.

This group was truly struggling to come to grips with the impact of the diagnosis, and trying to understand the impact it was having on their self-identity.

I'm giving up (N=2) The two women in this group could no longer grapple with the disease. Both were very strong women, but felt they could no longer continue their attempt to remain *who they were*. One, a 74-year-old retired owner of a large real estate company conceded: 'I am a fighter, but I am not an effective fighter with this. I was really an *independent* person. Now I am a *dependent one*. Nothing can compensate for the things I used to do'. The other woman, 77 years old exclaimed: 'I'm scared. I live in fear that at any moment someone is going to put me away because there is nothing left of me … being *dependent* that's the pits. I feel like I might throw in the towel … I … I'm a has been'.

The experience of living with progressive memory loss has deeply affected the lives of the 22 individuals, especially their self-identity and self-esteem. As evidenced above, they share many common experiences including a fluctuating self-concept, losses, emotions and strategies for coping, as they try to preserve their personal identity. However, there are often differences in the way they approach living their changing lives. As one 60-year-old man stated, 'It's like you just got born. I mean, this is the first day of the rest of your life. I don't need to hear that I am going to die. *I know that.* I don't need to be told that. What I need to know is how to live. That's my struggle'.

2. Core Values of Self-Identity: an Emerging Concept

The second research question focused on how an individual diagnosed with early stage AD defined the core values that comprised her/his definition of self. If we can better understand the *essence* of a person's sense of self or personal identity, then a milieu can be developed to affirm it. Of course then the question is, what needs to be provided? This section begins to tease out some of the dimensions related to self-identity.

These definitions of self unfolded during the interview, not through a series of responses to questions, but from each individual's narrative, as s/he shared her/his biography and the struggles of living with progressive memory loss. Individuals spoke of three major core values that helped define who they were, their selfhood, and what they felt was of prime importance to them and in consistency with their past. These were meaningful productivity, the primacy of autonomy, and the pre-eminent need for comfort and security. For 21 of these individuals, one or two of these themes appeared to dominate their discussions. The exception is one person who had completely accepted a changed definition of self.

Meaningful productivity (N= 7) The need to be meaningfully productive was a central tenet for seven individuals we interviewed, three men and four women. It helped them define who they were as they spoke to us; however, for each person it meant something different. For the 70-year-old lawyer, it meant continuing to practice law, though he knew he was having serious problems at work. He admitted:

> I'm still working and I'm becoming very, very conscious of how careful I have to be. I have been working on papers, and maybe I get a phone call, set the papers aside and I'll hang up and say, "Now what was I working on"? I start going through the papers on my desk, and I can't find things and get almost in a panic. Sometimes they are valuable papers not just my own notes. It's just that in the course of the phone conversation, I put it in the wrong file, but I don't know what file. Well, I'm not sure of myself on things that are complex; and I find I am proof reading like crazy; and it's very awkward and embarrassing for me. I've been at this for 45 years, though. I'm so used to being busy and active.

For a 73-year-old retired schoolteacher, it meant getting up early each morning and completing a word puzzle. She explained, 'Finding those little books where there are puzzles, and you are searching for words and going through the process of searching and looking, and when you find them and you've succeeded, it's a sense of accomplishment. It just makes you feel good, and so you get a good start to the day, and you don't feel like, I got Alzheimer's.'

For a 60-year-old self-taught computer programmer, meaningful productivity means learning a whole new line of work. She explained:

> I thought when the time comes to retire I would be a wedding planner. I've put on some weddings, and they turned out real nice. I started putting together flowers. I'm very creative, and I can put it together with a bang. Now, I don't want the bride to depend on me for everything, but the flowers I can manage. This is something you can do over a short period of time. You can see what you have done and what you haven't done, and I always keep the prototype to refer to it. If you had high productivity and suddenly you find yourself without it ... but when I create something of beauty, it fulfils me.

For this group of people with AD, meaningful productivity was a central part of their self-definition.

Primacy of autonomy (N= 7) For seven individuals interviewed, being independent was the critical feature that made them who they are. They valued their independence above everything else. For them, the struggle to maintain as much independence as possible was tantamount to survival.

The dominant theme throughout one 77-year-old woman's narrative was her need to be in charge of herself and her actions. She stated: 'You have to remember that I was no 1 and I don't like losing anything. I just want to be boss. I don't like being no 2'. Her daughter had hired a companion for her who likes to walk – an activity that gave her mother much enjoyment and stress release – but her mother resented it, stating angrily, 'I don't want to be walked with!' The daughter reminded her that the companion walked with her so she would not get lost. The woman responded (in a very small voice): 'I guess so ... I'm so independent, and I have to be so careful not to step on their toes or ... I have to do it her way. So, the minute that woman leaves, ten to one I'm out there, walking; I just stay to the area I know'.

Another woman, 55 years old, whose father was also recently diagnosed with AD, talked about how important it was for her to maintain her independence, acknowledging that it was within limits she may not like, but had to accept. However, when people stepped too far, taking away too much of her independence, she stood up for herself. She explained:

> Sometimes people try to do too much for you, and treat you like a moron. I do remember things. I can do things. I take baths. I read books. I read a pretty big newspaper. I go out for a walk. I can do things. I don't have to have everything done for me. I let people know I need help in this area, but leave me alone in this area. Within the limits that are placed on you, you have control.

Importance of comfort and security (N=5) Everyone has a psycho-social need for comfort and security. Yet, in listening to the narratives of these three women and two men we interviewed, these were of paramount importance to them, more than being independent, and, for some, more important than meaningful productivity. An environment that provided these values allowed them to be who they wanted to be. One 56-year-old retired businessman explained it this way:

> In my life, I've done a lot of letting people take care of me, so I am managing fine. I like myself. I accepted right from the beginning I had Alzheimer's. I wanted to be in the program (the drug trials for aricpet). I liked going to the doctor, cause I was being fussed over, every time I got all those MRIs, I liked that. I was always the kind of kid who liked getting his hair cut or going to the dentist. I'm a little strange, but it's helping me now with Alzheimer's. I don't feel like I am a burden. It's important for you to understand it, because I am enjoying life. Everybody's nice to me, and even my wife says nice things, I mean, how good can it get?

There appear to be certain core values which people hold dear that are essential to understanding how individuals define themselves. By listening to the narratives of these 22 people with AD, we have begun to identify three such values: meaningful productivity, autonomy and the need for comfort and security. All of these values are present in some form in the narratives, but often one or two of these values seemed to dominate the conversations as we listened to these individuals sharing their biographies and presenting their struggles when trying to cope with AD.

3. Impact of the Social-Psychological Milieu on the Concept of Self

The impact of the milieu on old people was first espoused by Dorothy Coons in her work with geriatric patients in back wards of state mental hospitals (Coons, Gottesman and Donahue, 1969). Kitwood, as has been mentioned, also has been a strong proponent (1990, 1993b) of the effect that a 'malignant social-psychology' can have on a diagnosed person's sense of self-esteem and personhood as the result of particular processes and interactions that people with AD have with others. He has identified some of these interactions as treachery, disempowerment, infantalization, intimidation, labelling, stigmatization, invalidation, banishment and objectification (see Kitwood, 1993b). Yet, as Adams (1996) has well elucidated, the empirical support for Kitwood's theories is weak. Sabat (2001), though, has demonstrated that these types of negative interactions can lead to excess disabilities.

The purpose of our study was not hypothesis testing, but the narratives of the 22 people we interviewed do lend support to aspects of Kitwood's theories about the importance of the social milieu. The social interactions of the people we interviewed affected their concept of self. Our findings do not support the idea that psycho-social factors contribute to the development of dementia, but psycho-social factors do appear to influence the person's self-identity. Two narratives illustrate this point. The first narrative is an example not of a 'malignant social-psychological' milieu, but an affirming one, one that values and supports the person's defined concept of self. Excerpts from the interview with Mrs Martin (M) completed with the two researchers (P. and G., who has AD) and her daughter (D) are illustrated below. Mrs Martin was one of the women discussed who defined autonomy as a core value of her self-identity. However, this disease has shaken her self-confidence and has almost made her give up who she is. She walked into the interview with eyes downcast and fearful, and an air of futility surrounding her.

P: What's the experience of living with Alzheimer's been like for you?
M: It can be down right scary (tears in her eyes and voice quivering). And then I think everyone else thinks I am out of wack … most of the time I'm fine. But, I do have memory loss, and when it comes, it comes.

(Much of the following conversation pertains to Mrs Martin's resentment of needing a companion when she walks, and her reaction to this infringement upon her independence. Walking has always been her major coping strategy. G. identifies very strongly with this situation.)

P: You have mentioned, Mrs Martin, how important it is for you to stay independent as long as possible. Have you taken any steps to help you stay independent, rather than having to rely on others?
M: Do I have any left?
P: What do you mean?
M: I feel like at times … I'm a has-been … But when that girl leaves, I get in there and I can start walking.
G: Does that girl give you the feeling of being taken over?
M: Sometimes she can.
G: Could you tell her where you want to go and how she could help you?
M: Gee, I don't know.
G: Yes! Tell her what you want to do and when you want to do it and you'll be in control.
P: She is really there only for you, and you are not using her right.
G: You know, you've got to think about it like you're taking her, not she's taking you.
D: Yeah … that's the idea.
M: (Beginning to agree) Right man!
D: (Clearly upset) I know that I wasn't thinking that hiring this girl was taking anything from you. I was thinking this was adding to you.
P: It's very difficult to accept that I can't do this thing I've loved all my life – walking by myself.
G: She's like your eyeglasses really; I can't read without my glasses. But they are my tool; they are not bossing me or telling me what to do … but I can't get along without them.
D: Sounds good doesn't it?
M: I guess so … I just feel I'm down at the bottom of the list.
G: But you're not! Now if you can find the tools that supply what you need, you can be a person again!
M: I'd like that.
P: And do you feel you're not a person?

M: Yeah.
P: You've given up too much; and you don't have to give up that much.
G: You are not as helpless as you think.
M: Oh! I like that; you mean I can still be a human being? (tears in her voice)
G: Of course you can! You just have to believe you are.
M: (still tearful) I guess I'll have to find out how to do it.
D: You know how to do it.
M: Just do it, huh?
D: Yes.
M: (softly with conviction) OK.
G: I know just how you feel. When I got this diagnosis, I was praying to die.
M: Yep ... yes ... ready to just ... give up!

Mrs. Martin stood up, gave G. a big hug, and she turned to her daughter and said, 'I'm ready to go'.

This dialogue is a good example of an *affirming* social-psychological interaction that supports the definition of self of a person with AD, in this case Mrs Martin's need to remain independent. Independence is her core value that makes her feel like a whole functioning human being. She walked into the interview very despondently, and at the end of the interview regained a sense of who she is and what she can do. She left the room taking control of the situation.

The second narrative confirms the effect of a 'malignant social-psychological' milieu and is an example of someone who is fighting against the 'label of AD' that can cause excess disability.

Mr Bear (B) was a 74-year-old retired travelling salesman who was diagnosed with probable AD two years ago. He was told recently by his doctor that he must give up driving, which has devastated him. He is extremely angry at the restrictions that have been placed upon him, since he has never had an accident or got lost. Driving was an integral part of his occupation, equated by him with independence and adulthood, so being forced to give it up, before *he believes* it is necessary has been a tremendous blow to his self-identity. During this interview it was extremely important for him to explain to us who he was and what he accomplished. He was a pilot in the Royal Canadian Air Force, and he showed us his uniform, which he keeps in the front hall closet, and as he proudly stated: 'It still fits'. Below are excerpts from the narrative in which he relates his reactions to his physician.

B: I find it very difficult: I'm told I can't do this and I can't do that, and it puts me on a negative feedback ... of a situation where I am no longer a human being. It's like a stigma, like carrying a sign that you are sort of demented, and you can't do this and you can't do that. They don't know if you can or can't because they don't give you a chance to try. This is the thing that actually annoys me the most. I feel like a prisoner in my own home.
Mrs. B: My husband was diagnosed last year by his doctor. It was a four-hour session to which his daughter took him; I did not go.
P: But this has much more meaning to you than just driving ...

B: (very angrily) Well the one thing they've actually taken is my self-esteem and my independence. I don't belong in society anymore. That is what they are telling me. The feeling I get is that I am incompetent. I shouldn't be living!

G: That's not equivalent though ... that they are saying you are incompetent doesn't make it so, you don't need to change your image of yourself.

B: Grant you; but it's actually the way it's expressed to me that you're addled ... get off to the side ... We don't need you anymore.

P: What is important is how you feel ...

B: I feel I have no worth.

This narrative illustrates well the impact of a 'malignant social-psychology' on a diagnosed person's sense of self. Mr Bear was able to verbalize aspects of this milieu delineated by Kitwood, disempowerment, labelling, stigmatization, and feelings of banishment. He is well aware of the labelling process that for him has resulted in his feelings, as he stated, pushed off to the side and no longer a part of society. For Mr Bear, the most devastating assault on his self-identity is the disempowerment symbolized by his driving privileges being taken away before he felt it was necessary. It is difficult to assess whether the doctor's evaluation of his driving skills was appropriate, but the way it was handled was destructive to Mr Bear's self-identity. If he accepted this definition of self, it certainly would result in excessive disabilities.

These two case studies suggest the important impact that the social-psychological milieu has on the self-identity of persons with early stage AD.

Conclusion and Implications

This study was undertaken to understand better what happens to the self-identity of an individual diagnosed with early-stage dementia, with the goal that out of this understanding can come suggestions for more person-centered care. It falls under a new paradigm of research that listens to and acknowledges the perspective of the person with dementia, seeing them as '*the experts*'.

In the study, we found that a diagnosed person's sense of self in the early stages of the disease is really in a state of flux. These individuals experience multiple losses related to that of the loss of significant roles, autonomy, respect, self-worth, and sense of competency. At the same time, they struggle to maintain core values, such as meaningful productivity, autonomy, and the need for comfort and security, which help define who they are. They experience a range of emotional reactions as they struggle to maintain their sense of personal identity, emotions such as frustration, embarrassment/humiliation, anger, despondency, and uselessness. They develop reaction patterns to the disease as they approach the daunting challenge of living with a dementing illness, while trying to maintain a sense of whom they are. Some individuals fight, as if this is their last battle; others accept the disease and can fit some of their new self-identity into their old one. Others must deny the reality of the diagnosis in order to maintain their self-concept. Others have given up and accepted a changed definition of self; the struggle is too hard and the battle is too difficult.

However, if we can better understand how a person with AD defines her/himself, and the difficulties they face in preserving who they are, then we can then assist in structuring a social-psychological environment that can affirm that person's sense of self. This is a critical factor in the early stages of dementia, as the individuals are at times disoriented and are questioning 'their held self definition'. In the two case studies presented in the paper, autonomy was the critical core value of self-definition for both individuals. These case examples show the impact of an affirming and devaluing social-psychological milieu. With an affirming milieu, the woman left the office with renewed hope, some restored self-respect, and feelings of empowerment. With devaluing social-psychological interactions, the man felt despondent, not respected, and disempowered. His need for autonomy was not being understood or addressed on any level. Only by truly listening to how people with AD define their sense of self in the course of their narratives/biographies can we build a supportive person-centered milieu.

Definitions of self are different and individuals define different core values. This study just begins to examine the self in early stage dementia, and ask questions such as, what happens to the self, how is it defined, and what affects it? This approach allows us to listen to the perspectives of the person with AD, so we can better understand and be sensitive to such issues. It leads to modified milieus that will preserve people's dignity and self-respect, crucial human needs necessary for all people. But perhaps most of all, this approach recognizes the person with AD as a partner in the quest for understanding the impact of this devastating disease.

References

Adams, T. (1996), 'Kitwood's Approach to Dementia and Dementia Care: A Critical but Appreciative Review', *Journal of Advanced Nursing*, Vol. 23, pp. 948-953.

Albert, S.M. and Logsdon, R.G. (eds.) (2000), *Assessing Quality of Life in Dementia*, Springer Publishing Company, New York.

Aneshensel, C.S., Mullan, J.T., Pearlin, L.I., Whitlatch, C.J. and Zarit, S.H. (1995), *Profiles in Caregiving: The Unexpected Career*, Academic Press, Inc., San Diego, CA.

Birren, J.E. and Dieckmann, L. (1991), 'Concepts and Content of Quality of Life in the Later Years: An Overview', in J.E. Birren, J.E. Lubben, J.C. Rowe and D.E. Deutchman (eds.), *The Concept and Measurement of Quality of Life in the Frail Elderly*, Academic Press, Inc., New York, pp. 344-360.

Brod, M., Stewart, A.L., Sands, L. and Walton, P. (1999), 'Conceptualization and Measurement of Quality of Life in Dementia: The Dementia Quality of Life Instrument (DQOL)', *The Gerontologist*, Vol. 39 (1), pp. 23-35.

Coons, D.H., Donahue, W. and Gottesman, L.E. (1969), *A Therapeutic Milieu for Geriatric Patients*, University of Michigan, Ann Arbor, MI.

Downs, M. (1997), 'Progress Report: The Emergence of the Person in Dementia Research', *Ageing and Society*, Vol. 17 (5), pp. 597-607.

Ernest, R.L., Hay, J.W., Fenn, C., Tinklenberg, J. and Yesavage, J.A. (1997), 'Cognitive Functioning and the Costs of Alzheimer's Disease. An Exploratory Study', *Archives of Neurology*, Vol. 54 (6), pp. 687-693.

Froggatt, A. (1988), 'Self-Awareness in Early Dementia', in *Mental Health Problems in Old Age: A Reader*, Open University Press, Buckingham, UK.

Glaser, B. and Strauss, A. (1967), *The Discovery of Grounded Theory*, Aldine Publishing Co., Chicago, IL.

Goffman, E. (1963), *The Presentation of Self in Everyday Life*, Doubleday Anchor Books, Garden City, NY.

Harris, P.B. (ed.) (2002), *The Person with Alzheimer's Disease: Pathways to Understanding the Experience*, The Johns Hopkins University Press, Baltimore, MD.

Kitwood, T. (1990), 'The Dialectics of Dementia: With Particular Reference to Alzheimer's Disease', *Ageing and Society*, Vol. 10 (2), pp. 177-96.

Kitwood, T. (1993a), 'Person and Process in Dementia', *International Journal of Geriatric Psychiatry*, Vol. 8 (7), pp. 541-545.

Kitwood, T. (1993b), 'Towards a Theory of Dementia Care: The Interpersonal Process', *Ageing and Society*, Vol. 13 (1), pp. 51-67.

Kitwood, T. (1997), 'The Experience of Dementia', *Aging and Mental Health*, Vol. 1 (1), pp. 13-22.

Kitwood, T. and Benson, S. (1995), *The New Culture of Dementia Care*, Hawker Publications, London, UK.

Kitwood, T. and Bredin, K. (1992), 'Towards a Theory of Dementia Care: Personhood and Well-Being', *Ageing and Society*, Vol. 12 (3), pp. 269-287.

Lawton, M.P. (1991), 'A Multidimensional View of Quality of Life in Frail Elder', in J.E. Birren, J.E. Lubben, J.C. Rowe and D.E. Deutchman, (eds.), *The Concept and Quality in the Frail Elderly*, Academic Press, Inc., New York, pp. 4-27.

Logsdon, R.G. (2002), 'Making the Best of Everyday: Quality of Life', in P.B. Harris, *The Person with Alzheimer's Disease: Pathways to Understanding the Experience*, The Johns Hopkins University Press, Baltimore, MD.

Logsdon, R.G., Gibbons, L.E., McCurry, S.M. and Teri, L. (1999), 'Quality of Life in Alzheimer's Disease: Patient and Caregiver Reports', *Journal of Mental Health and Aging*, Vol. 5 (1), pp. 21-32.

Lyman, K. (1989), 'Bringing the Social Back in: A Critique of the Biomedicalization of Dementia', *The Gerontologist*, Vol. 29 (5), pp. 597-605.

National Institute on Aging (2001), *Progress Report on Alzheimer's Disease 2000: Taking the Next Steps*, The Alzheimer's Disease Education and Research Center, Silver Spring, MD.

Post, S.G. (1995), *The Moral Challenge of Alzheimer's Disease*, Johns Hopkins University Press, Baltimore, MD.

Post, S.G. (2001), 'Comments on Research in the Social Sciences Pertaining to Alzheimer's Disease: A More Humble Approach', *Aging & Mental Health*, Vol. 5 (Suppl. 1), pp. S17-S19.

Sabat, S.R. (1994), 'Excess Disability and Malignant Social Psychology: A Case Study of Alzheimer's Disease', *Journal of Community and Applied Social Psychology*, Vol. 4, pp. 157-166.

Sabat, S.R. (2001), *The Experience of Alzheimer's Disease: Life Through a Tangled Veil*, Blackwell Publishers, Oxford.

Sabat, S.R. and Harre, R. (1992), 'The Construction and Deconstruction of Self in Alzheimer's Disease', *Ageing and Society*, Vol. 12 (4), pp. 433-461.

Snyder, L. (1999), *Speaking Our Minds*, Fallmen and Company, New York.
Whitlatch, C. (2001), 'Include the Person with Dementia in Family Care-giving Research', *Aging and Mental Health*, Vol. 5 (Suppl.), pp. S20-S22.
Woods, R.T. (1999), 'The Person in Dementia Care', *Generations*, Vol. 23 (3), pp. 35-39.
Woods, R.T. (2001), 'Discovering the Person with Alzheimer's Disease: Cognitive, Emotional, and Behavioral Aspects', *Aging and Mental Health*, Vol. 5 (Suppl. 1), pp. S7-S16.

Acknowledgements: This research was supported in part by grants from The Cleveland Foundation and John Carroll University. The author would like to acknowledge the invaluable research assistance of Gloria J. Sterin, Ph.D. and Casey Durkin, LISW, and the unwavering support of the Cleveland Area Alzheimer's Association, especially Sally Ollerton, LSW.

Chapter 8

The Social Construction of Older Women's Identities and Institutional Intervention[1]

Isabella Paoletti

Ageing is a complex phenomenon, socially constructed and as Barbato and Perse (1992:518) point out: 'characterized by biological, psychological, sociological and political elements'. The mental and physical decline observable in older people is anything but a mechanical process. This is clearly observable in the great differences noticeable in older people of the same age (Levin and Levin, 1980).

Today the world faces a radical change in the population structure, in Europe and the west in particular. This is the first time in history in which older people are close to representing 30 per cent of the population in many countries. Not only are we unprepared with regard to the organization of services and infrastructures suitable for handling the emerging needs, but there is also an urgent need for a cultural redefinition of the position of the elderly in our society, and to focus on gender issues, since two thirds of the older population are women.

Despite the fact that older women represent the great majority of the increasing older population, they are 'invisible' (Ginn and Arber, 1991; Harold, 1992) to legislation, service provision, research and even within the women's movement. The lack of research differentiated by gender is striking. Studies focused on older women are even fewer (Arber and Ginn, 1991; Ginn and Arber, 1992; Barer, 1994; Coopmans, Harrop, Hermans-Huiskes, 1988; Mengani and Gagliardi, 1993). However, interest in the issue is steadily increasing.

This study looks at how older women's identities are socially constructed, and in particular how they can be influenced by institutional intervention. Different perceptions of oneself as an older woman involve considerable differences in the definition of each person's possible spheres of action, and therefore of their life perspectives.

1 Author's Note: This chapter is based on excerpts from the author's earlier book *Being an Older Woman. A study in the Social Production of Identity* (1998). The chapter is adapted and published with permission of Lawrence Erlbaum Associates New York 0743.

In this chapter, in the first section of the analysis 'Membership categories in identity work' I show how age categories are used by older women in identity work in the course of ordinary activities. Older women's association with the category 'old' is seldom found in the data sets I have analysed. Distancing and denial of ageing are more frequently observed phenomena. However, association with the category 'old' is endorsed by the women when it becomes institutionally relevant and is giving them access to special activities and benefit. These later phenomena I describe in the second section of the analysis 'When being old matters'. In this section I also point out that if, in the one instance, institutional intervention creates new opportunities for women's active participation and protagonism, it imposes in the other instance the institutional agenda and its aims and procedures on older women's order of priorities and understanding of the issues at hand.

Background

In 1991 the Equal Opportunity Unit of the City of Perugia, in co-operation with similar units in England and Ireland, initiated an Action Project that was to establish a link between older women's groups across the European Community (EC) member states. The aims of the three-year project were to make visible older women's contributions to the community, as well as to point out their specific needs and problems. Funds were granted by the EC to cover international expenses of the project; but for initiatives carried out in each nation funds had to be sought locally. During the three years of operation, older women's groups from Germany, Greece, Portugal, Denmark and the Netherlands joined the project.

The women participating in the Action Project in Perugia were mainly members of Senior Citizen Centres. Users of these centres are generally working-class or lower middle class, self-sufficient people, ranging in age from 50 to over 90 years. The centres are run by a managing committee elected by the members, meeting regularly to make decisions about initiatives and events organized by the Centres. Women were generally scarcely represented on those governing committees, in fact older women, although in the majority as Senior Citizen Centres' members, were hardly using the centres when the project began.

During the three years of the Action Project, the older-women groups in Perugia carried out many activities in relation to the project. Theatre, singing and photographic workshops were organized. Educational initiatives showing solidarity between generations in schools, were undertaken. At a local level, radio and TV programmes, public meetings, exhibitions as well as exchange visits to various European countries were arranged. Some of these activities were shown to be particularly effective in getting women out of their houses, letting them meet, and showing their intelligence, initiative, commitment, stamina, solidarity and affection. Women became aware of new skills, opportunities, desires and life perspectives.

As a part of the Action Project in Perugia a research project was promoted: 'The social production of older women's identities and institutional settings'. This study was conducted, with EEC funding, in 1991-1994 in association with the European Older Women's Action Project for the Year of the Elderly, promoted by the Assessorato 'Progetto Donna' (Equal Opportunity Unit) of the borough of Perugia.

One of the main aims of the Action Project was to increase older women's participation in decision-making processes in their communities. For this purpose, older women were involved in the management the Action Project from the beginning. For example, in Perugia a committee was organized with women delegates from the Seniors Centres and other groups. The committee met monthly to take decisions about initiatives and events related to the Project. In taking part in the Project many women learnt, or more precisely, became aware of their skills in managing and organizing. Consequently their participation in decision-making, at various levels in their community, increased. Many of them became members of the management committees in their local Seniors Centres.

The end of the Action Project marked the beginning of two important initiatives: the constitution of the Italian Association of Active/Older Women (AIDA) in Perugia, and the creation of the Older Women Network (OWN) in Europe. In June 1995 the first meeting of OWN was held in Dublin, Ireland. Older women's groups from ten European countries were represented: Austria, Belgium, Denmark, Germany, Ireland, Italy, the Netherlands, Portugal, Spain and the United Kingdom. A draft constitution was discussed, and a resolution to be presented at the Fourth World Conference on Women in Beijing was agreed.

Sending delegates to the Fourth World Conference on Women in Beijing has been the first effort of OWN (Europe) in producing visibility for older women's needs and priorities on the international political scene. Some of the resolutions elaborated by older women in the NGO (Non-Governmental Organization) Forum were actually included in the Beijing Platform for Action.

The Study

This study explores the effects of institutional intervention in relation to the production of older women's social identities.

The study comprises a pilot and a main project. The pilot study was based upon interviews with older women of the Seniors Citizen Centres. The main action research project was based upon video recordings of the committee meetings of the Elderly Women's Group of Perugia and of the European Action Project for the Year of the Elderly (15 meetings were recorded for about 30 hrs recordings). Video recordings of theatre workshops (3 theatre workshops were recorded, about 6 hrs recordings) and of management committee meetings of Seniors Citizen Centres (3 meetings were recorded, about 4,30 hrs recordings) were also included in the data collection, as a source of comparison.

The women who were interviewed and participated in the committee meetings ranged between the ages of 50 and 85. They were all self-sufficient, and most of them lived in small villages on the outskirts of Perugia. Their educational background and economical status varied, but the majority had a primary level of education, and a modest income. The committee of the European Action Project met monthly to take decisions about initiatives and events related to the Project. Women representatives from the 'Seniors Centres' in Perugia, and officers of the Assessorato 'Progetto Donna' of the Commune of Perugia usually took part in the committee meetings and I, as researcher, was generally behind the video recorder, but at times I participated in the discussion.

The Social Construction of Identity in the Ethnomethodological Approach

In the ethnomethodological perspective, identity is understood as an interactional accomplishment, negotiated and achieved by members in the course of ordinary events, as constitutive features of their social encounters (Garfinkel, 1967; Schenkein, 1978; Watson and Weinberg, 1982). Therefore, any social interaction can be studied for its processes of identity production. Conversational membership categorization activities are particularly salient features of identity work (Baker, 1984; Coupland et al., 1991). Identification work is essential to social interaction. In producing and understanding utterances, members orientate their talk to the specific identities of the participants. Moreover, social interchange could hardly occur without reference to the context of interaction, and participants' identification work is a fundamental aspect of context. That is, reference to a common understanding of the specific motives or reasons for actions or accounts works in part through inferences about identity attributions.

Analysis

Through a detailed discourse analysis of the transcripts from the video material, within an ethnomethodological framework (Atkinson and Heritage, 1984; Garfinkel, 1967), this study describes the members' methods of negotiating different identities (Antaki and Widdicombe, 1998; Baker, 1983; 1984; Garfinkel, 1967; Paoletti, 1997; 2000; Watson and Weinberger, 1982). In particular the analysis considers the institutional influence on that identity work.

Membership Categories in Identity Work

Socio-linguistic studies (Coupland and Coupland, 1990; Coupland, Coupland and Giles, 1991; Taylor, 1992) have examined the conversational use of categories related to old age (which I will conventionally refer to as the category 'old'), in peer and inter-generational interaction in relation to identity-producing processes. In particular, the Couplands and their associates have pointed out the variability in the use of the category, and the different implications in identity work. In analysing the transcripts of audio- and video-data that follow, I wish to examine the embeddedness of the use of categories in practical activities. The use of categories is far from mechanical; rather, it is intertwined in a net of aims, motivations, moral relevance, social and institutional practices. Instances of either distancing from the category, or denial of ageing, as well as association with the detrimental characteristics of the category are reported in the literature, with different implications for identity projections.

Association is predominant in Taylor's data, which mainly refer to very old and frail elderly. Taylor offers an insight into the level of suffering and despair that old age can represent for some people, as we can read in the following transcript:

> ... I'm so tired of these days that are so long, and there's no end to them, and they just go stretching on and on and on and on. I, I, I'm even worried now about next week. What am I gonna do next week? You know. Beside to go to the doctor, n'two doctors in one day. So it's all kinda crazy. But I do, I wish to die all the time. (Taylor, 1992:506)

The data used in the aforementioned studies could be described as recordings of 'personal encounters'. The Couplands and associates' studies are based on intergenerational first-acquaintance conversations, whereas Taylor (1992) uses interview data of elderly, dependent homeowners and their student lodgers.

In the present study, the interactional encounters that were recorded refer to institutionally organized settings, that is, management committee meetings, and theatre workshops. It is noticeable that in about 50 hours of recorded data of activities in which 'elderliness' is central to the organizational feature of the setting (Committee meetings of the Older Women Group and of the Senior Citizen Centres), and to the definition of the task at hand (Older Women's Action Project and the theatre workshops), the terms '*old*', '*elderly*', '*pensioner*', and the like, are seldom used. Moreover, in this data, alignment with the category 'old', specifically with its negative attribution of decrement and ill-health (Coupland, Coupland and Giles, 1989), is absent, as are instances of self-handicapping (Coupland, Coupland and Giles, 1988) and self-stereotyping (Coupland, Coupland and Giles 1989; Coupland et al., 1988). The most common patterns of use of the category 'old', observable in the data, are distancing and denial of ageing. Association is limited to instances of use to justify limitations. However, association is also noticeable when the category 'old' assumes an institutional relevance.

I would like to argue that these women might have offered accounts on a more personal basis in different settings and activities, that may have occasioned contrasting self-images for the very same women. Therefore, I aim to highlight the occasioned nature of the accounts. That is, accounts are produced by members with reference to specific situations, motives and settings. It is difficult to imagine that painful self-disclosures such as those reported in Taylor's study could have occurred in the course of a committee meeting or during a theatre workshop. They would have been incongruous given the occasion and the task at hand. The occasioned nature of accounts does not pose only epistemological questions on how they can be analytically treated, but it also has very powerful practical implications. That is, certain social environments and interactions can mobilize positive self-image, and foster healthy and active ageing.

Justifying Limitations

Disclosure of chronological age is often reported to be used to account for ill-health (Coupland, Coupland and Giles, 1989). Old age and consequent frailty and decline are also used by caregivers to account for 'questionable behaviour' amongst older people (Taylor, 1992). In this study, the membership category 'old' is rarely used by the women to refer to themselves. When used, it is generally implied more than expressed explicitly. In some instances, reference to old age is used to justify the women's perceived limitations.

The following passage is a long and complex transcript, where age and social class identities are projected in the context of a very animated discussion. The women are evaluating the latest public performance of their singing group. Lidia has reported negative comments from the public and is now envisaging future prospects for the singing group.[2]

Lidia	we could turn, towards for example choir, not a real choir, no pop song, so just to sing, and who sings must be able to sing,
Researcher	well no
Lidia	you need [( )
Ilda	[you cannot demand this
Alma	[madam ((raising her hand)) this this this I take the floor I am sorry, consider madam once I told a lawyer, madam I don't understand you, that I don't understand you, it could happen, right but that you don't understand me you are a great ignorant, excuse me, here we are all,
Ilda	elderly
Alma	no one is a singer ((Ilda nods)) and who does not understand us ((sign with her hand meaning "to go away"))

2 Transcript notations:

. or ,	stop or pause in the rhythm of the conversation
?	rising intonation
!	excited tone
( )	word(s) spoken, but not audible
(dog)	word(s) whose hearing is doubtful
((laugh))	transcriber's description
[	overlapping utterances at this point
=	no gaps in the flow of conversation

Lidia I didn't make myself understood
Alma ((Alma turns)) ( ) eh [because you cannot throw away a word ((sign with her hand that means "throw away"))
Lidia [I don't mean that you don't understand me,
[I didn't make myself understood
Ilda [( ) it's not possible
Lidia madam not everyone can write poetry
Alma umh ((Alma nods))
Lidia [is that right?
Ilda [OK [no that's right
Lidia [therefore you cannot pretend that a person that cannot write poetry ((Alma nods)) will start writing poetry
Alma umh
Lidia voice, is a gift just like that of writing poetry who hasn't got it cannot invent it then since it is not compulsory to sing the singing group should
[be made of persons ( )
Alma [I don't no no no I don't agree [I don't no no no I don't agree then we bury the group here I am sorry
Ilda [no no no

There are some comments exchanged on the necessity of rehearsal for all the groups together before performances, then Alma continues to express her disagreement with Lidia's proposal:

Alma it's the only thing that would keep me away ever if you say to do discriminations, no way we are all a group, for the good and bad fortune and all a group we have to remain
Officer ss sss ( ) just a moment just a moment
Clelia there is another thing, that whoever didn't like it. Can shut up that I mean we are not young any more [( ) ((everybody talking))
Ida [the voice collapses, as everything else
Clelia am I right? and everyone tries to do her best
Ida certainly
Alma [I cannot sing, I only went up to grade four, I cannot write poetry ( )
[are you joking
Clelia [( ) for older people, we should consider that
(12/18/1992 Committee meeting of the Action Project)

Lidia proposes a new composition of the singing group based on ability, those *who sings must be able to sing*. The researcher signals disagreement, *well no*. Other negative comments follow, *you cannot demand this*; in particular Alma comes out with a passionate protest *((raising her hand)) this this this I take the floor*. Not only the contents, but also the style, the argumentative structure, the use of gestures and the use of regional dialect (unfortunately impossible to render in the English translation) all contributes to producing different social class identities for Lidia and Alma.

Alma starts her speech reporting an episode of misunderstanding, between herself and a lawyer. The sentence, *you don't understand me you are a great ignorant*, is constructed against the background of common knowledge of a lawyer as a supposedly highly educated person. Alma argues that the lawyer was not justified in showing inability in understanding a less educated person as herself. However, the reverse would have been admissible, *that I don't understand you, it could happen*. In this way Alma projects her own identity as less educated, a significant attribution for 'social class' identification. Her next argumentative move is to include 'being able to sing' in 'being educated', consequently implying that more musically educated people should be able to understand less musically educated people. In an instant of hesitation, *here we are all*, Ilda completes the sentence with, *elderly*, introducing for the first time the use of the category 'old', apparently to justify the unsuccessful performance.

Finishing each other's sentences is a practice widely used by the women, as will be obvious in the course of the analysis. In this case Alma sticks with her argument, *no one is a singer*, and is sustained by Ilda *((Ilda nods))*, and finishes establishing the exclusion of the dissident, *and who does not understand us ((sign with her hand meaning 'to go away'))*. Notice that logical connections are never made explicit: sentences are juxtaposed in a strictly consequential sequence though, and gesture is used as a structural component of the sentence, not as simply an emphatic device.

The distinction proposed by Lidia, *I don't mean that you don't understand me, I didn't make myself understood*, seems to endorse Alma's argument that more educated people have to make a special effort in explaining themselves to less educated people, signalling consequently her higher level of education. Moreover, in Lidia's arguments all logical connections among sentences are made explicit, and no gesture substitutes for talk. It is particularly in contrast to Alma's expressive strategies that Lidia appears 'more educated', with clear implications for class identification.

Ambiguity is produced through the use of the term *pretend*, in relation to writing poetry and singing, a term that can mean either to allege falsely or to demand, *you cannot pretend that a person that cannot write poetry ... will start writing poetry*. The real argument proposed by Lidia is excellence of the product. She appears to be saying: '*if we want a good performance we need good singers*', but that is not stated openly. Instead she says that singing, like writing poetry, is a gift. Consequently nobody is obliged/has to pretend to be able to write or sing *(it cannot invent it/it is not compulsory to sing)*. But, just as a person who is not skilled in writing poetry can still want to do it, so it is for singing. Excellence of the product remains a hidden agenda.

Alma continues expressing her strong disagreement, *I don't no no no I don't agree*, and she threatens to dissolve the partnership, *we bury the group here*. Then after a brief discussion on the importance of rehearsals, she continues her argument, using biblical overtones. She threatens again to leave the group; *it's the only thing that would keep me away*, i.e. if discriminatory criteria were established in the composition of the singing groups. She underlines the moral character of the enterprise, *we are all a group for the good and bad fortune, and all a group we have to remain*.

To support Alma's argument against discrimination, Clelia joins in, using reference to old age to justify limitations in the performance. It is necessary to point out that Clelia is among the youngest in the group, being in her 50s. It recurs throughout the data, that reference to the category 'old' is more frequently used by younger group members. Indirect reference to 'old age', *we are not young any more*, is used to account for the inadequacy of the performance of their singing groups. Ida reinforces Clelia's statement, mentioning various negative aspects of elderliness: *the voice collapses, as everything else*. The image of collapsing can be associated with bodily appearance, which is particularly salient to women's picturing of old age (Kamler and Feldman, 1995:9).

Alma continues with her protest, this time explicitly stating her limited education, *I was in the fourth class of primary school*. She rebels *are you joking*, to the implications of Lidia's argument, *I cannot sing, I cannot write poetry*. In fact, Alma also likes to write poetry. In the next turn old age is mentioned again as a sufficient justification for special consideration, *for older people, we should consider that*.

In this transcript we have seen how age and class identity are constructed in and through the argumentative feature of the exchange. Limitations due to old age are used as an argument to sustain an inclusive policy in group composition. Moreover, lack of education, a social class identifier, is applied for the same purposes. Identity work is achieved in relation to the occasion, the committee's evaluation of the singing performance. The outcome of the discussion has possible concrete implications for the women's lives: exclusion or inclusion in the singing group. Age as well as social class identities are produced in the process of dealing with practical ordinary events as serious matters that have concrete consequences for the participants.

In this transcript, the use of categories and identity projections, is strictly connected to the activity that is being carried out in the specific occasion: 'arguing'. From this perspective, the detrimental attributions that come with the category 'old' are in some way bracketed, in the sense that they can be mainly interpreted as moves in a specific argumentative strategy. Consequently, it is understandable that, on other occasions, these very same women forcefully refuse to use the category 'old' to refer to themselves, or that they attribute negative aspects of old age to 'out-group' member (Coupland et al., 1991), an interactional approach described in the following paragraphs.

Distancing

Instances of the use of the category 'old' to designate 'the others' (the very old) are reported in the literature: 'Very often "old" is invoked as an outgroup category, even by speakers we are referring to as elderly' (Coupland, Coupland and Giles, 1991). Distancing is achieved by association of the category 'old' with its negative stereotypical attributions (frailty, dependence, ill health, and loneliness), but also by designating other members with it. By not advocating co-membership in this category, such speakers project a positive personal identity for themselves.

The gradeable properties of age categories (Coupland, Coupland and Giles, 1991) are particularly evident when out-group members can be designated within the same membership category. A decremental perspective is evoked with the out-group member occupying the very end of the scale. Decline however, remains impending for any member, as can be seen in the next transcript.

In the last meetings in 1993, before the summer break, the discussion developed around the following year's programme. Rita mentioned activities aimed at bringing solidarity among generations. Here, she is explaining why she thinks they are relevant:

Rita	I'd like from the young people a bit more sympathy for the elderly ( ) we can still defend ourselves
Officer	[please, please ((the talking stops))
Rita	[but the elderly who stay inside the house and do not go out any more, and they marginalize themselves because, there is no communication we as much as we can do the children one, either because you are busy or because you are in a hurry or you have to run here and well sometimes the elderly stay alone for hours, inside the house, the memory fades more and more, who can offer a bit of of, of comfort perhaps make them speak about the old days, eh only the young people

(5/10/93 Committee meeting of the Action Project)

The word 'elderly' is followed by a distancing move, *we can still defend ourselves*, that projects a differentiation among two different groups of older people. Consequently, the negative attribution of marginalization *(do not go out any more, no communication)*, loneliness *(the elderly stay alone for hours)*, forgetfulness *(the memory fades)*, do not refer to the in-group, but to the 'others', the very old. Nevertheless consider that '*we can still defend ourselves*' conveys a temporary status that projects similar negative perspectives onto Rita's future life (Taylor, 1992). Thus, the passage through 'natural lifetime' (Baker, 1984) is used as a resource in the talk, projecting decrement as a natural development (Coupland and Coupland 1989). Moreover, different degrees of business are distributed in relation to the different 'stages of life', *either because you are busy or because you are in a hurry or you have to run*. This account can be heard as a moral tale (Silverman, 1987; 1993), in which different moral duties are allocated and suspended. In particular, the care and support of the very old, a woman's duty (Facchini and Scortegagna, 1993/1994; Laws, 1995; Mengani and Lamura, 1995; Paoletti, 2001), is alleviated from the busy adult, and the responsibility of communicating with the elderly is passed on to the supposedly disengaged young.

Similar attribution of sadness and solitude are projected onto institutionalized elderly, depicted in the next excerpt. The group is discussing activities of solidarity among generations to be carried out in relation to the Action Project.

Tina I'd also like to go to this little old people [( ) I'd like it
(Delia) [eeh I have
Alba did you read it Irma, [Irma
Tina [because we also need to think about them,
Diana this with the elderly (I say) something we did it more than with the children=
Officer =eh yes
Tina but not I was saying
Diana we too we too
(Ida) our Centre too
Woman [poor elderly
Officer [( ) at San Marco they said [(that they did it)
Researcher [but this is an excellent idea
[because if there isn't
Ida [of course of course
Researcher soli solidarity among older people
Ida yes yes
Tina I'd like [(very much)
Woman [( )
Tina to do something because they go there, they do some, [something for example
Researcher [that's great
Tina [I saw a sketch (there was)
Nina [I also went (to) to to perform (to the older people).
[Aaat, aat, at Fonte Novo
Tina [there was one already (usually) for Christmas all these sketches are performed and we could also do go to once [to these
Ida [to bring a bit of,
Tina of cheerfulness
Ida of consolation
Tina to bring something and to bring a bit of cheerfulness to this little old people don't we
Researcher of course ((whispering general comments))
Tina I'd like I'd ( )
Officer well oh, there is this to say too, that it is true that the solidarity among generations,
Omitted turns
Officer then, solidarity among generations it istrue does not mean only [(between older people)
Woman [with young people ( ) ((whispering))
Officer because moreover the (fourth) age is not who knows which therefore it can also be solidarity with the more [old
Nina [with the more old
(10/9/1992 Committee meeting of the Action Project)

Tina expresses the desire, *to go to this little old people*. Notice the expression 'little old people'. There is a blurred distinction between a patronizing tone and a caring content. This ambiguity has been noticed in studies of baby talk to the elderly (Caporael, 1981; Cohen and Faulkner, 1986; Caporael and Culbertson,

1983). Specifically, Caporael and Culbertston (1986) notice that, although baby talk can be heard containing 'depreciatory message ... the register is primarily associated with nurturing affect' (p. 100). Also, considering the good intention of the speaker, talking of '*little old people*' may nevertheless predict and produce dependency. The whole discourse in the preceding passage is strongly inscribed in a moral universe. Tina presents visiting the elderly as a moral duty, *we also need to think about them*, and in doing so she is actually constructing 'them' as an out-group. Some lines later, this sense of compassion and moral obligation is increased by a woman saying, *poor elderly*. Many interjections state how Senior Citizen Centres have participated in activities involving the elderly, *this with the elderly (I say) something we did it more than with the children; our Centre too*. The researcher's turn introduces a different perspective. By talking about, *solidarity among older people* she, in fact, includes present group members as well as the 'others' in the one category. This is not picked up until the end of the passage, except by the officer, another younger group member.

Tina goes on to describe a possible activity, a theatre performance, to be carried out for the older people. By saying, *I also went ... to perform ...at Fontenuovo*, Nina makes explicit, for the first time in this sequence, who the 'elderly' being discussed are: they are 'institutionalized elderly' (Fontenuovo is a geriatric home in Perugia).

The reference to Christmas serves to inscribe the issue of 'visiting the elderly' in a moral and religious context: doing-good-deeds-for-Christmas, *for Christmas all these sketches are performed and we could also do go*. In this passage, in which Ida and Tina finish each other's sentences, *to bring a bit of ... cheerfulness ... of consolation*, 'the elderly' are constructed as in need of being cheered up and comforted, thus implying their sadness and suffering. In particular, the expression, *to bring a bit of ... consolation*, may remind participants of the Christian precept of 'comfort the suffering'. I believe that this discourse of providing assistance would be a lot less salient if the speakers had been men, who are not generally perceived as caregivers.

At the end, the officer expresses the policy of the group in relation to solidarity among generations by naming 'the others' as, *the more old*. This formulation is supported by Nina. It is important to point out that chronological age is not the main issue here in determining the difference between older people and 'the more old'. Although in the group there are many women in their 50s and 60s, there are also many in their 70s and some in their 80s. It is the 'institutionalized elderly' who are being treated as a homogeneous group with typical – that is, stereotyped – needs.

This stereotypical view of the 'very old' or 'institutionalized old people', who are constructed as an out-group, has double implications for identification work. On the one hand, distancing themselves from the category allows the women to project positive self-images of effective adults. On the other hand, decrement is still impending and, as in the first transcript analysed, it is managed as a threat to positive self-projection, *we can still defend ourselves*. Thus, it appears that stereotyping, and consequently the marginalization of older people is not only an issue at an intergenerational level, but it can occur among older people themselves (Levin and Levin, 1980).

The accounts analysed here are constructed against the background of a moral order; they are primarily moral accounts (Silverman, 1993) in which the 'sad', 'suffering' and 'lonely' elderly must be assisted. It is a moral order that is more relevant to women than to men; in fact, the care of the elderly is considered a woman's duty (Facchini and Scortegagna, 1993/1994; Rose and Bruce, 1995). This has a correspondence in actual gender composition in the profession of caregivers: by and large, formal and informal care of the elderly are carried out by women.

Distancing from the category 'old' allows members to project positive self-image, attributing negative characteristics to the category to out-group members. 'Denial of ageing', as we will see in the following paragraphs, has similar effects on identity projection; that is, presenting positive self-image, while postponing decline.

Denial of Ageing

The explicit rejection of membership in the category 'old', is a widely documented phenomenon in the literature (Bultena and Powers, 1978; Coupland, Coupland and Giles, 1991; Kamler, 1995). Old age is often seen as a natural process of decrepitude, an ineluctable decline in health and competence (Coupland and Coupland, 1990; Bultena and Powers, 1978). Gerontological studies contribute to this view of ageing as a deviant phenomenon (Green, 1993), by characterizing it primarily in terms of senescence and ill health.

In Bultena and Power's ten-year longitudinal study, intended to measure age identity through self-age categorizations, age categories are considered discrete well-defined categories. However, when I use the term 'denial of ageing' as a descriptor of various members' activities, I refer to substantially different conceptions of age categories as blurred, fuzzy-edged and interactionally defined (Hester and Eglin, 1997; Sacks, 1992). Such categories constitute background knowledge, and their specific management in conversation allows members to negotiate personal identities in, and through the unfolding of the conversation (Antaki and Widdicombe, 1998; Baker, 1983; 1984; Paoletti, 1997; Watson and Weinberger, 1982; Schenkein, 1978).

There are some examples in the data where the category 'old' is explicitly rejected by the women as a term properly referring to them. A particularly relevant instance is offered by a discussion of the choice of the name of the women's group in Perugia that had to be officially constituted. Names that would include the word '*old*' were only proposed by younger group members; these were decisively rejected by the older women. The discussion lasted for about 15 minutes. The following transcript is the most significant part of that interactional sequence.

Social worker	international Italian solidarity association or group women or older women right?
Woman	yes women
Women	women
Teacher	women
Social worker	older women is not that great
Women	no no [no ((aloud speaking altogether))
Woman	[are you joking?
Alba	[(they are not old at all) her her her they are all young
Officer	older women
Sonia	eh that's right ((smiling))
Alba	the ladies, [are all young
Pietro	[where are the old people ((smiling))
Officer	over 50 years [(they are not a lot)
Pietro	[eeh! ( ) ((gesture to indicate exaggeration))
Elia	(my husband's grandmother) would saywhat old, old is the shell

(2/5/1994 Committee meeting of the Action Project)

'Women' is explicitly stated as the preferred word for the participants to refer to themselves. When the social worker proposes 'older women' as a less preferred term, *older women is not that great*, she is strongly supported, *no no no ((aloud speaking all together)); are you joking*. A quite intricate series of terms in the discussion follows. Alba's remark *(they are not old at all) she she she they are all young*, lists the women considered young in the group, but she excludes herself. This is a move in a 'ritualistic sequence' (Coupland et al., 1991) to elicit protest and therefore her inclusion, as can be seen from the following dialogue. Sonia comments on Alba's remark, *eh that's right ((smiling))*, with an ironical inflection; she can be seen doing 'pretending' (Baker, 1984:313), that is, Sonia is signalling pretended membership of the 'young' category with respect to lifetime positioning. In this way she is actually distancing herself from it. This is not what Alba was expecting, therefore she produces the next significant move restating, *the ladies, are all young*, apparently including herself this time. As others have noted, being considered young is particularly salient for women in relation to the importance bestowed on bodily appearance (Kamler and Feldman, 1995:9). Meanwhile, the officer proposes the use of the term '*older women*', but she is not supported. This is noticeable, because she generally has a large following in the committee. Pietro replies ironically to the officer, *where are the old people ((smiling))*. The gradeable qualities of the category 'old' (Coupland et al., 1991) are made explicit in the next turns in the excerpt: the officer defines elderliness as starting after 50 years of age, *over 50 years*, but Pietro does not agree, *eeh! ( ) ((gesture to indicate exaggeration))*. To determine when old age does start is a problem for all practical purposes, whether on a personal, social or institutional level.

Finally, Elia reporting the saying, *what old, old is the shell*, at the same time negates and affirms membership in the category 'old'. In Italian there are several expressions similar to 'old is the shell', for example, 'old are the clothes'. They all refer to the distinction between appearing old physically and being young in energy and spirit.

This duplicity in association and rejection of the category results very clearly in the name that was finally chosen for the older women's group in Perugia: AIDA, that is (Associazione Italiana Donne Attive/Anziane, in English it reads: Italian Association of Active/Older Women). The final 'A' of the association name carries this duplicity. The decision to include the word '*older*', despite the aversion expressed by the women, was due to institutional reasons, such as prospective links to European elderly networks, access to special funding and the like. The word '*active*' allows the camouflage; in fact, the word could be omitted since a second 'A' has not been added to the acronym.

The distancing previously mentioned from the category 'old', as well as denial of ageing, have been shown to be used conversationally by members, to project images of themselves as effective adults proposing positive self-identifications. A similar combination of association and dissociation from elderliness is achieved in the talk reported in the next transcript. In this case, a criticism of the negative characterization of the category is attempted.

Deconstructing Ageing

The women are planning a TV programme for a local station in, which they were invited to take part. In this excerpt Rita strongly supports the idea of including the topic of solidarity among generations.

Rita	I felt my only satisfaction, these days going to visit schools with these youngsters
Alba	that's true that's true ((all talking at once commenting))
Lola	[( )
Rita	[( ) with these generations with these discourses of the youngsters with the elderly [to limit a bit this elderliness to take out a bit
Emma	[(to overcome the generational)
Rita	the old from the word because, because we are, we are old well but with a lot of experience that we, one could, one could give a lot yet you know, a lot of teaching

(10/5/93 Committee meeting of the Action Project)

Rita starts with a mild dissociation from the category, *to limit a bit this elderliness*; then she specifies: *to take out a bit the old from the word*. This very vividly expresses the dissociation from the detrimental attribution of the category, 'old' as the word 'negative' could be substituted. She seems to be proposing to take out the negative aspect from the word '*elderliness*'. She accepts membership in the category, *we are old*, but wants to dissociate herself from the detrimental characterization of the term and to highlight, instead, its positive aspects. In fact, the explicit association with the category is immediately followed by its commonsense positive characterization, *with a lot of experience*. Denial of ageing is not the only means of projecting a positive social image: subversion of the category has been attempted as well.

Positive characterizations of the category 'old' are quite rare. The next transcript can certainly be considered one such exception. Generally, positive self-appraisals as an older person are constructed through comparisons with negative stereotypic constructions of old age (Bultena and Powers, 1978; Coupland, Coupland and Giles, 1991). In the following case, a more positive life situation is directly experienced by the subject: relationally, economically and socially, life is said to be improved with increased age. This is a rather funny and provocative transcript, the only one in the data in which association with elderliness is invoked and where it is constructed positively. It sounds like a manifesto.

Lola	listen, I the people of my age ( ) now the, we older people have come out of our shells and we are beautiful strong and spunky and not any more with lice on our heads but well-groomed by the hairdresser,
Emma	I said it also [in my programme
Lola	[we have started to experience this after we were 60 years old, and we are ready to help the young people boys (girls) everybody who needs it

(10/5/93 Committee meeting of the Action Project)

Lola is in her 70s and she feels she is, together with other older people: *beautiful strong and spunky*. She describes these positive connotations as the outcome of a process, *we older people have come out of our shells*. The whole passage gives a sense of progression from a negative to a positive condition, in particular, *not any more with lice on our heads but well-groomed by the hairdresser*, hinting at improved economic as well as social situations. The present positive condition is explicitly associated with elderliness, *we have started to experience this after we were 60 years old*.

This passage projects a very different life perspective from Rita's, in which marginalization, loneliness, and fading memory were ahead of her. Here, solidarity with young people is the prospect. In order to help them to reach the same positive situation she has obtained after many struggles during the course of her life, *we are ready to help the young people*. In this way, Lola also gives a non-traditional twist to the womanly caring role for the young, that is, a 'political' inter-generational solidarity.

Despite the overall trend of dissociation from the category that has been illustrated herein, there are occasions in which 'being an older woman' is endorsed and becomes significant. In the next section I will examine how the category 'old' is used when it becomes an institutionally relevant category.

When Being Old Matters

In this section I examine how age categories are treated differently by the women when they are institutionally relevant. On the one hand, institutional intervention can positively mobilize women's perceived identities, opening new opportunities of action for them. On the other hand, institutional terms of relevance can prevail negatively on older women's understanding of the issues in relation to a particular interaction. Institutional influence on identity production appears to be complex and multi-faceted.

When Elderliness is Assuming Character of Prestige

In the analysis of the transcripts which follow, I will point out how 'elderliness' can assume a character of 'prestige' when it gives access to special institutionally designed activities, or to particular benefits or services. In these instances, it is endorsed by the women with no hesitation.

In the course of the Action Project there were numerous occasions in which interest was expressed by various institutions about the Older Women's Group in Perugia. The group was invited to international conferences, magazines for older people called the women for interviews; local radio shows and TV programmes sought their contributions; their singing and theatre groups were invited to perform in geriatric homes, schools and senior citizen centres; and nursing schools sought contact. Through the Action Project, 'being an older woman' became an object of interest for a series of different institutions. This interest contributed to defining what 'being an older woman' meant and can mean, and projected new, different, and appealing life perspectives for the women involved.

Requests for contributions by the Older Women's Action Project to various local, national or international events were routinely presented and discussed in the committee meetings. The following transcripts offer two examples. In the first, the officer is soliciting the women's participation in an international EC initiative.

Officer within the initiatives for the
European Year of the Elderly, a train is organized that will leave from Paris and will reach I don't know how many European countries how many countries will it reach Mira?

Mira sixteen

Officer sixteen European nations, eee, among
which Milan I mean Italy through Milan it will be in Milan the eighth of October. We sent a bit of our things because we thought to interpret the will of all of you that the European Action Project was represented in this train

Nina yes

Officer isn't it? oh, uum we made the impossible
there too because they wanted it so but not really so, not too much but not too little, eee and well we tried to content them this morning in their last phone call they said that they will show a poster, with some photos of the main stages of the Project and also the material that I sent them that is the booklet

	the booklet with the contact with the other Nations the booklet of Perugia of course the research of Isabella Paoletti all that (which), they will show all that we sent them. It wouldn't be a bad idea that on the eight of October [someone went to Milan
Ida	[(someone)
Women	[( )
Officer	well for for the Office Mira will go. That's it that's it, think about it
(15/9/93	*Committee meeting of the Action Project)*

The use of the category 'elderly', in designating an international event, *the European Year of the Elderly,* here looses all its negative connotations. In fact the women are asked to take part, *It wouldn't be a bad idea that ... someone went to Milan*, in a prestigious initiative, *a train is organized that will leave from Paris and will reach ... sixteen European nations*, that will draw attention to their work. This request implies travelling and being a spokesperson, both activities that are quite unusual for most of the women in the group. Membership in the category here allows access to a desirable activity, and a very unconventional image of older women is projected.

International events such as this one, or such as participation in conferences and exchange visits among groups of older women in various European countries, were seen as desirable and prestigious by the women. At the same time many local initiatives were appreciated. These too were designed to bring out women's experience and their contribution, as it clearly appears in the next transcript.

The women associated with the Action Project were asked to intervene in a training course for nurses and various personnel working with elderly people, to bring their perspective on the condition of elderly people. In the following excerpt they are discussing how to participate. The officer suggests taking a slide show, the result of a photographic workshop in which the women were invited to reminisce about some old photos of theirs.

Officer	it's, a, a programme of stories of memories knowledge through memories from eeem, us to the young the young, in this case are, above all, persons who will then work with older people, eh therefore [from nurses
Woman	[they are students
Office	to social worker,
Woman	students
Officer	or students of of of of various
	disciplines who then either from a cultural or physical caring point of view might work with older people in short the intention is to make aware these persons that's of the, true, reality I mean the true meaning
	[( ) the older person therefore is not only a ( )
Women	[( )

(10/12/1993 Committee meeting of the Action Project)

The hesitation, *eeem, us*, in pronouncing the pro-term can be interpreted as signalling disturbance in the categorization process. The category 'old' is clearly implied in the use of the pro-term, because of the presence of the category 'young', both of which are drawn from the same 'stage of life' membership categorization device (Sacks, 1972). It is also part of the category-bound activity (Sacks, 1972:222) 'passing on memories'. In particular, Boden and Bielby (1983; 1986) have pointed out the relevance of the past as a topic and a resource in elderly talk. Therefore, the officer might have hesitated in including herself in the category, being a younger group member.

No association is produced between present group members in relation to '*older people*', constructed as beneficiaries of review services and assistance offered by the students and professionals who will be in the slide presentation audience. Instead, expressing the aim of the event, *the intention is to make aware these persons that's of the, true, reality I mean the true meaning ... older person*, the women's possible potential contribution is broadened out, and they are constructed as the repository of the 'true' knowledge about older people's condition. Two differentiated groups of elderly people are projected: in-group knowledgeable elderly, out-group sick and dependent elderly (Coupland, Coupland and Giles, 1991). No explicit use of old age categories is made in the transcript to designate the in-group, which allows the participants to conversationally produce the distinction between in-group and out-group, while at the same time avoiding negative association for the in-group. In other instances, association with the category 'old' is seen positively.

Older People as Beneficiaries of Government Services and Specific Legislation

Older people as a group are the beneficiaries of government services and specific legislation. They are the objects of interest of several different institutions and in various ways. For example, older people represent a conspicuous part of the electorate, and for this reason they are of interest to political institutions. In the course of the last committee meeting, Enza is reporting news of a political action from a local Member of Parliament:

((all the women are talking together))

Enza ((talking softly to the officer)) Rossi told me that, the Government the Italian Parliament (the new Italian Parliament) is creating a commission
Officer excuse me she is saying an important thing
Enza very important that, the Member of Parliament Rossi, told me that the Parliament the new Government is looking into the possibility of letting us have back the international card for elderly people for us elderly people a card, um an international card that we can travel in various countries=
Nina =with special discounts for elderly people good
Enza ((nodding)) it's doing, everything to let us have it back (this card)

(2/5/1994 Committee meeting of the Action Project)

Notice that Enza is not only describing what she sees as important news, but is also constructing it as such. She reinforces the officer's statement, *she is saying an important thing*, with, *very important*, and she changes from the informal whisper to the Officer, *Rossi told me*, to the public announcement to the group, *the Member of Parliament Rossi, told me.* 'Older people' is constructed here as a homogenous group, as a recipient of favours, *letting us have back the international card for elderly people*, that persons with specific institutional roles are able to obtain through effort and strife, *it's doing, everything to let us have back (this card).* Membership in the category here is not questioned, but is rather underlined*, the international card for elderly people for us elderly people a card*; the pro-term *us* makes explicit membership in the category 'old', and Enza is thus clearly 'doing inclusion' (Watson, 1987). Further, Nina comments positively on the prospect, *special discounts for elderly people good.*

Travelling is made relevant to 'older people' by this discussion; the elderly are treated as a homogeneous group, and they are constructed both as a recipient of favour and as actively engaged in life. Could the above passage be heard as a piece of electioneering propaganda for the Member of Parliament Rossi? There is no evidence that the audience heard it this way, and I am in no way attributing such intentions to the speaker. By asking such a question, however, I wish to draw attention to the possibility that if older people can find 'elderliness' appealing, in relation to the grant of special benefits by some institutions, then they become of interest to these institutions in various ways.

The next paragraphs focus precisely on how specific institutional aims, procedures and discourses are made relevant to the women in the course of the committee meetings, and how they interfere with older women's definition of the situation.

Institutional Definition of the Subject

Institutions have not only specific agendas, but also 'needs' of their own that have nothing to do with their functional aims: their management and organization impose on members' attention, issues that very often obscure the needs and priorities of the persons for whom they are supposed to be caring. This section illustrates how institutional 'needs' and priorities assume a level of relevance, which is greater than the older women's agenda and expectations.

In the next transcript, a social worker is introducing a new service that has just been established in the district, a centre for menopause, what we could call 'a gender and age specific institution'.

Social worker	I have still, a, message to give, (a different subject at three o'clock) it opens it was opened today for the first time this centre for menopause [in San Marco
Berta	[where where
Lidia	oh! [this is something we wanted to hear about
Social worker	[in San Marco

Lidia	[( )
Social worker	[(today)
Researcher	[sss ssss
Social worker	I chose you instead of going to participate innn this opening,
Alma	but where is it
Social worker	so there is this centre for menopause,
Alma	yes
Social worker	in San Marco,
Alma	eh
Alba	by now it is over for us
Alma	[ssss
Social worker	[in San Marco there is a gynaecologist there are, three social workers,
Alma	yes
Social worker	I mean I too am in the, little group…
Lidia	what are the characteristics of this centre
Social worker	well what are the characteristics this centre there is the possibility to have a gynaecological visit, em with this doctor who is specializing in this sector when I say doctor I mean a gynaecologist but she is a woman her name is …, … and this possibility to have this medical examination, will then allow privileged routes, for the clinical examination in the hospital, because for the first time the local services will be in contact with the hospital in fact I'll be working inside the hospital with, … … I think this is his name who is the gynaecologist who works in this sector, of menopause then meetings will be organized.

(22/2/1994 Committee meeting of the Action Project)

The social worker introduces the news, *it was opened today for the first time this centre for menopause*, welcomed by Lidia, *oh! this is something we wanted to hear about*, while Alma seeks an explanation, *but where is it*, and general comments are expressed. In this way Lidia and Alma contribute to construct the news as relevant to the group.

Alba's remarks, *by now it is over for us*, that correspond to reality for most of the women in the meeting, are not picked up by anyone. In this case the pro-term *us* is used to signal exclusion (Watson, 1987:282). At the institutional level, menopause is defined as relevant to older women, constructed as a homogenous group, by a powerful, credible and competent member: the social worker from the menopause centre, *there is a gynaecologist there are, three social workers, … I mean I too am in the, little group*. Members' relevance is obscured, and this becomes particularly evident in the description of the menopause centre produced.

Lidia solicits information about the centre, giving the social worker the opportunity to point out its relevance to the women. This explanation, though, is constructed around organizational structural problems, *for the first time the local services will be in contact with the hospital.* In fact, the social worker points out how the use of this centre (*this possibility to have this medical examination*), will facilitate access to hospital examination (*will then allow privileged routes, for the clinical examination in the hospital*). It is not clear what types of need on the part of the women could be answered, although there is a reference to the organization of informational meetings (*there will be meetings organized*). What is highlighted is not how the centre could be useful to the women, but how it can be used by the women from the standpoint of organizational procedures; its relevance is taken for granted. It appears as if the institution is useful in that it exists.

Just from this passage we can glimpse the immense institutional machinery, particularly within the medical and caring system, hiding behind the category 'old'. This machinery contributes to the definition of what 'being old' means in relation to powerful institutional practices and discourses. In the next transcript, institutional conflicts among two different Units of the Commune of Perugia, are made relevant to the women; also in this case differences among women's and institutional 'needs' are evident. It is the institutional ones that prevail.

Two departments of the Commune of Perugia: the Equal Opportunity Unit and the Social Services Unit, are discussed, and conflicts between them are revealed in the course of the conversation in the committee meeting. The topic of the conversation is the organization of an exhibition of older people's work, in which the older women's group will participate. Lola is asking whether they are talking of the same exhibition being organized by the Social Services Unit. Lola explains that she has just been asked by an officer of the Social Services Unit to bring her poetry to an exhibition.

Lola	is it the very one in the Commune? still this one
Officer	yes
Lola	or is it a different one
Officer	no (it is still that one at Rocca Paolina)
Lola	it is still this one, yes OK that one up there at the Commune (told me), if I could bring them to her, ( ) poetry and photos (on) the poster. That one at the Commune
Officer	but who who is she ((Lola turns around without replying)) but lets not make a muddle ladies ((with her voice slightly altered)) excuse me ladies here we are talking about the Action Project, ((background noise stops))
Lola	eh eh [(of the Project)
Officer	[well this work, this work that you were talking about of which you are talking about Lola, is it the work that you have done for the Action Project?
Lola	eh eh
Officer	and so if you (have done it) with the Action Project eh eh that too whom are you giving it [(what are they doing with it)
Lola	[it's said it was together ((turning towards Nina))
Nina	she wanted to bring it, to show it, at the Rocca Paolina
Officer	I understand it but you will bring it with all the things of the [Action Project
Nina	[and then you bring it with [all the things of the Action Project
Lola	[(but) this morning that lady at the Commune told me,

Officer yes
Lola [( )this thing that's why I saying it
Nina [( )listen to Irma ssss
Officer since you have always participated in the Action Project haven't you? and so. Is this material the drawings the tales the poetry the photos or what it is for the Action Project [(we don't want to hang it)
Lola [(certainly)
Officer well but if you give it [(to the lady)
Lola [(eh I know it) eh I found out just now that you were involved in it what can I know she told me this morning about it I don't know anything now another time, (that's why I was asking) explanations
Nina well we solve it
(2/5/1994 Committee meeting of the Action Project)

With the question, *but who who is she*, the officer signals trouble, that is understood as such by Lola who does not treat the question as a proper question, not answering to it *((Lola turns around without replying))*. The officer makes explicit the problem, *lets not make a muddle ladies*. The tone of her voice *((with her voice slightly altered))*, together with the content of her words, produce immediate attention from the group *((background noise stops))*.

The officer is now asking Lola to define the institutional attribution of her work, *is it the work that you have done for the Action Project?*; Lola gives her assent, *he he*. Lola is made morally accountable in reference to the institutional ownership of her work (Silverman, 1993:108). The officer's sort of inarticulate remark, *and so if you (have done it) with the Action Project eh eh that too whom are you giving it*, signals the ordinariness, common sense, facticidity of her work belonging to the Action Project, and the moral sanctions implied in upsetting such order (Cuff and Payne, 1979:164). Nina attempts an explanation of Lola's intention, highlighting Lola's intentions and order of relevancy, *she wanted to bring it, to show it, at the Rocca Paolina*. The Officer twice underlines the importance of the institutional attribution of the older women's work, *I understand it but you will bring it with all the things of the Action Project; Is this material the drawings the tales the poetry the photos or what it is for the Action Project*. Lola feels the need to justify herself, *I found out just now that you were involved in it what can I know she told me this morning about it I don't know anything now another time*, and assert her right to ask for explanation, *that's why I saying it, (that's why I was asking) for explanations*. Both Nina and Lola contribute in this way to construct the moral accountability of the issue at hand.

The older women's work appears here to be constructed as an institutional possession. This is not a trivial issue. Institutions must be seen to be doing things, they do not only have to produce services but they must be seen to perform them. As a serious matter of social and political accountability they have to document their activities, and make them visible, understandable, and tangeable. When Lola expresses her idea to offer her poetry for the Social Service Unit's exhibition, the officer expresses disagreement and anger. This is because the officer sees the risk that work carried out under the auspices of the Action Project will be credited to the Social Service Unit and not to the Equal Opportunity Unit. But this issue is irrelevant to the women, who want mainly to see their work exhibited, as Nina explains it: *she wanted ... to show it, at the Rocca Paolina.* Between the two forms of relevance, it is clear that the institutional one prevails.

This interactional episode shows how specific institutional priorities, such as making the production of services publicly witnessable, are made relevant to the women in the course of ordinary events. On the one hand, such institutional activities as the organization of the exhibition allows women's work to be brought forward, thus producing positive and effective identities for them. On the other hand, institutional priorities establish the organization of activities. Institutional aims and procedures are made relevant to the women, creating a different order of priorities. The institutional influence on the social construction of identity is thus complex.

In the above paragraphs the association with the category 'old' has been highlighted in relation to its institutional relevance. Access to prestigious events, benefits, and services were implied in such association. In particular, institutionally organized activities can positively mobilize women's perceived spheres of action and life perspectives, adding new possibilities to what being an older woman can mean. In contrast to this positive institutional influence however, the needs, priorities, procedures, and discourses that belong exclusively to specific institutional settings, may impose on the understanding and perception of older women.

Conclusions

From the analysis of the above transcripts, we gain an idea of the degree of variability in the use of the category 'old'. It has been shown how the use of the category is specifically related to the occasion, the setting of the encounter, and the conversational purposes of the interlocutors. Use of categories is not clear cut, nor mechanical, but achieved through interpretative work by members, in producing as well as in understanding, talk. In fact, categories could be considered as background knowledge, by which actual states of affairs and identities are managed on the ground, through step by step interactional production (Antaki and Widdicombe, 1998; Schenkein, 1978).

The stable character of membership categories is in contrast with the variability of their conversational use. That is, their common sense meaning stands in opposition to their malleability in allowing members to produce highly individualized and differentiated identities. Both the possibility of mere reproduction of typified and stereotypic categorization, as well as distancing and differentiation from them, are conversationally available. It is through the variability of the use of categories that either marginalization and exclusion of older people, or, instead, integration and social resourcefulness, are conversationally produced.

The analysis has shown how the women project positive personal identities, differentiating themselves from old age categories and from related category-bound activities. The images of older women emerging from the transcripts analysed, are ones of busy and effective adults. Images of dependency, sickness and loneliness are not part of the picture. On the other hand, these women construct stereotyped identities for the 'other', the very old or institutionalized elderly. It is in this double-faceted character of categorization processes that complex interactional phenomena at a group level, such as marginalization or racism, can be understood. It is the association with stereotyped meanings of the category that produce de-individualization and therefore exclusion.

This study has not only a theoretical interest in relation to the description of processes of identity production, but a very practical aim. Politicians, legislators, social workers have to become aware of the effects that the provision of services has on the older population. Services can foster older people's independence, active and healthy life-style, or can foster their dependency and frailty. To consider the gender differences and cultural particulars that make gender differences relevant is also very important, since the large majority of older and frail people are women.

Further studies should in particular explore how institutional organizational needs such as personnel shifts, specific routines etc impose on processes of identity production in the institutionalized elderly, with devastating psychological effects. Awareness of the processes of identity production of elderly people would undoubtedly be very useful in the training of personnel working with older people, showing in detail the effects on identification processes of ordinary institutional practices in hospitals and nursing homes, as well as in common sense discourses and practices related to the fact of being old.

References

Antaki, C. and Widdicombe, S. (1998), *Identities in Talk*, Sage, London.

Arber, S. and Ginn, J. (1991), *Gender and Later Life*, Sage, London.

Atkinson, M.J. and Heritage, J. (eds.) (1984), *Structures of Social Action. Studies in Conversation Analysis*, Cambridge University Press, Cambridge.

Atkinson, P. (1985) 'Talk and Identity: Some Convergences in Micro-Sociology', in H.J. Helle and S.N. Eisenstadt (eds.), *Micro-Sociological Theory*, Vol. II, Sage, London, pp. 117-132.

Baker, C. (1983), 'A "Second Look" at Interviews with Adolescents', *Journal of Youth and Adolescence*, Vol. 12 (6), pp. 501-519.

Baker, C. (1984), 'The "Search for Adultness": Membership Work in Adolescent-Adult Talk' *Human Studies*, Vol. 7, pp. 301-323.

Barbato, C.A. and Perse, E.M. (1992), 'Interpersonal Communication Motives and Life Position of Elders', *Communication Research*, Vol. 19 (4), pp. 516-531.

Barer, B.M. (1994), 'Men and Women Aging Differently', *International Journal of Aging and Human Development*, Vol. 38 (1), pp. 24-90.

Boden D. and Bielby, D. (1983), 'The Past as a Resource: A Conversational Analysis of Elderly Talk', *Human Development*, Vol. 26, pp. 308-19.

Boden D. and Bielby, D. (1986), 'The Way It Was: Topical Organization in Elderly Conversation', *Language and Communication*, Vol. 6, pp.73-89.

Bultena, G.L. and Powers E.A. (1978), 'Denial of Ageing: Age Identification and Reference Group Orientation', *Journal of Gerontology*, Vol. 33, pp. 748-754.

Caporael, L. (1981), 'The Paralanguage of Caregiving: Baby Talk to the Institutionalized Aged', *Journal of Personality and Social Psychology*, Vol. 40 (5), pp. 876-84.

Caporael, L. and Culbertson, G.H. (1983), 'Baby Talk Speech to Elderly. Complexity and Content of Message', *Personality and Social Psychology Bulletin*, Vol. 9 (2), pp. 305-312.

Caporael, L. and Culbertson, G.H. (1986), 'Verbal Response Modes of Baby-Talk and Other Speech at Institutions for the Aged', *Language and Communication*, Vol. 6 (1/2), pp. 99-112.

Cohen, G. and Faulkner, D. (1986), 'Does "Elder's Speak" Work? The Effect of Intonation and Stress on Comprehension and Recall of Spoken Discourse in Old Age', *Language and Communication*, Vol. 6 (1/2), pp. 91-8.

Coopmans, M., Harrop, A. and Hermans-Huskies, M. (1988), *The Social and Economic Situation of Older Women in Europe*, Joint Report of Two Research Project, Commission of the European Communities, Directorate-General Employment, Social Affaires and Education, Brussels.

Coupland, J. and Coupland, N. (1994), '"Old Age Doesn't Come Alone": Discursive Representations of Health-in-Aging in Geriatric Medicine', *International Journal of Aging and Human Development*, Vol. 39 (1), pp. 81-95.

Coupland, N. and Coupland, J. (1989), 'Age Identity and Elderly Disclosure of Chronological Age', *York Papers in Linguistics*, Vol. 13, pp. 77-88.

Coupland, N. and Coupland, J. (1990), 'Language in Later Life', in H. Giles and W.P. Robinson (eds.), *Handbook of Language and Social Psychology*, Wiley, Chichester.

Coupland, N., Coupland, J. and Giles, H. (1989), 'Telling Age in Later Life: Identiy and Face Implications', *Text*, Vol. 9, pp. 129-151.

Coupland, N., Coupland, J. and Giles, H. (1991), *Language, Society and the Elderly*, Blackwell, Cambridge, MA.

Coupland, N., Coupland, J., Giles, H. and Henwood, K. (1988), 'Accomodating the Elderly: Invoking and Extending a Theory', *Language in Society*, Vol. 17 (1), pp. 1-41.

Coupland, N., Coupland, J., Giles, H. and Henwood, K. (1991), 'Formulating Age: Dimensions of Age Identity in Elderly Talk', *Discourse Processes*, Vol. 14 (1), pp. 87-106.

Coupland, N., Coupland, J., Giles, H., Henwood, K. and Wiemann, J. (1988), 'Elderly Self-Disclosure: Interactional and Intergroup Issues', *Language and Communication*, Vol. 8 (2), pp. 109-133.

Coupland, N., Coupland, J. and Grainger, K. (1991), 'Intergenerational Discourse: Contextual Versions of Ageing and Elderliness', *Ageing and Society*, Vol. 11 (Part 2), pp. 189-208.

Cuff, E.C. and Payne, G.C.F. (eds.) (1979), *Perspectives in Sociology*, George Allen and Unwin, London.

Faccehini, C. and Scortegagna, R. (1993/1994), 'Italia: Alterative allístituzionalizzazione e ruolo centrale delle donne', in F. Leseman and C. Martin (eds), *Assistenza a domicilio, famiglia e anziani. Un confronto internazionale*, Angeli, Milano, pp. 33-69.

Garfinkel, H. (1967), *Studies in Ethnomethodology*, Prentice-Hall, Englewood Cliffs, N.J.

Ginn, J. and Arber, S. (1991), 'Gender, Class and Income Inequalities in Later Life', *British Journal of Sociology*, Vol. 42 (3), pp. 367-396.

Ginn, J. and Arber, S. (1992), 'Towards Women's Independence: Pension System in Three Contrasting European Welfare States', *Journal of European Social Policy*, Vol. 4 (2), pp. 255-277.

Green, B.S. (1993), *Gerontology and the Construction of Old Age*, De Gruyter, New York.

Harold, S. (1992), 'Education in Later Life: The Case of Older Women', *Educational Gerontology*, Vol. 18 (5), pp. 511-527.

Hester, S. and Eglin, P. (eds.) (1997), *Culture in Action. Studies in Membership Categorization Analysis*, University Press of America, Washington.

Kamler, B. (1995), *From Autobiography to Collective Biography: Writing Workshop Practice with Women 60-80*, Paper presented to the American Educational Research Association Annual Meeting, San Francisco, California.

Kamler, B. and Feldman, S. (1995), *Mirror, Mirror on the Wall: Reflection on Ageing*, Australian Cultural History, no 14, Deakin University, Geelong.

Klein, G. and Paoletti, I. (eds.) (2002), *La costruzione conversazionale dell'inclusione e dell'esclusione*, Edizioni Scientifiche Italiane, Napoli.

Laws, G. (1995), 'Understanding Ageism: Lessons from Feminism and Postmodernism', *The Gerontologist*, Vol. 35 (1), pp. 112-118.

Levin, J. and Levin, W.C. (1980), *Ageism: Prejudice and Discrimination against the Elderly*, Wadsworth, Belmont, Californa.

Mengani, M. and Gagliardi, C. (1993), *Older Women in the European Community: Social and Economic Condition*, Italian Report, INRCA; Ancona.

Mengani, M. and Lamura, G. (1995), 'Elderly Women, Family Structure and Care Patterns in Italy', in G. Dooghe and N. Appleton (eds.), *Elderly Women in Europe*, Centrum vor Bevolkings, Bruxelles.

Paoletti, I. (1996a), 'La produzione dell'identità nell'intervista con anziane', in A. Macarino (ed.) *Analisi della Conversazione e prospettive di ricerca in etnometodologia. Atti del convegno internazionale*, Universitá di Urbino, 11-13 luglio 1994, Edizioni Quattroventi, Urbino.

Paoletti, I. (1996b), 'La costruzione sociale dell'immagine dell'anziana', *Oggidomani Anziani*, Vol. IX (1), pp. 21-35.

Paoletti, I. (1997), 'La produzione dell'identità nell'intervista con anziane', in A. Macarino (ed.), *Analisi della Conversazione e prospettive di ricerca in etnometodologia*, Edizioni Quattroventi, Urbino.

Paoletti, I. (1998a), *Being an Older Women: A Study in the Social Production of Identity*, Lawrence Eribaum Associates, Hillsdale, N. J.

Paoletti, I. (1998b), 'Handling "Incoherence" According to the Speaker's On-sight Categorisation', in C. Antaki and S. Widdicombe (eds.), *Identities in Talk*, Sage, London, pp. 171-190,

Paoletti, I. (2000), 'Being a Foreigner in Primary School', *Language and Education*, Vol. 14 (4), pp. 266-282.

Paoletti, I. (2001), 'The Forgotten Majority: Images of Older Women and Their Lives in Italy', *Indian Journal of Gerontology*, Vol. 15 (1-2), pp. 198-220.

Rose, H. and Bruce, E. (1995), 'Mutual Care But Differential Esteem: Caring between Older Couples', in S. Arber and J. Ginn, (eds.), *Connecting Gender and Ageing*, Open University Press, Buckingham, pp. 114-128.

Sacks, H. (1972), 'On the Analyzability of Stories by Children', in J.J. Gumperz and D. Hymes (eds.), *Directions in Sociolinguistics: The Ethnography of Communication*, Holt, Rinehart and Winstone, New York and London, pp. 216-232 (Reported in Coulter 1990).

Sacks, H. (1992), *Lectures on Conversation*, vol I and II, Blackwell, Oxford.
Schenkein, J. (1978), 'Identity Negotiation in Conversation', in J. Schenkein, (ed.), *Studies in the Organization of Conversational Interaction*, Academic Press, New York, pp. 57-77.
Silverman, D. (1987), 'Constituting the Subject', in Silverman, D., *Communication and Medical Practice*, Sage, Newbury Park, pp. 134-190.
Silverman, D. (1993), *Interpreting Qualitative Data*, Sage, London.
Taylor, B. (1992), 'Elderly Identity in Conversation. Producing Frailty', *Communication Research*, Vol. 19 (4), pp. 493-515.
Watson, R. (1987), 'Interdisciplinary Consideration in the Analysis of Pro-Terms', in G. Button and R. E. Lee (eds.), *Talk and Social Organization*, Multilingual Matters Ltd, Clevedon, pp. 261-289.
Watson R. and Weinberg, M. (1982), 'Interviews and the Interactional Construction of Accounts of Homosexual Identity', *Social Analysis*, Vol. 11, pp. 56-78.

Chapter 9

Old People, New and Old Artefacts – Technology for Later Life

Jan-Erik Hagberg

Lengthening the Normal Life Span with the Help of Technology

How should old people live in a society characterized by advanced technology and rapid technical development? Should they use technology as a tool in order to maintain the same kind of life they themselves lived when they were younger, or in order to live as the younger generation does today? Do old people need access to modern technology to a greater extent than young people do?

Should society build the care and welfare sector for the elderly based to a greater extent on advanced technological systems that can give a control function, and facilitate communication and the mediation of knowledge? Or should old age be a period in life when the technological society fades into the background, when life becomes more tranquil and material things are therefore less essential?

These questions lead to existential and moral standpoints. What does it mean to grow old? How do we want life's different stages to relate to one another? By increasing or changing our use of technology can we remove the reasons for having to change as we grow old? What does rapid technological change mean with regard to everyday life? Can new technology level out the differences between the old and the young, or does it instead highlight generation differences? In that case, is there anything that we value? What answers we give depend on how we view technology's relation to social life and what we perceive as the meaning of being old.

It is not possible to specify a definite age limit for when a human being is old, in the sense that I attach to the concept in this chapter. I deal with the stage of life when an individual's room for action and ability to act are influenced by a biological and/or social ageing that is connected to great age. I use the concept of elderly in a broader sense, referring to the period that is entered when one leaves the social context that dominates everyday life during the early adult period, until one is old. One can refer to the concepts of the third and fourth ages, respectively. The third age is that time in life when one, after the adult period, still is, wants to be, and can be, active in life in society. The fourth age is the time when life is adapted since the ability to act which one previously had, is impaired by biological, social or cultural circumstances. The chapter revolves around the question of technology's importance at the boundary between the third and fourth ages.[1]

On a general level most people are probably of the opinion that it is natural to stimulate the development of technology which can postpone the fourth age and facilitate life for those who reach this age. Thus we commonly believe that the technology of the future should certainly be able to compensate for lack of physical power, decreased mobility or failing memory. Old people certainly should have access to communication technology that makes it possible for them to maintain contact with others, even when they are physically bound to their homes. It would certainly be a good thing if old people themselves could monitor their health with the aid of intelligent knowledge systems supported by the Internet. Old people should certainly be able to continue to participate within life in society by using interactive media and communication systems.

In the political debate both in Europe and Japan, great importance is attached to technological development in order for society to take care of a rapidly growing group of old people. The political interest is primarily focused on creating prerequisites for old people, to be able to take care of themselves with the aid of new technology, and perhaps with the help of relatives or the public care sector. But in the broader debate there are also visions of new technology enriching the life of old people, and placing new dimensions on old age's special quality of life. The expectations are concerned with everything from better aids for doing everyday tasks, to sophisticated intelligent homes that both make it possible for community care to be carried out there and for those who live at home to make excursions into a virtual world.

R&D-systems are complex, and it would be naive to believe that development and technological research would be directed with particular energy towards old people's special needs without vigorous steering on the part of society. Attempts to do this are visible in the European Union's Framework Programme for Research.[2] There is also growing research concerned with technological development for old people's specific needs, but only recently can one speak of more unified attempts to systematically stimulate broad technological development and research which emanate from the entirety in the lives and problems of the elderly.

One fundamental problem both in the public debate and in research is, however, that knowledge concerning old people's needs of, readiness for, and interest in using new technology is very poor. Attention so far has, as a rule, been directed at specific, technological solutions for clearly defined needs. How is life affected by the broad technological changes in society? How should new technology be combined with existing technology? What does it mean for the overall picture to make use of new technology? These questions have hardly been addressed at all. Nor is there other than sporadic knowledge of how old people actually use the everyday technology they have, and what technology means to different age groups and at different stages of life.

We find ourselves, therefore, faced with a paradox. A very rapid technological development, foremostly of communication and media technology, is ongoing. This will utterly change the foundations of our daily lives. In spite of the fact that technology's potential in relation to old people's needs is great, the risk is also great that old people's everyday life will become more complicated instead of being facilitated and that old people will therefore to a greater extent be left out of the social life of the other generations. Technology can strengthen age discrimination and become a tool in a socially created dependency for old people. Thus a very important political question should be how old people's and the older generation's living conditions can be fortified by the process of technological change. Yet how this is to take place has hardly been discussed at all.[3]

In this chapter I establish some different perspectives on the question of technological development for old people's needs. I approach these complex problems by linking up with the humanistic and sociological scientific research orientation which views technology as a social phenomenon.[4] My point of departure is thus to regard the use of technology as a part of everyday social and cultural life which is not only important because of its functionality, but also because of its capacity for the creation of meaning.

One aim of this chapter is to contribute to the discussion on new information and communication technology and its possibilities in relation to what old people want and need. I will also deal with the pre-requisites for conducting research on technological development in relation to the needs of the elderly.

The Technological Landscape's Unevenness

We live both literally and metaphorically in a technological landscape. In this landscape we find the artefacts – tools, appliances and machines – that we need in our everyday life. They are incorporated in complex, socio-technological systems. The technological landscape has dimensions of time and space; the artefacts take up a place in space and the use of them is linked to where we are and how we use time. But they are also a means for us to liberate ourselves from deadlocks in time and space by facilitating our movements in the space, bridging over distance and being a storeplace for what we produce and experience. The technological landscape is uneven. Within certain areas the technology is advanced and the technological systems change rapidly. Within other areas the landscape is sparser and the artefacts' and the systems' stability more evident. Our individual technological landscape (or how we have access to and use the technological landscape's different parts) is different and reflects both the individual's choices and interests and the social structure's limits and possibilities.

Old people have, of course, in many respects the same relationship to everyday technology as others have. They are in themselves very different and they have different interests in and attitudes towards technology. The fact that old people are at the end of their life does, however, bring about their age-specific relationship to everyday technology and they are influenced by changes in the technological landscape in different ways from younger people. Decreased physical powers, sometimes also decreased mental ability, and a sparser social network can, for example, lead to a dependence on, what is to them, new technology. Thus through technology, age-related 'losses' in ability to act and other abilities can be compensated for. In a similar way established technology can gain new importance and new usage as a result of changed living conditions. But when technological development leads to the technological landscape changing, then this can result in activities that are well known to old people becoming difficult to maintain. The changed technological landscape places demands on new knowledge and adaptations. Thus, a person who does not want, or is not able to afford, the new appliances or the changed technological system, can become marginalized.

It is partially an open question whether great age makes the adaptation to new technology especially difficult. Old people should find it easier than young people to handle the technology shifts, because of their long experience of using different kinds of technology, and during their lives having experienced a great number of changes.[5] Several conditions speak in favour of the contrary, however. Putting new technology into use means that one must unlearn the use of procedures connected with older technology. This is in all likelihood more difficult for old people than for young ones. Another circumstance that constitutes an obstruction for old people is that new technology often is introduced in situations where old people are not present, for example in working life or communal planning. Marcellini et al. (2000) have, by means of investigations in several European countries of old people's acceptance and use of new technology, found strong support for the fact that old people have special difficulties in using new technological systems that are introduced into the local environment.[6]

My conclusion is that old people, more tangibly than others, have to live with the complications that arise by the spread of new technology and thereby the changing of their technological landscape. At the same time their dependence on new technology can increase in order for them to maintain their ingrained everyday lifestyle. Thus, there is every reason to discuss how everyday technology will develop in relation to old people and to ageing. Is there an ongoing radical change of everyday technology's fundamental systems? Many people maintain that this is the case, and mean that information and communication technology is integrated in almost all kinds of everyday technology. Society becomes a network society, the houses are intelligent, the homes are smart and the individual places that we arrange our existence around, obtain a changed functionality.

New Technology Changes, But What?

Hopes that new technological developments will solve the ageing society's social and economic problems correspond well with how we in general regard new technology. Many people have a technology-optimistic basic outlook that leads to an unreflecting faith in new technology, and hopes of rapid changes in its wake. At the same time we know that the reality is more complicated. New technology both solves and creates problems. The diffusion of innovations takes a long time, the effects are complex and those who are socially and economically weak often stand on the sidelines when new technology is spread.

One important insight from the last 20 years of research on technological changes is that of the duplicity of technology. New technology *both* changes and preserves. New appliances and technological systems can give completely new prerequisites for activities in which we are involved, and thereby give rise to large changes in society. However, the same or other new appliances and technological systems can also bring about strenghtened established social conditions and compensate for effects caused by another new technology. A common theme in research has been to remove technological-determinative assumptions and conclusions, i.e. that a certain technology has inevitable effects on society and the individual. Instead an emphasis has emerged on the social and cultural processes' importance in crystallizing which technology will be implemented, and how it will be used.[7] Sometimes the actual content of the technology has been kept in the background i.e. what is actually possible (and not possible) to achieve with a certain technology or a technical solution. The American technology historian Thomas Hughes has made a valuable distinction when he pointed out that technological development certainly is not deterministic, but the technological systems, the tangible and realized technology, has a *momentum*.

Technology is used and developed in a certain way that depends on its content *and* how the dominating actors act. Thus we must conduct the discussion on two levels. One level is concerned with the social, economic, political and cultural factors that give the technological development orientation and content. Another level concerns how different kinds of technology are developed and acquire their characteristics and how this takes place in relation to the users of the technology, and which choices and what room for action individuals actually have when new technology is spread in society.

Social scientists have seldom dealt with the latter perspective i.e. the technology's social micro-world, which happens when individuals of flesh and blood meet new technology and put new appliances or machines into use and incorporate them into their everyday life. Nowadays there is certainly considerable empirical research on the effects of the introduction and spread of technological innovations in concrete social environments. However, many of these are concerned with changes in working life and in the production of goods and services. Fewer are concerned with new technology in relation to the activities of households, family life or the individual's everyday life. The few examples of such studies that do exist start out, as a rule, from the distribution of the new technology and contemplate what occurs in direct connection with this.[8]

New technology is the observation platform used for increasing knowledge about how new technology should be designed. I wish to claim that a change of viewpoint is necessary. The course of events must also be regarded with a starting point from the individual and the social multiplicity that forms the entirety for those individuals who make use of (or do not use) the different innovations. It is this entirety that should form the framework for understanding the importance of the new technology, and getting guidance as to how the new technology should be designed. Thus, in traditional studies of users, the new technology and its possibilities as seen by developers, are in focus. In reverse studies the users' whole field of appliances and machines i.e. their technological landscape, is in focus, and the new technology's possibilities are seen in relation to this entirety. It is, therefore, not sufficient to follow the new technology's roads into the living room from production to consumption, or from development to usage. New technology must also be viewed from the entirety of everyday life to the specific events involved in making use of new appliances and systems: from the needs the user has, to the technical developer's attempts to anticipate these.[9]

From the reverse perspective it is easier to see that new technology is always exposed to double competition. Firstly, an innovation must manage to assert itself in relation to other new products. These can be alternative solutions to the same or similar problems, or other products that compete for the customers'/users' time, attention or money. Secondly, an innovation must meet competition from the existing material structure that the users live in. A space must be created for the innovation at the cost of something established being used to a lesser degree, taking up less space or disappearing altogether. This process is hardly paid any attention in research on the spread of innovations. The Swedish social geographer Torsten Hägerstrand has likened the course of events to a carpet being rolled out in front of us at the same time as it is rolled up behind us. Objects become obsolete and perhaps unusable because the infrastructure that they require disappears. During the 'rolling up', knowledge that is linked to the different objects disappears too.[10] Each one of us who visits an auction of the estate of a deceased person can, in the flow of objects the auctioneer puts under the hammer, observe the movements that our materialistic everyday culture undergoes. A weird mixture of objects goes under the hammer. Some can still be used and are regarded as more or less new. Others can certainly be used but do not reach up to the demands of normal standards. Certain objects have been given a new lease of life and are loaded with new values such as being beautiful or typical of a period. Others have been transformed from utility goods into ornaments and can command high prices. At the end of the auction the auctioneer usually has a, surprisingly small, odd collection of objects that nobody has found to have any value.[11]

Our by degrees old-fashioned materialistic surroundings are winnowed out from our daily life in many ways. The auction illustrates a process that contains many steps before a category or a generation of objects has become rolled up at the rear end of Hägerstrand's carpet. The existing objects put up fierce resistance to the new ones. To refer back to the metaphor of the technological landscape; the spreading of new technology thus means that the landscape is changed not only by the innovation's placement but also by other parts of the landscape changing shape or disappearing. Appliances, machines, tools and systems are transformed into artefacts that have lost their previous functional meaning.

The winnowing out of the artefacts has an elusive but distinct connection with our ageing process. In certain stages of life we acquire new artefacts, and in others we get rid of obsolete or worn out ones. One hypothesis is that a generation takes with it a certain kind of technology and ages alongside it. This does not, however, apply to all kinds of technology, perhaps not even specific areas of technology, but is more of an attitude towards everyday technology and what it is good for and when it is motivated to trust technically based solutions to problems. To what extent we are prepared to change an attitude already established earlier in life when we grow old, is an open question. Research is needed on individuals' courses of life where individuals' and the artefacts' 'biographies' are woven together.

The Blind Spot in Everyday Studies

The potential in the reverse perspective is great, but at the same time the difficulties in answering the questions of needs and effects that technology developers pose, are obvious. Herein lies a call to social scientists to concretize in a better way within their research, the everyday importance of technology, but also to us all as members of society to place demands on technology and its developers.[12] Social scientists do not, however, have much to say about everyday technology.

It is seldom the case that everyday *materiality* is included in studies of how individuals live and experience their lives. The technological landscape is taken for granted.[13] This blindness is obvious too in research on old people's everyday life. Research on the ageing process has developed extensively during the last 10-15 years. Previously a medical perspective, in which ill-health and illness dominated was emphasized. A result of this was that 'misery pictures' of old people's existence were strengthened, and society's problems in arranging care and welfare ended up being the focus of interest.[14] Being old was equated with being ill. By research showing how old people actually do live, other aspects and conditions have been given attention. Research on old people and ageing today is concerned with the whole spectrum of conditions that are important to the lives and life quality of older people, but with one exception: old people's technological landscape is seldom, or never, put in problematic focus.[15]

A swift survey of the literature is sufficient to be able to confirm that the material dimensions of existence are seldom visible in gerontological research. One exception is possibly an interest in housing's, or rather accommodation's, importance for old people's quality of life. The studies most often deal with how apartments and other types of special accommodation for older people should be designed in order for them to meet with old people's need for security, care and social relations. There is, however, a growing interest in how ordinary housing should be designed in order to function for old people who are in need of support and help and yet who are able to retain their independence.[16]

There are of course also examples of more specialized studies on technical products in relation to the elderly and older people's needs. One orientation can be given the designation *assistive technology*. This deals with the development of technical aids, which can alleviate daily life for those who find it difficult to use standardized equipment and appliances. Mainly this is a question of different types of disability aids. Criticism has been directed against some of the technological developments for old people, because they have emanated from needs that have been stated by relatives and carers, rather than the older people themselves. The products that have been developed have had a stigmatizing effect i.e. have accentuated that it is not normal to grow old.

A broader perspective on technology for the elderly has developed within a network of *gerontechnology*.[17] The term was coined as a collective concept for research and development that aims at achieving improvements for the elderly by means of technology.[18] Within the network for gerontechnology there are distinct ambitions to develop a framework of analysis in order to better understand technological development and technology's possibilities to make life easier.[19] Gerontechnology is defined by Harrington and Harrington as research, development and design within engineering sciences, based on knowledge of the ageing process. The aim is to achieve good health, full social participation and an independent life-style even during the later part of life. What can be achieved by technological solutions? Five different kinds of effects are mentioned in particular: technology can prevent age-related illnesses and thereby connected losses in physical and mental capacities; technology can compensate for declines in capacities that have already taken place; technology can facilitate different activities, technology can facilitate the care of the elderly and technology can improve research on the elderly.

The network for gerontechnology has, without doubt, advanced the position for research on, and the development of, new technology that can improve everyday life for the elderly and old people. Until present times, technological development has principally been steered by acute problems and circumstances. 'Gerontechnologists' wish to achieve a systematic stocktaking of how different technological fields can contribute with products that facilitate living, and increase the quality of life. There is of course, no reason to criticize these ambitions. But the basic problem concerning a lack of knowledge about the connection between technological research and the users' needs and everyday life, remains. In line with moving from technological development for concrete well-defined needs (assistive technology) to technological development for more complex needs, the demands on an understanding of how technology actually is used, increase. The discrepancy between the ambitions to solve problems with the aid of new technology, and knowledge as to how the technology can, and should, be used to strengthen the quality of life in step with our ageing, is an obvious one.

Old People in a New Technological Landscape

Technological development on a broad basis, directly oriented towards the elderly's special needs is naturally of importance. Sometimes, however, hopes of success are built upon an unrealistic view of how technological research is transformed into tangible results. It is hardly as simple as this. If we only knew the technological needs of old people then technology researchers, who were willing to satisfy each and every one of them, would be on hand. Technological research is at all times interested in certain issues and is thus engaged in certain defined areas and possibilities for application. There is a research frontline, and it is decided what is of interest and feasible to execute in relation to it. In a similar manner, the technological development of companies is linked to specific areas, applications and market segments. To a large extent it is within the dynamic fields of R&D that the frameworks for future everyday technology are formulated. If we, as researchers of the elderly, want to influence the most powerful technological development then we must concentrate on areas that are engaged in technological research. One of the hot spots is easy to identify: the development and implementation of information and communication technology (ICT) in old and new technological systems. I shall therefore, in the rest of this chapter, deal with this field in relation to old people's everyday lives.

The development of ICT systems intended for use in different everyday situations is extensive, but difficult to comprehend. The entirety can be summarized by the concepts: networking society, and 'intelligent', or 'smart', homes.[20] The network society stands for the way in which institutions and units in society are bound together in new ways. 'Intelligent houses' and 'smart homes' stand for the individual places around which we arrange our life, and which obtain a changed functionality. The vision is that appliances and systems that are in the home will be able to gain new strength and be linked to each other, and to the surroundings, through versatile communication and control functions. The 'intelligent home' thus implies that household appliances, computers, networks and mobile phones amalgamate.[21]

At a more general level, the core factor is that the boundaries of the home in relation to its surroundings change. The communication area between the home, the neighbourhood, the local community, and the national and the global world expands. Each home can be part of a large number of networks, and reach an almost limitless number of others. The 'intelligent home' gives us a new precision in gaining access to activities and phenomena that are located outside the home.

It gives us increased scope, helps us to plan our time, and provides an increased and more accessible layer of information and knowledge. But what applies in one direction also applies in the opposite one. The 'intelligent home' supports our environment's ability to orient itself in our home and thereby increase the range of others in our private sphere. The first highway, from the home and to the outside world, mainly changes activities already in existence.[22] The other highway, from society and into the home, entails great possibilities, but also risks; the home can become an arena for a number of activities which up to now have been both physically and organisationally incorporated in different social institutions.

When the homes of the future are described, much is cloaked in darkness. The impression is one of a number of actors with great capacity to develop applications, searching for an area of use from what they wish to produce. This vagueness is especially applicable to what will happen to household technology. One example mentioned is a fridge that can keep a check on the stores and give support for shopping lists and food recipes. The possibilities to move new forms of entertainment, education and experiences into the home are described with great enthusiasm. In spite of the vagueness, it is possible to mention some new features in the development of a new generation of everyday technology:

- The home is linked up to a network that is comprised of other homes, schools, day care centres and workplaces – new forms for exchanges and insights can develop.
- New forms for participation in communal decision-making are developed via interactive media.
- Household, and other, appliances already in the home are developed and incorporated in networks that make new functions, communication and controls possible.
- New appliances with functions hitherto meaningless in the home environment are developed and brought into the home. An example is appliances for one's own care and welfare, and also for that given by others.
- The home becomes an arena for individually chosen entertainment by means of interactive media.
- The home can become a base for the production and distribution of services.

Linked with each and every one of these lines of development are hopes that new technology will be able to improve old people's lives. Old people themselves, or old people with the support of others, should be able to maintain their everyday lives even when their physical, and sometimes even mental, powers decline. Of course, the leading actors are not driven by the ambition to create new technology for old people, but in the wider debate on the ageing society the new ICT is regarded as a key tool to save society and individuals from the consequences of the ageing explosion.[23]

It is possible to identify a number of different categories of expectations that concern old people in particular:

- Social networks can be set up and maintained with the new communication systems in spite of increasing physical distances between old people and their children, other relatives and friends. An old person with a need for activity and an interest in keeping in contact with others can, with the help of the intelligent home, maintain long-standing relationships and develop new social ones.

- Entertainment and recreation can be stimulated, and participation in social life can be strengthened by new media.
- Virtual experiences can replace real experiences, and virtual movement in time and space can replace physical moves. The effects of the body's ageing process can be alleviated.[24]
- The pre-requisites for carrying out household chores (cooking, personal hygiene, cleaning, washing, walks, telephone calls etc.) can be strengthened by new knowledge and ordering systems.
- Care and welfare can be decentralized to the individual homes and the need for help from others can decrease through new knowledge and communication systems.
- Control over everything functioning properly in old people's accommodation, and the old people themselves, can be improved through new surveillance systems.
- Old people themselves can obtain appliances that prevent them getting into difficulties such as falling or getting lost.

Intelligent Homes for Old People

Many old people worry about their inability to manage the practical chores necessary to sustain their homes. 'Intelligent homes' can mean that difficulties increase because the home contains more complex technological systems, but can also facilitate the running and maintenance of the home. That the home can be maintained, even when it becomes intelligent, as the place where one has control over one's existence is of absolute central importance.[25]

A decisive question is how older people control their homes and how the local environment is influenced. If this control is to be retained, then the 'intelligent homes' must contain and make possible many degrees of freedom and space for individual life-styles or, expressed differently, that which is 'intelligent' and 'smart' must increase both the individual's room for action[26] and ability to act.

I wish to draw the following conclusions from the discussion that I have conducted so far on the 'intelligent' home in relation to old people. A large number of actors develop a new generation of appliances, machines and systems, that together can change the fundamental structures in the technological landscape. It will take much longer than these leading actors expect, but homes will change. A number of activities both in homes and in society will eventually be adjusted for the majority of people living in 'intelligent homes'. Applications will develop and spread, not as a result of an inherent logic in the technology, but as a result of the different actors' actions. As different closures take place, certain solutions will be executed and others will not be. Gradually as the 'intelligent home' gains more solid contours then its compelling content, the momentum of technology to use the term coined by Thomas Hughes, will assert itself. Everyday life will become difficult to handle for those who find themselves left by the wayside. Will old people be the winners or the losers?

One first answer depends on whether one believes that the 'intelligent home' presents aspects from which old people in particular gain a special benefit, or with which older people have special difficulties. Here we touch upon a widespread complexity of questions that demand both a deeper analysis and empirical studies. An obvious risk is present of course; the 'smart homes' are developed by young persons, engineers, behavioural scientists and architects, with little understanding of the life of the elderly.

A second answer worth bearing in mind is that the growth of the 'intelligent home' is a process that takes time. It will become part of everyday life and be incorporated in the technological landscape in parallel with life going on as usual. Each generation will stamp its mark on how the intelligent home is used. An interesting research question is how middle-aged generations prepare the way for their future lives as old people, amongst other things through the design of their homes and their everyday technology.

A third answer can be sought by questioning to which specific generation and age group old people belong. What does the fact that a person in the final stage of life, who has lived a long time and has a relatively short life span left, mean for his or her relationship with the objects and other material structures present in his or her surroundings? Can older everyday technology be replaced by new without an old person's habits, values and identity undergoing a change? These are questions that are well worth investigating empirically, but for the answers to be qualified, a theoretical development is needed which combines perspectives from research on ageing with research on the use of technology in everyday life.[27]

I will, in the following section, outline the contours of such a theory.

Old People in the Technological Landscape's Outer Zones?

That research on how we use everyday technology is conspicuously undeveloped is surprising, not least considering how prominent consumption and materialistic conditions are in modern society. However, several interesting studies exist regarding the question of how individuals and households are beginning to use new media and communication technology.[28] A summarizing concept that indicates the character of the process that takes place when new appliances are incorporated into everyday life and made into something that can be used, is that they are 'domesticated'. Appliances are given a place in the household's time and space and become part of its social and cultural capital. The process is not merely, or even mainly, internal, but is part of the household's relationship with its surroundings. By the 'domestication' of a new appliance, the members of the household change their contact areas with other people, and express values and meanings that are important for their relationships with relatives, friends and the neighbourhood. Thus the acquisition of new technology contributes to the creation of and recreation of the home, the household, the family and relationships with others.[29] The degree of openness is adapted to the new technology's character; the household will be eager to show off some technology and to hide other kinds. For many old people the introduction of technology that is specifically intended for old people has a stigmatizing effect, which is typical for 'domestication'.[30]

It is reasonable to suppose that 'domestication' has different meanings for older people and for younger ones, and that a new technology can therefore have completely different connotations and meanings for these groups. The meaning that different age groups assign to the use of computers and the Internet would be, for example, well worth investigating. In a German study, which deals with projects that aim at the elderly using the Internet to educate themselves, amongst other things, the old people's duality stands out. Older people have notions such as: 'the Internet is only for young people'; 'everything is in English'; 'the costs are beyond control'; 'one becomes isolated'; 'one wastes time'; 'one does not wish to show one's ignorance about computers'; 'one's integrity is threatened'. Yet the study does report a growing number of old people who have stepped over the threshold and use home computers and the Internet and thereby have come to belong to new groups and networks.[31]

That different groups ascribe different meanings to the Internet is part of its 'domestication'. The Internet becomes 'alive' through being used and given meanings, by individuals who have different interests and experiences. The broader technological landscape can be regarded from this perspective too. The landscape changes over time – appliances, machines and systems are brought into the landscape, used, gain social and cultural attributes, change, are transformed, become marginalized and disappear. Thus the technological landscape has a distinct character, which is typical of the period. It is renewed at the same time as it ages. Each generation has a unique relation to the technological landscape because the individual's life course runs parallel to the changes in technology. How we use the technological landscape is part of our ageing process. Here we can anticipate a key question in order to understand old people's need of, and interest in technology. During their lifetime they have experienced how everyday technology has changed. They have used, and still use, different generations of appliances and machines. Older people's technological landscape is therefore more 'long drawn out' than younger people's in the sense that older people's landscape contains many parts with a function and character from an earlier period, parts which in return are well-known and bound to memories and experiences.

How and when we make use of new technology and how and when we retain older technology, has an elusive but distinct connection with our ageing. In certain stages of life we procure new technology, and in others we get rid of obsolete or worn out technology. One hypothesis is that such technology, and use of technology that has an impact on everyday life during an age group's younger years or period of early adulthood, in later life is regarded as being important and natural to use. To make use of new technology and be in command of it, for example, contributes to the distancing from parents who did not have access to that specific technology when they were at a corresponding stage in life.[32] The new technology is incorporated into the age group's collective identity and memory, and is part of tales of how things used to be.[33] Experiences contribute to çharacterizing a generation. One can speak of 'the radio generation', 'the car generation', 'the TV generation'. New technology can define both a period of time, social conditions and a generation ('defining technology'). For old people today the telephone is such a 'defining technology'. They have used the telephone to communicate during the whole of their adult lives. The telephone has achieved a reinforced form of importance in old age, and become of almost vital importance in maintaining their social life. In an English study of elderly people's family and neighbourhood contacts (Phillipson et al., 2001) carried out at the beginning of the 1990s in four cities, the importance of the telephone for maintaining and widening old people's contacts with others stands out as being completely decisive. That old people of the 1990s could rely on the telephone is therefore one of the most significant differences in relation to how old people lived in the England of the 1950s. The researchers' conclusion was that old people's daily telephone calls brought about social closeness and integration in the community, and gained a new meaning since the 1950s. Physical proximity was completely decisive for participation and security.[34]

My point is not to plead the case for the importance of the telephone to old people in particular. That is obvious to everyone. The telephone as an example does, however, show that a certain technology definitely can have different meanings to different age groups, but at the same time, in other respects can contribute to integrating these age groups. The telephone is 'generation comprehensive'; it includes and mixes children and old people, grandmothers, daughters, grandchildren and sons. The modern telephone the mobile phone, does not have this general character if one regards how it is used. Very few old people today use a mobile phone and probably will not use one as an appliance one carries around wherever one is. They do, however, derive an advantage from the mobile phone system's existence, by their being able to reach other people in principal whenever and wherever they want to.[35] For the next generation of old people the mobile phone will be an obvious tool for communication, and contribute to increasing their possibilities of being outside the home.

The different generations of telephone systems (an appliance fixed in the home for old people and one in the hand for young people), illustrate how the technological landscape has different layers for the old and the young. The two aspects that I have touched upon above – each generation's specific relationship to ongoing changes in everyday technology, and differences in attitudes towards everyday technology during different stages of life – are decisive for understanding the prerequisites for the spread of new technology, and therefore also, for technological development. If we depart from the standpoint that technological development leads to the technological landscape's older parts losing their functionality both absolutely and in comparison with newer parts, then continuous change means that old people are left by the wayside more and more. An old person moving around in parts of the technological landscape that younger people have left, or seldom visit, can strengthen the identity of being old. Such a division corresponds well with theories that state that old people are separated from society with increasing age. According to the so-called disengagement theory, it is a double-barrelled process, which means that both the individual and society prepare for a retreat. The old person who chooses, or is forced to choose because of a sparser network, to retreat from active social life and society, cuts him/herself off from opportunities to participate in social life in many ways.[36] One way of expressing this detachment could be that the technological landscape changes, and that the ageing individual consciously chooses to abstain from innovations at the same time as little consideration is taken to old people's needs when new technology is being developed.

One side of this detachment is that old people are, or are regarded as being, more and more obliged to spend their lives in their own homes. Old people retire, or are forced to stay at home because of a loss of mobility and sparser contact networks. The home is perceived by their relatives, authorities and politicians as the old person's natural habitat .

The fixation on the home as decisive for quality of life is not unproblematic. The risk exists that romanticized pictures of home life hide many old people's loneliness and vulnerability. The scientific basis for faith in the importance of home for the welfare of old people is also relatively weak, amongst other things because it has been taken for granted that being housebound increases with increasing age and loss of mobility.[37] Consequently, this leads to a limited field of vision, so that only old people who share the majority's life-style are visible. Thus, there is reason to expand the concept of the home, and place the focus on how old people create their own security through the construction and defence of the place they regard as their home. Everyday technology therefore must be regarded as forming a part of a physical place (locale), in a social place (location) that provides room for socializing and is the starting point for participation in the neighbourhood (local community) and as a mental phenomenon that is designated subjective meaning and contributes to identity with meaning.

Marbach (1993) has, in a study of older Germans' social networks found that the degree to which degree old people are bound to their homes, depends on which lifestyle habits they have developed when they were young. Even if advanced age means increasingly being housebound, many people who have developed a social faith in others during their lives, do maintain an active life outside the home. Marbach puts forward the hypothesis that an important difference is if one has the ability to establish contacts with younger people, when old people's peer networks become sparser.[38]

Technology in Harmony with Old People's Everyday Life

Up to now in this chapter I have, from some of many possible angles of approach, discussed the relationship between new technology and that already in existence, and between technology developers and users. If nothing else, this chapter shows that the question of how technological and material structure influences everyday life is extremely complex, and, that there are no simple couplings between the development of a new technology, ready-to-use products, the actual usage and the multitude of events and thoughts that everyday life entails for each and every one of us.

Does this mean that it would be impossible to achieve a better link between technological development and users' needs and interests? Are the processes so complicated that it is just as well to let them run their course? Few people would advocate such resignation. In the same way as Thomas Hughes, I have argued for technological systems to be understood as charged with energy that makes them develop in certain ways but not in others. The momentum of systems is derived from persons and organisations who with different interests are tied to systems, inventors, engineers, marketers, politicians, manufacturing companies, R&D laboratories, research institutions, financiers, authorities, standardizing institutions and interest groups.[39]

From this viewpoint, the question of how technological development, better than at present, can be brought to satisfy old people's needs and interests becomes a question of how the systems' actors can be influenced, and how new knowledge can be introduced into their activities. I will plead the case for technological development having to be supported by and based on four qualitatively different levels, which represent different perspectives on the user.[40]

- The first, and most obvious, is that design and development of new technology must be based on knowledge of the users' needs, interests and knowledge.
- The second, and more difficult, is that technological development must be based upon knowledge of social and cultural conditions that are of importance to the entirety of the users' everyday life.
- The third, somewhat more difficult, is that innovations are placed in relation to the entirety of the materialistic conditions in which old people live, i.e. the technological landscape of old people.
- The fourth, and most difficult, is that technological development must be confronted by perspectives that question whether it is needed at all.

At the *first level*, a fundamental demand is that distinct user perspectives are constructed early on in technological development, and then followed during the innovation and distributive chain of events. The user perspective at this level can support itself on a long tradition that has been especially strong in the development of household appliances and the designing and decorating of housing.[41] In established lines of business, studies on needs and testing are self-evident. Lately, the insight to integrate user perspectives in the development of technology-based products has increased among most manufacturers. Nowadays there are also a number of engineering courses that aim at giving a broader competence, with the ambition of integrating technological, psychological/cognitive, design and linguistic knowledge.

Especially in the case of older people, however, the difficulties are obvious and demand the development of methods which facilitate old people being included in the specifications of needs and tests.[42] Of strategic importance is such technological research and development that can lead to standardization or platforms that are general ones, and can be used in many different applications.[43] One important aspect is that old people themselves are allowed to have a voice and are not hidden behind their 'ombudsmen' in the care sector, research or politics. At the first level the given perspective is to follow and guide new technology 'into everyday life', what I previously have described as 'to see what happens through what is new'. As a rule those who are involved at this level of R&D share this perspective regardless of their professional identities.

At the *second* level, technology development for old people may meet with difficulties because ignorance about old people's conditions is great and a number of stereotypes and myths flourish.[44] At present there is a rather large amount of comprehensive empirical and theoretical research concerned with old people's lives, how the elderly create meaning and identity in their existence, as well as social pictures and conceptions of the elderly and ageing which can be used to improve the quality of technological development. In many cases this knowledge is necessary in order for new technology not to cause more damage than good when seen from the perspective of old people.

It is unrealistic to believe that it would be possible to develop this knowledge within the technology developing organizations. Demands are therefore placed on researchers of the elderly to account for knowledge of older people's lives in such a way that a discussion can be conducted, which includes technology developers, technology researchers, decision-makers, and not least, old people themselves. Thus the goal is to achieve meeting places for discussion as to what is possible and important. A central task is to stimulate and 'institutionalize' a dialogue between technology developers and researchers of the elderly. Since the two categories partly belong to different knowledge cultures some 'translation work' is necessary. A dialogue can only take place if the co-operation is long-term and useful to both parties. The two groups do, however, tend to view the problems from different perspectives. Those who are primarily interested in technology development view what is new and likely to become important as the given starting point, while researchers of the elderly find their frame of reference lies in the opposite direction, i.e. they evaluate what is new in relation to that which already exists.

The *third level* considers that everyday life takes place within a material structure that I have here called the technological landscape. From this perspective the need for and development of new technology, are regarded in relation to everyday life and the technological landscape's entirety and how changes in the technological landscape influence old people's lives. I have pointed out that the interest in studies on the importance of technology for the activities of everyday life and social relations hitherto has been small, and basic sociological research is needed.

At this level, the problem of dialogue between different researchers probably increases. They are interested in different problems and see solutions from different viewpoints. The technology developers have a technology, and seek its use. Researchers on everyday life defend themselves against a role which entails their legitimizing a certain technological solution. Research that deals with the 'domestication' of new technology can be a bridge between these perspectives, as it can provide knowledge that is of interest from both points of view.

The *fourth level* starts out from the perspective of an outsider. The entirety in old people's existence (including what technology can and cannot achieve), must be examined by researchers and others who are neither associated with, nor have links to, the actors who develop, support and distribute new technology. The questioning of the institutionalized power relationships is of course a fundamental element in social and humanistic research, and this perspective's importance for understanding old people's lives is obvious. I emphasize this here because of the reason that research on older people for a long time has had, and to a great extent still has, a pronounced normative aim. The common point of departure is to improve conditions for old people or for society and to solve problems. The space available for alternative solutions, other problem formulations or perspectives is limited. Research that does not take the 'system's' problems and solutions for granted is necessary both to avoid the problem scenario being one-sidedly endorsed, and to give inspiration and ideas.

Research *on* technology, and not *in* or *for* new technology, can seldom contribute concrete answers to questions that technology developers and the professional actors in the field of ageing pose. Often this research can also be experienced as irrelevant or counter-productive. In spite of this it can have great importance when applied.[45] Those who make decisions on new technology and who carry out development need to be inspired, guided, tempted (and sometimes deterred), and learn from what users ask for and value. The political debate needs the influx of knowledge on old people's living conditions in relation to technological development, and the general public needs better possibilities to place demands on and influence technological development.

At the beginning of this chapter I called attention to the complexity in the growth of large technological systems. These systems must be developed both as infrastructures and as concrete applications for different users. The change that is now taking place in everyday technology, by means of information and communication technology, has this character. How the technological landscape will change is to a great extent still an open issue. Closures of different kinds take place, i.e. certain alternatives are executed and others are rendered impossible. These closures are of decisive importance for everyone, but of special importance to those who find it difficult to change their everyday life and who put their trust in well-known everyday technology. This is the case for many old people. Older people themselves and researchers of the elderly must, if not for any other reason but this, interest themselves in how the everyday technology of the future is to be designed.

This attitude involves not affirming or denying that new technology is a solution to the specific problems that old people meet as a result of their being old. It becomes a question of the possibilities and limitations of different technologies in the social and cultural context that they are to be incorporated in. And it also means that old people's lives must be regarded as being special in many ways and that each generation is unique in relation both to previous and forthcoming generations of old people.

Long Life with Technology

I began this chapter by asking if we should regard technology as a tool for keeping ourselves young, despite the years passing by and our growing old. Should technology lengthen the normal life span? My different threads of reasoning lead to several answers. New technology can both lengthen life and shorten it. New technology can both make the old and the young more similar and more dissimilar. I have with reasonable credibility shown that whatever form of everyday technology one allows into one's life, has to do with who one is and who one wants to be as an individual, and is also linked to the way in which the age group to which one belongs perceives itself and is perceived by other age groups. The category of 'older people' consists of several generations ordered according to increasing age. These different generations can vary greatly amongst themselves in their attitude towards technology in general, or towards a specific appliance or technological system, as a result of their previous experiences and the fact that each generation finds itself in a fixed chronological stage of the life course. Old people have a unique position. They are age pioneers for new everyday technology. They are the first generation (and only one) that at an advanced age comes into contact with exactly that technology when it is unproven and at the start of its distribution. They are at the same time the last defenders of the older parts of the technological landscape.

Notes

1 The concepts of third and fourth ages are impaired by their containing normative statements on how the elderly and old people should live. The conception of a fourth age mainly departs from a biological view on ageing.
2 The Fifth Framework Programme 1998-2002, Key Action 6: The Ageing Population and Disabilities. (Work Programme, 2000). However, in the preliminary documents concerning the Sixth Framework Programme (2002-2006) there are no direct references to ageing and the specific needs of elderly users of technology. (Priority Thematic Areas of Research, Proposal for Council Decision, March 2002), EU Cordis.
3 A Swedish example is the parliamentary committee Senior Citizen 2005 (Äldre, 2005) which has as its mandate to draw up a national policy, which is durable when a growing percentage of the population is old. In a Green Paper the committee emphasizes the importance of technology for the elderly's security and independence. The committee attaches, amongst other things, great hopes to the possibility of achieving new information technology that can correspond with the elderly's special needs. The

committee has, however, not suggested any special measures to increase knowledge of old people's use of technology and needs for it. Source: 'Riv ålderstrappan!' Livslopp i förändring (SOU, 2002:29), www.senior2005.gov.se.

4 Bijker, Huges and Pinch, 1987; MacKeinzie and Wajman, 1985; Hektor, 2001.

5 Östlund, 1995, page 230 and Östlund, 1999, page 27.

6 Marcellini et al., 2000. The study deals with the use of ticket machines, automatic teller machines and telephone cards. It was carried out in Mannheim, Chemnitz, Ancona and Jyväskylä.

7 Amongst others: MacKeinzie and Wajman, 1985; Bijker, Hughes and Pinch, 1987; Hektor, 2001.

8 Swedish examples are Östlund, 1995; Sturesson, 2000; Hektor, 2001.

9 An early Swedish appeal for the necessity of studies on technology, individuals and society containing this perspective is found in Ingelstam and Schiller, 1981.

10 An outline of Torsten Hägerstrand's time-geographical concept in relation to individuals' actions and projects is found in Åquist 1992. An almost opposite way of looking at how new technology relates to our knowledge is put forward by the Swedish social scientist Roger Säljö. He stresses that a central feature in the development of technology is that new appliances and systems contain a larger layer of knowledge than the appliances and systems they replace; know-how and capacities that earlier were necessary to perform a certain activity are 'built in' and not needed later on. Thus, while Hägerstrand emphasizes modern technology's discontinuity in relation to the technology of older times, Säljö stresses its continuity, new artefacts are built upon and include earlier artefacts. Säljö, 2000.

11 It seems to me as if this collection of leftovers has increased through the amount of electronic appliances that rapidly become completely unusable. Yet there is a market for older electronic appliances, for example radios and gramophones.

12 An early appeal on Swedish soil to regard technology from the 'bottom-up', i.e. to start out from its usage is found in Ingelstam and Hasselrot, 1983.

13 My point is that individual and family lives and the activities of groups are not seen in relation to their interaction with the materialistic structure and that analytical accounts are lacking. One exception is the Danish social scientist Tarja Cronberg (1986). She presents a model that emphasizes the ability of individuals to take action in relation to the technology that the individual can use (room for action). There is a tradition in philosophy with an interest in the materiality of existence with its roots with Husserl and Heidegger. The latter's discussion on objects' being (in German Zeug) is of direct interest in a perspective that stresses that everyday technology consists of systems of tools and appliances. Heidegger is interested in the built-in usable features of the objects. The everyday, and therefore hidden, quality becomes visible when an object is put into use. Each tool or utility object is always functionally connected to other objects. We see this quality most obviously when an object fails to work or disappears from use. See Cornell, 1993. The social science that most distinctly deals with everyday and material conditions is ethnology. A Swedish example is Kjellman, 1993.

14 Jönson, 2001, pages 26-30; Gubrium and Holstein, 2000, pages 2-11.

15 In Gubrium and Holstein, 2000, which is a modern reader on classic and contemporary research on the elderly's everyday life, the technology perspective is missing. In none of the book's 30 essays is the question of everyday technology's importance dealt with. In Featherstone and Wernick, 1995 there is an interesting essay with a technological visionary content: Featherstone, Mike: Post-bodies, Ageing and Virtual Reality. See also Östlund, 1995.

16 Heywood, Oldman and Means, 2002, pages 30-39.
17 Some of these studies have been published in connection with two international conferences, the first in Eindhoven in 1991 and the second in Helsinki in 1996. Both conferences were connected with a network supported by the EU within COST 5.
18 The concept was introduced at the end of the 1980s by Jan Graafmans at Eindhoven University of Technology. Graafmans, Taipala and Charness, 1998.
19 Graafmans, Taipala and Charness, 2000; Harrington and Harrington, 2000, pages 1-17.
20 Castells, 1996. Castells asserts that one of the coming network society's characteristic features is that chronological ageing will decrease in meaning for what way of living and which living conditions individuals and groups have.
21 Hagberg, 2001.
22 For example, activities that are based on the use of radio, telephone, TV, the Internet etc.
23 Amongst others: Ageing, Care and Welfare for the Elderly and How IT Can Improve Quality of Life. A report from a Swedish/Japanese seminar in Stockholm 2001, arranged by the The Knowledge Foundation, The Vardal Foundation, and Swedish Council for Working Life and Social Research.
24 Featherstone, 1995.
25 Kontos, 2000.
26 In the room for action is also included not doing anything.
27 Östlund, 1995.
28 Silverstone and Hirsch, 1992; Lie and Sörensen, 1996.
29 Silverstone, Hirsch and Morley 1992.
30 Marcellini et al., 2000; Mollenkopf et al., 2000b.
31 Stadelhofer, 2000; Czaja and Lee, in Charness, Parks and Sabel, 2001, present a survey over research on the elderly's use of the Internet and discuss how an increase in user-friendliness can be achieved.
32 Corsten (1999) accounts for a theory-based argument for events during growing up being crucial for how an age group will regard itself, and be regarded by others, as a generation or not. He does not, however, explicitly include the spreading of new everyday technology as being such a decisive event. My hypothesis is that the situation where one forms one's own household indicates the major orientation of the technological landscape that one has during one's later life.
33 Eyrman and Turner, 1998, make use of Bourdieu's concept habitus to account for how common experiences form the members of a generation's actions and attitudes and how certain conditions can create solidarity between different groupings that belong to the same age group. New technology can be such a common experience, but a generation's identity can also be expressed by how it uses technology (for example the post-wartime consumer generation). Technology can also be a means to remember and depict generation identities.
34 Phillipson, Berhard, Phillips and Ogg, 2001, pages 256-259; Östlund, 1995, pages 151-168.
35 Less than five per cent of those who are 75 or older have access to a mobile phone (Germany). Mollenkopf, H. et al., 2000a, page 162.
36 Cumming, 1963/2000, conducts an extensive discussion on the usefulness of the disengagement theory, which is partly commented upon in Gubrium and Holstein. The theory is obviously functionalistic in its construction; the separation is a result of on-going adjustments to future illness and death. The parallels to Karl Mannheim's (1952) classical theory on the inevitability of the generation change as part of each society's renewal are obvious.

37 Heywood et al., 2002, pages 30-32.
38 Marbach, 2001. Marbach makes a connection to a developmental psychology attachment theory but one can also, by means of Bordieu's concept, see the differences between individuals that is connected with differences in what social capital one owns.
39 Hughes, 1987, pages 76-78.
40 Östlund, 2000.
41 Hagberg, 1986.
42 Östlund, 2000. Spiltze and Moulton, 2001.
43 One example of obvious importance to the elderly is different research programmes that aim at developing platforms that mean that computers can 'speak' in mother tongues such as Swedish.
44 Hazan, 1994; Sawchuk, 1995, page 173.
45 Östlund, 2000, page 47.

References

Ageing, Care and Welfare for the Elderly and How IT Can Improve Quality of Life (2001), Report from a Swedish/Japanese Seminar, Stockholm 2001, Arranged by the The Knowledge Foundation, The Vardal Foundation, and Swedish Council for Working Life and Social Research.

Åquist, A-C. (1992), *Tidsgeografi i samspel med samhällsteori*, Notes from Lund University's Geographical Departments, Dissertation 115, Lund University Press, Lund.

Bijker, W., Hughes, T. and Pinch, T. (eds.)(1987), *The Social Construction of Technological Systems*, The MIT Press, London.

Castells, M. (1996), *The Information Age. Economy, Society, and Culture*, Vol. 1 The Rise of the Network Society, Blackwell, Oxford.

Charness, N., Parks, D.C. and Sabel, B.A. (eds.) (2001), *Communication, Technology and Aging. Opportunities and Challenges for the Future*, Springer Publishing Company, New York.

Cornell, P. (1993), *Saker. Om tingens osynlighet*, Gidlunds, Hedemora.

Corsten, M. (1999), 'The Time of Generations', *Time and Society*, Vol. 8 (2), pp. 249-72.

Cronberg, T. (1986), *Teorier om teknologi och hverdagsliv*, Nyt fra Samfundsvidenskaberne, Copenhagen.

Cumming, E. (1963/2000), 'Further Thoughts on the Theory of Disengagement', in J.F. Gubrium and J.A. Holstein (eds.), *Ageing and Everyday Life*, Blackwell, Oxford.

Czaja, S.J. and Lee, C.C. (in press), 'The Internet and Older Adults: Design Challenges and Opportunities', in N. Charness, D.C. Park and B.A. Sabel (eds.), *Aging and communication: Opportunities and challenges of technology*, Springer Publishing Company, New York.

EU Cordis: ‹http://www.cordis.lu/fp5› and ‹http://fp6.cordis.lu/fp6›.

Eyreman, R. and Turner, B.S. (1998), 'Outline of a Theory of Generations', *European Journal of Sociology*, Vol. 1 (1), pp. 91-106.

Featherstone. M. and Wernick, A. (eds.) (1995), *Post-Bodies, Ageing and Virtual Reality: Images of Ageing, Cultural Representation of Later Life*, Routledge, London.

Graafmans, J., Taipala, V. and Charness, N. (1998), *Gerontechnology. A Sustainable Investment in the Future*, IOS Press, Amsterdam.

Gubrium, J.F. and Holstein, J.A. (eds.) (2000), *Ageing and Everyday Life*, Blackwell, Oxford.

Hagberg, J-E. (1986), *Tekniken i kvinnornas händer. Hushållsarbete och hushållsteknik under tjugo- och trettiotalen*, Linköping Studies in Art and Science no 7 (summary in English), Linköping University, Linköping.

Hagberg, J-E. (2001), 'Ett smart hem för en bättre vardag', in G. Blücher and G. Graninger, (eds.), *Från våra sinnen: en antologi om sambandet mellan den fysiska miljön, hälsan och sinnesintrycken*, Stiftelsen Vadstena forum för samhällsbyggnad, Linköping.

Hagberg, J-E. (2002), 'Teknikens vardagliga panorama' in L. Sturesson (ed.), *Spänningsfält: Tekniken – politiken – framtiden*, Carlsson, Stockholm.

Hagberg, J-E. and Johansson, B. (1990), *Vardagsteknikens dynamik. Forskningsfrågor om teknikutveckling, teknikspridning och sociala effekter*, Technology and Social Change, Working Paper; 70, Linköping University, Linköping.

Harrington, T.L. and Harrington, M.K. (2000), *Gerontechnology. Why and How*, Shaker, Maastricht.

Hazan, H. (2000), 'The Cultural Trap: The Language of Images', in J.F. Gubrium and J.A. Holstein (eds.), *Ageing and Everyday Life*, Blackwell, Oxford.

Hektor, A. (2001), *What's the Use? Internet and Information Behavior in Everyday Life*, Linköping Studies in Arts and Science, 240. Linköping University, Linköping.

Heywood, F., Oldman, C. and Means, R. (2002), *Housing and the Home in Later Life*, Open University Press, Buckingham.

Hughes, T. P. (1987), 'The Evolution of Large Technological Systems', in W. Bijker, T. Hughes and T. Pinch (eds.), *The Social Construction of Technological Systems*, The MIT Press, London.

Ingelstam, L. and Hasselrot, T. (eds.) (1983), *Skruven. En diskussionsbok om tekniken i vår verklighet*, LiberFörlag, Malmö.

Ingelstam, L. and Schiller, B. (1981), *Teknik och social förändring*, Liber, Lund.

Jönson, H. (2001), *Det moderna åldrandet. Pensionärsorganisationernas bilder av äldre 1941-1995*, Dissertations in Social Work, 2, Socialhögskolan, Lund.

Kjellman, G. (1993), *Varats oändliga tinglighet. En studie av föremål som kulturbärare*, Carlsson, Stockholm.

Kontos, Pia C. (2000), 'Resisting Institutionalisation: Constructing Old Age and Negotiating Home', in J.F. Gubrium and J.A. Holstein (eds.), *Ageing and Everyday Life*, Blackwell, Oxford.

Lie, M. and Sörensen, K. (1996), *Making Technology Our Own. Domesticating Technology into Everyday Life*, Scandinavian University Press, Oslo.

MacKeinzie, D. and Wajman, J. (1985/1999), *The Social Shaping of Technology*, Open University Press, Buckingham.

Mannheim, Karl (1952/1972), *Essays on the Sociology of Knowledge*, Routledge and Kegan Paul Ltd, London.

Marbach, J.H. (2001), 'Aktionsraum und soziales Netzwerk: Reichweite und Ressourcen der Lebensfürung im Alter' *Zeitschrift fur Gerontologie und Geriatrie*, Vol. 34, pp. 319-326.

Marcellini, F., Mollenkopf, H., Spazzafumo, L. and Rupilla, I. (2000), 'Acceptance and Use of Technological Solutions by the Elderly in the Outdoor Environment: Findings from a European Survey', *Zeitschrift für Gerontologie und Geriatrie*, Vol. 33, pp. 169-177.

Mollenkopf H., Meyer S., Wurm S. and Friesdorf W. (2000a), 'Technik im Haushaltz zur Unterstützung einer selbstbestimmten Lebensfürung im Alter. Das forchungsprojekt „sentha" und erste Ergebnisse des Sozialwissenschaftlichen Teilsprojekts', *Zeitschrift für Gerontologie und Geriatrie*, Vol. 33, pp. 155-168.

Mollenkopf H., Wahl H-W. and Reichert M. (2000b), 'Neu Technologien im Alltag Älterer', *Zeitschrift für Gerontologie und Geriatrie*, Vol. 33, pp. 153-154.

Östlund, Britt (1995), *Gammal är äldst. En studie av teknik i äldre människors liv*, Linköping Studies in Arts and Science, 129, Linköping University, Linköping.
Östlund, Britt (1999), *Tekniska möjligheter & sociala begränsningar – om äldre människors väg in i IT-samhället*, Rapport & dokumentation, 89, Hjälpmedelsinstitutet, Vällingby.
Östlund, Britt (2000), *Svensk forskning om användning av informations- och kommunikationsteknik*, KFB-note 2000:2, Kommunikationsforskningsberedningen, Stockholm.
Phillipson, C., Berhard, M., Phillips, J. and Ogg, J. (2001), *The Family and Community Life of Older People. Social Networks and Social Support in Three Urban Areas*, Routledge, London.
Sawchuk, K.A. (1995), 'From Gloom to Boom. Age, Identity and Target Marketing' in M. Featherstone and A. Wernick (eds.), *Post-Bodies, Ageing and Virtual reality: Images of Ageing, Cultural Representation of Later Life*, Routledge, London.
Senior 2005 (2002), 'Riv ålderstrappan: Livslopp i förändring', Statens offentliga utredningar, SOU 2002:29, Fritzes, Stockholm.
Silverstone, R. and Hirsch, E. (eds.) (1992), *Consuming Technology. Media and Information in Domestic Spaces*, Routledge, London.
Silverstone, R., Hirsch, E. and Morley, D. (1992), 'Information and Communication Technologies and the Moral Economy of the Household', in R. Silverstone and E. Hirsch (eds.), *Consuming Technology. Media and Information in Domestic Spaces*, Routledge, London.
Spilze, C. and Moulton, G. (2001), 'Design Challenges Associated with Longevity: The View from Industry. Opportunities and Challenges for the Future' in N. Charness, D.C. Parks and B.A Sabel (eds.), *Communication, Technology and Aging. Opportunities and Challenges for the Future*, Springer Publishing Company, New York.
Stadelhofer, C. (2000), 'Möglichkeiten und Chancen Internetnutzung durch Ältere', *Zeitschrift für Gerontologie und Geriatrie*, Vol. 33, pp. 186-194.
Sturesson, L. (2000), *Distansarbete: teknik, retorik och praktik*, Carlsson, Stockholm.
Säljö, R. (2000), *Lärande i praktiken. Ett sociokulturellt perspektiv*, Prisma, Stockholm.

Chapter 10

Biographical and Strategic Issues in Research about Ageing

Kees Knipscheer

1. Introduction

After having been involved in research about ageing for more than 30 years it still happens when I talk to people about my research, that they all of a sudden give me a bemused look and say: 'Oh, that sounds interesting'. However, their faces tell me they think I am from a different world. 'Who is crazy enough to study ageing?' By the end of the sixties, it was very unusual to study ageing, and even today it is only a small minority of people who have consistent scientific commitment to the study of the ageing population, although the older people soon will make up more than one-third of the total population in western countries. Sometimes even your nearest colleagues seem to consider researchers of ageing as infected by some kind of disease, which has to be kept at a distance. Apart from the fact that being involved in the study of ageing is seen as exceptional, it also proves to be very demanding. Once baptized in 'the world of the aged' one's unlimited commitment is required. An interdisciplinary perspective is required which involves the danger of being overruled by the medical 'Mafia'. The study of ageing also implies a permanent struggle against myths about the phenomenon of ageing.

In the first section of this chapter, I will discuss a few key issues in the study of ageing that I had to address when they came up during my career in research about ageing. These issues turned out to be crucial in shaping and enlarging my gerontological expertise. Four concepts will be selected: age, generations, time and context. In the second section I will look at the elderly in the system of the modern welfare state, and at the paradoxes created by its approach to ageing and older people. In the third section several topics will be discussed, which may be considered to be interesting for new research about ageing with an emphasis on a qualitative approach.

2. A 'Biography' in Gerontology

This is about a special kind of autobiography. How did it come about, my career in gerontology? What were the stepping stones to bring me where I am now? I will try to identify the issues that shaped my scientific work in ageing. Looking back now I am surprised to see what a nice sequence the issues that I got involved in form.

2.1 Age. The Meaning of Age and its Sociological Role

At the end of the sixties I was asked to write a masters thesis about the sociological role and meaning of age. At that time 'age' seemed to me a very abstract concept, which was hard to tackle with a sociological vocabulary. However, by studying the sociological, historical, anthropological and psychological literature I became more and more intrigued and gradually aware of a few key-points in the sociological meaning of age. Three points seemed to be the most important ones (Knipscheer, 1971).

Firstly, on the one hand, age by itself is related to the structured character of the continuum of individual human life from birth to death and on the other hand it is also embedded in the socio-historical process of the continuance of generations during human history. Being of a certain age makes one a member of a certain generation, which in turn locates one in human history.

Secondly, as a sociological concept, age is linked with an ascription orientation. That means it ascribes to persons of a certain age a specific social position with its rights, expectations and norms, whether it is used in an age-heterogeneous or an age-homogeneous context. In some societies it may be more explicitly expressed and in others less.

Thirdly, the sociological meaning of age in a specific society is embedded in its culture, i.e. it is coloured by the orientations, expectations, norms and values specific to that culture, and it is connected with its societal institutions. In general, modern western societies are much less governed by age-related institutions than some earlier societies with age-driven regimes. Nevertheless, industrial societies have some quite strict age-related institutions, such as legal adulthood and retirement age, and also several informal age-related patterns of behaviour, such as visiting house music parties, or belonging to women's bridge clubs.

Such a reflection on the sociological meaning of age made me from the very beginning aware of the possible sociological impact of age, of the cultural diversity of age norms and expectations, and the strengths and weaknesses of formal and informal age norms and expectations. For example, while the legal retirement age has not changed over the last 50 years in most western societies, only a small minority in these countries continue working until they are 65 years of age. But at the same time, most people live five to ten years longer than they did 50 years ago.

At the beginning, my approach to research was limited to a sociological one. Despite the fact that I became aware of the cultural diversity in age differences (in fact almost all cultures have specific cultural 'rites de passage'), it was not until after more interdisciplinary research I discovered that age was in some sense a 'non-variable'. That is to say many, maybe the majority of the phenomena which are age-related are not related to a specific age. Most specific age-related phenomena appear to be socially constructed. For example, the onset of chronic disease is definitely age-related but sometimes it starts at 40 and sometimes at 70 years of age. Widowhood is age-related, however, compared to the early twentieth century it has in most cases been postponed for several decades of a lifetime. The onset of the retirement process may nowadays start when people are in their forties, while the formal retirement age has not changed.

To sum up, age appears to be a key concept in studies about ageing, however it seems to be much more the age-relatedness of the phenomena that is of importance, not the specific age per se.

2.2 Generations. The Meaning of Generation and its Role in the Ageing Process

During the 1980s my research about ageing was moving on and I spent some years studying the meaning of generation and its role in the ageing process (cf. Hammarström and Närvänen in Chapters 3 and 4 respectively). As mentioned earlier, age locates people in the historical process of the continuance of generations in human history. The notion of generation refers to two, quite distinct sociological contexts: the family and kinship relationships (Hagestad, 1983, 1985; Plath, 1980) and the society at large (Mannheim, 1952; Ryder, 1965). Within the family and kinship context the notion of generation refers to the succession of parents, children, grandchildren etc. The parental generation is responsible for the education and socialization of the younger generation, for economic support, and for the continuity of the kinship system. The relationships between the generations are strongly institutionalized by norms and legal rules, by informal traditions and emotional bonding. Ageing in this context means moving from childhood, to parenthood and grandparenthood, with all the rituals and life events implied in these transitions. This includes intergenerational reciprocity and exchange, intergenerational concerns and conflicts, tensions between individual ambitions and normative obligations. Ageing in this context means moving gradually from, as a child, looking up to the older generations to, as an older person, looking down upon the younger generations (cf. Plath, 1980). Saying 'Ageing is a family affair', acknowledges that ageing brings about a gradual but crucial shift in position and perspective, which takes place in the context of a kinship system.

Sociologically, the notion of generations has also been linked to birth-cohorts. That means that birth-cohorts (those who are born over a period of five to ten years) are sometimes considered as a generation, e.g. 'the baby boom generation' after World War II. While the notion of birth-cohorts refers to the birth in the same period, Mannheim in his treatise on *The Problem of Generations* stresses the importance of 'the common location in the historical dimension of the social progress', particularly referring to people's passage of the formative socialisation years during the same historical period. They have a common location in human history. 'This location as such only contains potentialities which materialize, or are suppressed, or become embedded in other social forces and manifest themselves in a modified form' (Mannheim, 1952: 303). Birth-cohorts as a generation have a common historical location, and as such a common start of their lifecourse. Apart from their specific individual characteristics, they grew up with comparable structural opportunities, limitations and contextual conditions. They may have developed a kind of common cohort biography (Knipscheer, 1991) and this common set of experiences may have implications for the rest of their life. As such it has to be accounted for when studying the ageing of members of a specific cohort/generation (cf. Uhlenberg and Riley, 1996).

2.3 Time. The Meaning of the Past, Present and Future as Constructed in the Individual and the Social Context

A few decades later I reflected more deeply on the temporal embeddedness of human life and explored its contribution to the change of people's perspectives while ageing. Temporal embeddedness refers to the permanent location of human life in a temporal order of past, present and future and to the specific way human beings are related to this order. Although human lifetime has an irreversible character, it does not mean that human beings must always remain in the present. The human mind allows people to go forward and backward perceptually in lifetime; however, they always start from the mental and physical present, here and now. Thus human beings have the capacity to transcend the irreversibility of time continuously, and simultaneously relate the present to the past and the future. The focus here is on the social dimension of this temporal embeddedness, that is to say on how the meaning of the past, present and future is constructed in the interrelatedness of the individual and the social context (Knipscheer, 1988).

On the basis of an in-depth analysis of George Herbert Mead's work presented in an article from 1983, Maines et al. elaborated Mead's 'theory' of time in order to explore the potential of time as a theoretical construct to contribute to sociological investigations. They refer to several areas in the sociology of ageing where such construct can be useful, for example, 'midlife-crisis' and 'life review'. Maines, Sugrue and Katovich stress that the strength of Mead's time-related theory can be seen in the way this theory fully takes into account the subjectively perceived reality of the present, as expressed and experienced in the process of human behaviour. That means that the theory acknowledges both the socio-structural connections of this perceived reality, i.e. its relationship to the actual socio-structure of the present, and its personal experienced and perceived reality. However, at the same time Maines et al. stress, in line with Mead, the importance of the temporal dimension of the theory in linking past experiences and future-oriented options to the present. For Mead (1932: 9), 'presents [are] sliding into each other, each with a past which is referable to itself, each past taking up into itself those back of it and in some degree reconstructing from them its own standpoint'. Presents are emerging events.

In line with Mead's time-related theory, Eames (1973:72), another follower of Mead, refers specifically to two aspects of this emergent process: 'One aspect ... is that it is not reducible to its conditions (as given in the present, it is qualitatively unique). The second aspect of the emergent event is that it is a present, and as such it is the starting point of its own perspective from which the past and the future are constructed'. This emergence process of the present calls for the 'social nature' (i.e. sociality) of the present; the social nature is implied in the process of adjustment of the emerging present in the flow of presents. Thus, 'the qualities carried over from the past present must be brought into harmony with the new qualities of the present present' (Eames, 1973: 72). In the emerging present, the past has to be reconstructed and the future anticipated (this is called temporal sociality, as it refers to the merging of the individual and social experiences of the past and future options), while other perspectives, i.e. the actual social context of the individually experienced present, is taken into account simultaneously (this is called structural sociality, as it refers to the embeddedness of the individual emerging present in the actual social context).

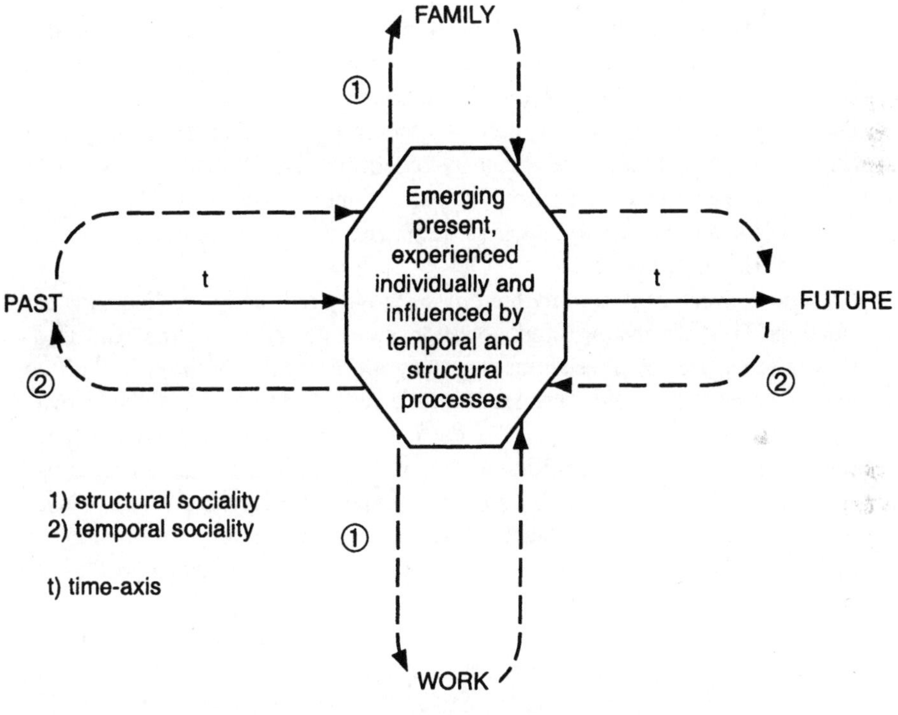

Figure 10.1 Flow of presents influenced by structural and temporal sociality processes

After a general introduction of Mead's time-related theory Maines, Sugrue and Katovich (1983) focused their analysis of Mead's theory on the meaning of the past. Because this has a special relevance for ageing issues, we follow the analysis by Maines, Sugrue and Katovich. They identified four dimensions in the meaning of the past, which have special relevance in Mead's theory. The first dimension, and the most easily recognized, is the symbolically reconstructed past. This involves redefining the meaning of past events in such a way that they have meaning and utility for the present (Mead, 1929: 238), as the updated meaning of the past is implied in the emergent present. For example, a person's perspectives on the past of his/her primary education will change several times while moving up to secondary school, college and university. A woman's perspective on her husband may change after his death and it may change again after remarrying, and even over time when the relationship in the new marriage is evolving.

The second dimension, the social structural past, has not been dealt with explicitly by Mead, but is found in the literature on his theory. It refers to the notion that the social context is structured in the past and conditions future activities. Thus, the anticipation of the future as given in the present must take the preconditions of this context into account, settled in the past. Someone who leaves a professional educational programme as an adolescent before passing the examinations for example, limits his or her future professional options when he or she is 25 years old.

The third dimension, is the implied objective past. This past can be best explained by a simple example given by Mead himself. When he arrives in his office he becomes aware of an implicit past: 'I must have arisen and eaten my breakfast and taken the car, to be where I am. The sense of this past is there as an implication' (Mead, 1929: 238).

The fourth dimension, the mythical past, is only indirectly implied in Mead's formulation. This dimension refers solely to symbolic creations that are used to direct or manipulate social relationships; they are fictitious, but real in their consequences. Once these 'pasts' are legitimated, they start to work in social reality. For example, as a former prisoner of the conservative regime Nelson Mandela became a symbol of the peaceful revolution in South Africa, in that he became the first president of the new regime. As such he obtained a mythical role because he descended from the black population. Sometimes grandmothers can obtain a kind of mythical position in a similar way by keeping a family together just by their presence.

As an example of several meanings of the past we can refer to the lifecourse of a woman in her 70s, who began to work as a maid at the age of 12, married and started a family at the age of 18, and remained a housewife throughout her life. The need for an important reconstruction of her past arose when her daughter entered the workforce again after the birth of her second child. A second reconstruction of the meaning of her life course was needed when her granddaughter started academic studies in geography at the age of 18. The grandmother's experience of her adolescence and her family household work had not changed, but her interpretation of it changed several times, stemming from her family history. In reference to her socio-structural past, she may have experienced several times in her life when she felt she had limited future options just because of structural limitations in her past, i.e. having no professional education. However, when she has been able to get a kind of mythical position as a grandmother among her children and grandchildren, she may claim that in spite of her limited opportunities, she has been able – although unaware of it – to manage a creditable family life (Knipscheer, 1988).

2.4 Context. The Environmental Docility Hypothesis

A fourth issue came up when I became involved in the work of Lawton (1980). A number of years ago Lawton (1985) approached the issue of ageing as a question of person-environment interaction. He launched the environmental docility hypothesis, suggesting that the more an individual's physical capacity decreased in functioning, the more demanding the living environment became. For example, older people who develop difficulties in walking, have problems coping with staircases and traffic lights.

The focus of the original model (Lawton and Nahemow, 1973; Lawton, 1980) is on the mechanisms through which transactions between the person and the environment occur, especially among older persons. Such transactions are based on a specific fit between the capacity of the person and the more or less demanding characteristics of the environment, called environmental stress. Older people with a decreased competence in (I) ADL (Instrumental Activities of Daily Life, such as cleaning, walking, washing, eating) develop a need for a lower level of environmental stress in which adapted behaviour is expected to promote subjective well-being. In such a way, environmental changes which lower the level of environmental stress may facilitate coping with decreased (I) ADL capacities. This interactive mechanism between personal competence and environmental demands, referred to as the 'environmental docility hypothesis', has become an important tool in environmental planning activities for functionally dependent older people. It has been used in many ways in the development of housing facilities for handicapped older people. However, this model, as it was launched originally, stresses the passive environment-dependent role of the older adult, and neglects the needs and preferences of the person involved. It was criticized by Carp and Carp (1984), who argued that the environment not only raised demands but in many cases also offered resources and opportunities. These may challenge people to develop new ways of autonomous behaviour, and initiate proactive environmental changes. In response to the criticism of his model, Lawton (1989) elaborated his original model with the concept of 'efficacy', a concept indicating whether the relationship between person and environment was effectively managed or not. This 'efficacy', and the subjective experience of being efficacious, is considered to mediate person-environment transactions. This means that given a certain level of efficacy, people who take an active stance will show proactive person-environment behaviour, while those who take a passive stance will show docile person-environment behaviour and will become constrained by environmental demands. In other words, in person-environment interaction it is not only a question of individual capacities and environmental conditions, but also a question of the individual willingness to profit from available opportunities and challenges, which determine adaptive behaviour and well-being (Knipscheer et al., 2000).

3. The Social Construction of Paradoxes about Ageing

Being involved for decades in research about ageing, one of the most penetrating insights that I have gained is that the way we deal with older people is to a large extent a product of changing societal institutions and structures, and as such a part of the modernization of society. In order to develop a kind of gerontological sensitivity it was extremely important to understand the notions of age, time, and generation. However, to understand older people and their situation these notions have to be geared to the actual societal context and be interpreted from the social and cultural mechanisms, which help to form the identity of older people. Looking around in the 'world of the elderly' over the last decades I have identified several remarkable paradoxes. As Baltes and Carstensen (1996) note, although influenced heavily by the cultural context of the historical era, a deep ambivalence about ageing can be traced from ancient to modern times. With the advent of industrial capitalism, human value became equated with productivity and, at the same time, retirement was institutionalized as a symbol of non-productivity. Ironically, this more negative view of old people and ageing was facilitated by scientific attention to ageing. By focusing almost exclusively on the problems of older people – their isolation, dependence, role-loss and illness, researchers reinforced a very negative portrayal of ageing. The view of ageing as a time of decline was further reinforced by well-intentioned advocates and politicians who, in order to win support for the infirm elderly, portrayed them as sick and needy. The implementation of the *Older Americans Act* and similar policies in the United States and other countries functioned as a two-edged sword by providing protection but also endangering individual autonomy and integrity (Estes and Binney, 1989; Guillemard, 1992; Baltes and Carstensen, 1996: 400). (Cf. also Macnicol in Chapter 2.)

In the expansion of the welfare state after World War II, western countries constructed a kind of iron fence as a protection shield because older people were considered to be at risk. The older people were liberated from the obligation to work, they became supported by housing facilities, guaranteed an income, and were served by health maintenance and care. Categorical social security measures, public pension systems and health and long-term care institutions were established. In some way two categories, the working people and the dependent ones constituted society at that time. However, in the meantime the social category of older people was changing considerably. Life expectancy increased and earlier retirement did largely evolve. Most older people had more money available, were healthier and created a category of the older leisured. Nevertheless, the institutional approach to the elderly remained settled in the old system!

However, not only the social approach to older people has become obsolete and seems to run behind the societal changes. Also our cognitive perspectives on ageing appear to be caught in a sort of raster as Levenson and Crumpler (1996) demonstrated recently. In discussions about ageing among ordinary people, as well as among scientists studying ageing, it seems evident that the discussants are guided by specific underlying principles and preconceptions about the process of ageing.

Recently, Levinson and Crumpler identified in the scientific literature, three specific raster or models concerning lifespan developmental approaches to ageing. The first one they call the ontological model. For pure ontogeneticists, such as Erikson (1963), adult development and ageing is driven and constrained by age-linked intrinsic imperatives, basically given in biological determinants such as genes. Of course, a number of them e.g. Baltes and Nesselroad (1984), are cognizant of the social forces that aid or hinder developmental achievements, but the main point of the approach is to discover a universal invariant sequence of development. Ontologists look for lifespan changes common to adults across culture, sex and social class. In this perspective ageing is to a large extent a pre-programmed process and in this sense it easily demonstrates a kind of fatalism. Such a perspective on ageing will not inspire the professionals to a creative and stimulating approach when tackling the problems of ageing, neither will it push older people themselves to a proactive attitude to optimize their own ageing process. It may be tempting to take a resigned attitude and to convey this message to others at an early stage.

The second model contains notions that reflect a sociogenetic perspective. It emphasizes a multitude of developmental pathways that depend on the social context. This point of view is as old as sociology itself. The lifecourse is shaped by social forces, with biology being far less deterministic than is suggested by ontogeneticists. Cross-cultural comparison studies in particular seem to confirm the strengths of this perspective.

The third model is labelled the 'liberative' perspective (cf. Loevinger [1977], talking about development as liberation). The 'liberative' approach acknowledges determinism but does not treat adult development and ageing as entirely being subjected to biological or social forces. Instead, adult development and ageing is 'characterized by a reduction in the extent to which one's motives, states of mind, and behaviour can be explained deterministically' (Levenson and Crumpler, 1996: 61). The third model does not deny that ontogenetic and sociogenetic forces are at work, they are however much less deterministic than is often assumed. For older people it opens up the perspective of not in advance letting themselves be dictated by physical and/or mental decline ('deficit model') and accepting strongly institutionalized pathways of late-life transitions and ageing.

Already 13 years ago, Kohli (1988) wondered to what extent the ageing of society would be a challenge for sociology. His argument was that the traditional issues in sociology, such as social inequality, social stratification and socialization were studied within the context of a 'work' society. The way sociology has dealt with these issues up to now will not fit the study of the future organization of society. From Kohli's arguments we can conclude that many sociological issues that have been raised concerning the 'traditional working adult world', will become invalid when studying older people of tomorrow. Their world will *not* turn out to be a replica of the adult working world of today. Recent decades have shown how these two worlds develop into a split, in which the adult world is becoming more and more demanding, and the 'world of the older people' is becoming a strange mixture of leisure, self-interest, volunteering, and material and emotional need, demonstrating a deepened ambivalence about ageing and towards older people in society.

4. Anchor Issues for a 'Qualitative' Research Programme about Ageing

In this section I will try to raise some suggestions for topics in research programmes about ageing; topics, which seem to be of special interest in the context of research, which has its main focus on qualitative research. However, in saying this I would like first to warn against making a strict separation between quantitative and qualitative research. On the contrary, in order to strengthen empirical evidence, it may be very productive to start with one research method and continue with the other. As a newcomer in a special area of research it may be worthwhile to have an exploratory qualitative orientation in this area before preparing an elaborated survey study. On the other hand, when already having the outcomes from a large-scale survey, making in-depth studies on specific sections of the sample or on specific issues, will help strengthen the empirical evidence and contribute to the understanding of the results.

4.1 Talking about Ageing

One of the first topics I would start studying is 'talking about ageing'. How do people talk about ageing, and what do they mean when they have something to say about ageing in general, and about their own ageing specifically? In itself it would be very interesting to see how people in society in general talk about ageing. Taking it a step further, I suggest it would be interesting to study to what extent talking about ageing among people aged 50 differs from talking about ageing among those aged 75 years. What does healthy ageing mean to those who are 50 and to those who are 75 years of age?

In a national representative study among 4,494 older adults (55-90 years old) in the Netherlands, the respondents were asked to assess, on a five-point scale, their health in general, their health compared to age peers, and their health compared to their health ten years previously.

The questions posed and the range of the answering categories were:

- How is your health in general (poor to very good)?
- How is your health compared to that of other people of your age (much poorer to much better)?
- How is your health now in comparison to what it was like ten years ago (much poorer to much better)?

In this study an interesting finding in the measurement of subjective health was made (Liefbroer and de Jong Gierveld, 1995). The empirical results were that two out of the three health measures showed a decline with increasing age, as was expected. However, the positive evaluation of their own health in comparison to that of their peers increased, the older the respondents were. Those between 55 and 60 evaluated their own health as poorer as compared with the health of other people of the same age, while those between 85 and 90 evaluated their own health as better than the health of those of the same age. So, the older people are, the more they consider themselves as much healthier than their peers. Apparently, the standards people use at different ages to compare their health with that of their contemporaries change. How does this come about? Can this be clarified in talking with older people about age, ageing and health?

Another direction would be to compare talking about ageing among people of different professions e.g. nurses, sport professionals and teachers. Understanding how people, old and young, talk about ageing seems to be of fundamental importance for any researcher in gerontology, in qualitative and quantitative research. Also, we have to discover how to talk with older people about ageing, how to understand them, and from this understanding to learn how to phrase standard questions, unambiguous stimuli, for interviews. In many cases, researchers in their thirties make questionnaires for people in their eighties. That makes an age difference of half a century. Their cultural, social, economic and historical experience differs so much that mutual understanding is not at all a matter of course.

4.2 The Meaning of the Post-Retirement Period

One of the most intriguing issues in ageing nowadays seems to be the ambiguous and paradoxical situation of the early-retired persons in western industrial society. What does it tell us about the meaning of ageing, about the notions these people have about the second half of life? While life expectation was increasing up to the last decade of the twentieth century and is expected to continue to increase slowly, the working life is ending earlier and earlier in most western countries since 1980. From a societal perspective this situation created, as Riley and Riley (1989) phrased it, a 'structural lag'. While these people aged between 55-60 and 70 have a lot of capabilities, there are no structural role models, no societal acknowledged positions to fill the gap.

Perhaps we do not have to make a 'problem' of it. Most people seriously tell us they look forward to stop working, to have time to travel and to relax from a demanding job. However, what does it mean to people to have 20 or 30 years for leisure, while society is not waiting for them, does not need them and offers them neither acknowledgement and respect, nor any opportunities for them to contribute to society?

Peter Laslett (1991, 1993) suggested that the Third Age, the age between 55-75, should be the Crown of Life. However, it seems rather to have become the Age of the Great Invisibility. People of this age live in a kind of 'time-out position' until they sooner or later come into the situation, when they have to accept societal care and yet claim respect for their wish for independence.

To interview in depth a representative sample of older persons of different socio-economic levels about their meaning of life around five years after retirement would be an interesting and rewarding project. To what extent do they have a notion of their contribution to society? Do they miss a societal role as a citizen? When there is a certain kind of emptiness in their life, does it appear to be related to the 'Great Invisibility'? How do they cope with it, to what extent are they able to compensate for it, and to what extent do they experience these compensations as surrogate solutions?

4.3 The Meaning of the Parent-Child Relationship in Old Age

Thousands of studies – and I have been involved in a number of them – have confirmed over the last fifty years that industrialization, urbanization and modernization have not destroyed family and kinship relationships. Certain changes have been identified. However, the continuity has been greater than was expected in earlier apocalyptic scenarios. Two shifts seem to have taken place. Firstly, the focus on the maintenance of the continuity of (either masculine or feminine) kinship over centuries has been replaced by a downward orientation with a focus on the next generations (children, grandchildren, great grandchildren). Partly, this seems to create a 'relative structural isolation from the kinship' (Parsons, 1943, 1965) and is to be related to a more balanced relationship between husband and wife, while the previous priority for one of the kinship systems of origin is becoming increasingly less important. Secondly, the husband-wife relationship has comparatively decreased in importance while the parent-child relationship has increased in importance. This means the downward relationship within the kinship has become relatively more prominent. Whether this is also the case for the parent-child relationship from the perspective of the child is a question to which there still is no definite answer. Probably it depends to a large extent on the previous relationship between parent and child in each individual case. Independently of these two major shifts in the kinship orientations, within a large majority of families 'keeping in touch' is still a very important adage in most western European countries. Visiting patterns and the exchange of help and support remain strong, even under changing living conditions and individualization in housing facilities. This situation leaves the questions open as to why the impact of the macro changes in western societies appears to be much less devastating than expected? What makes the family and kinship relationships resistant to macro attacks? More specifically, what is the meaning of the parent-child relationship, which seems to be the cornerstone in this kinship building, both from the parent's point of view as well as from the children's? How does this relate to the meaning of ageing itself?

4.4 Frame of Reference Related to Age

An individual's frame of reference may be age-, period- and cohort-related, as may be understood from the generation theory of Karl Mannheim (see above). However, the relatedness of people's standards and expectations to age may be very special. For example the older people become, the more they consider themselves healthier than their contemporaries. Also, when older people suffer chronic conditions, the fact of good health becomes less expected and therefore of lower priority in life. Such findings may be considered not so much as the outcomes of the actual conditions but much more as the consequence of a shift in age-related standards. It seems to be of crucial importance to explore the age relatedness of people's frame of reference as a key issue in establishing an understanding of the meaning of ageing in society.

4.5 Myths about Ageing

I don't know of any period of life, which is 'infected' with as many myths as old age. The proverbial wisdom is just one of the less disastrous examples, other examples are the paradoxical situation of older workers, the linkage between depression and old age, and between old people's need for security and their dependency on others.

About 15 years ago the leader of the Dutch Ballet Dance Company made an impressive effort to destroy one of these myths. In contrast to the normal procedure up to that time, when dancers retired at the age of about 35, he put together a team of people over 40 – between '40 and death', as he used to say – and started to develop special choreographies for them. While the first period was very challenging for the team as well as for the choreographers, the special strengths of this team were discovered and the choreographers succeeded to explore the special expressive abilities of these dancers. Later on, in a special television documentary 'Pas-de-vieux', the team and the choreographers demonstrated the success of this initiative and the group has now obtained international acknowledgement.

This example shows at least two things. Firstly, apparently 'mythical' fixed age boundaries can be broken down. Secondly, there is a need for special approaches to find out what the specific strengths of 'older' people are. The ageing society has a need for a special type of 'choreographers' who can discover the special strengths of older people and initiate new challenging approaches in order to 'liberate' these strengths (compare, 'development as liberation' above, Loevinger, 1977).

4.6 Cross-Cultural Qualitative Studies

Each of the issues raised above as anchor topics for ageing research – talking about ageing, meaning of life after retirement, meaning of parent-child relationship, frame of reference related to age – may be extended by taking on a cross-cultural approach. Our understanding of these phenomena will be deepened cumulatively by adding specific cultural contexts because it will enable scholars to separate cultural-specific hypotheses and more general hypotheses.

5. In Conclusion

In writing this I intended to show how my own gerontological interest came about over time and how intriguing issues came up and caught my interest. In between, I tried to add some hints from my own experience, which may make sense to people who intend to develop their own expertise in research about ageing. In the final section I suggested a number of topics or issues, which may be worthwhile starting points for new research. Some of them are key issues in understanding ageing from a sociological point of view and some of them are of societal relevance in the context of a changing society.

References

Baltes, M.M. and Carstensen, L.L. (1996), 'The Process of Successful Aging', *Ageing and Society*, Vol. 16, pp. 397-422.

Baltes, P.B. and Nesselroad, J.H. (1984), 'Paradigm Lost and Paradigm Regained: Critique of Dannefer's Portrayal of Life Span Developmental Psychology', *American Sociological Review*, Vol. 49, pp. 841-846.

Carp, F. and Carp, A. (1984), 'A Complementary Congruence Model of Well Being on Mental Health for the Community Elderly', in I. Altman, M.P. Lawton and J.F. Wohlwill (eds.), *Elderly People and Environment*, Plenum, New York, pp. 279-336.

Eames, E.R. (1973), 'Mead's Concept of Time', in W.R. Corti (ed.), *The Philosophy of George Herbert Mead*, Amriswiler Bucherei, Winterthur, Geneva, pp. 59-81.

Erikson, E.H. (1963), *Childhood and Society*, Norton, New York.

Estes, C.L. and Binney, E.A. (1989), 'The Biomedicalization of Aging', *The Gerontologist*, Vol. 29 (5), pp. 587-596.

Guillemard, A.M. (1992), 'Europäische Perspectiven der Alterspolitik' (European Perspectives of Politics in Ageing), in P.B. Baltes and J. Mittelstra (eds.), *Zukunft des Alterns und gesellschaftliche Entwicklung* (Future of Ageing and Societal Development), De Gruyter, Berlin, pp. 614-639.

Hagestad, G.O. (1983), 'The Continuous Bond: A Dynamic, Multigenerational Perspective on the Parent-Child Relations between Adults', in M. Perlmutter (ed.), *Parent-Child Interaction and Parent-Child Relations in Child Development*, (The Minnesota Symposia on Child Psychology, Vol. 17), Lawrence Erlbaum Ass., Hillsdale N.J., pp. 129-158.

Hagestad, G.O. (1985), 'Continuity and Connectedness', in V.L. Bengtson and J.F. Robertson (eds.), *Grandparenthood*, Sage, Beverly Hills, CA, pp. 31-48.

Knipscheer, C.P.M. (1971), 'Leeftijd als sociologisch gegeven', *Sociale Wetenschappen*, Vol. 14, pp. 20-45.

Knipscheer, C.P.M. (1988), 'Temporal Embeddedness and Aging within the Multigenerational Family: The Case of Grandparenting', in J.E. Birren and V.L. Bengtson (eds.), *Emergent Theories of Aging*, Springer Publishing Comp, New York, pp. 426-446.

Knipscheer, C.P.M. (1991), 'Het leeftijd-cohort-periode model als heuristisch hulpmiddel', in P. Ester and J.A.M. Wezel van, *Sociale aspecten van modernisering*, Tilburg University Press, Tilburg.

Knipscheer, C.P.M., Broese van Groenou, M.I., Leene, G.J.F., Beekman, A.T.F., Deeg, D.J.H. (2000), 'The Effects of Environmental Context and Personal Resources on Depressive Symptomatology in Older Age: A Test of the Lawton model', *Ageing and Society*, Vol. 20 (Part 2), pp. 183-202.

Kohli, M. (1988), 'Ageing as a Challenge for Sociological Theory', *Ageing and Society*, Vol. 8 (4), pp. 367-394.

Laslett, P. (1991), *A Fresh Map of Life; The Emergence of the Third Age*, Weidenfeld and Nicholson, London.

Laslett, P. and van der Kamp, M. (1993), *The Third Age, a Fresh Map of Life*, LSOB/NIG, Bunnik.

Lawton, M.P. (1980), *Environment and Aging*, Brooks/Cole, Monterey, California.

Lawton, M.P. (1985), 'The Elderly in Context: Perspectives from Environmental Psychology and Gerontology', *Environment and Behaviour*, Vol. 17, pp. 501-519.

Lawton, M.P. (1989), 'Behavior-Relevant Ecological Factors', in K. Schaie, W. Schooler and C. Schooler (eds.), *Social Structure and Aging: Psychological Processes*, Lawrence Erlbaum, Hillsdale, New Jersey, pp. 57-78.

Lawton, M.P. and Nahemov, L. (1973), 'Ecology and the Aging Process', in C. Eisdorfer and M.P. Lawton (eds.), *Psychology of Adult Development and Aging*, American Psychology Association, Washington DC, pp. 619-674.

Levenson, M.R. and Crumpler, C.A. (1996), 'Three Models of Adult Development', *Human Development*, Vol. 39 (3), pp. 135-149.

Liefbroer, A.C. and de Jong Gierveld, J. (1995), 'Living Arrangements, Socio-Economic Resources and Health', in C.P.M. Knipscheer, J. de Jong Gierveld, T.G. van Tilburg and P.A. Dykstra (eds.), *Living Arrangements and Social Networks of Older Adults*, VU University Press, Amsterdam pp. 15-36.

Loevinger, J. (1977), *Ego Development: Conceptions and Theories*, Jossey-Bass Riley, San Franscisco.

Maines, D.R., Sugrue, M.N. and Katovich, M.A. (1983), 'The Sociological Import of G.H. Mead's Theory of the Past', *American Sociological Review*, Vol. 48, pp. 161-173.

Mannheim, K. (1952), 'The Problem of Generations', in K. Mannheim (ed.) *Essays on the Sociology of Knowledge*, Routledge, London.

Mead, G.H. (1929), 'The Nature of the Past', in J. Coss (ed.), *Essays in Honor of John Dewey*, Henry Holt, New York, pp. 235-242.

Mead, G.H. (1932), *The Philosophy of the Present*, Open Court, Chicago.

Parsons, T. (1943), 'The Kinship System of the Contemporary United States', in T. Parsons (ed.), *Essays in Sociological Theory*, Glencoe, IL., pp. 177-196.

Parsons, T. (1965), 'The Normal American Family', in S. Farber, P. Mustacchi and R.H. Wilson (eds.), *Man and Civilisation: the Family's Search for Survival*, McGraw Hill, New York.

Plath, D. (1980), 'Contours of Consociation: Lessons from a Japanese Narrative', in P.B. Baltes and O.G. Brim (eds.), *Life-Span Development and Behavior*, Academic Press, New York, pp. 287-307.

Riley, M.W. and Riley, J.W. (1989), 'The Lives of Older People and Changing Social Roles', *The Annals of the American Academy of Political and Social Science*, Special Issue, The Quality of Aging: Strategies for Interventions, Vol. 503 (May), pp. 14-28.

Ryder, N.B. (1965), 'The Cohort as a Concept in the Study of Social Change', *American Sociological Review*, Vol. 30, pp. 843-861.

Uhlenberg, P. and Riley, M.W. (1996), 'Cohort Studies', in *Encyclopedia of Gerontology: Age, Aging, and the Aged*, Vol. I, A-K, Academic Press, San Diego, pp. 299-310.

Index

Made in the USA
Las Vegas, NV
30 October 2024

10652739R00127